garden your city

garden your city

Barbara Hobens Feldt

Illustrations by Paula Brinkman

taylor trade publishing

Lanham • New York • Dallas • Boulder • Toronto • Oxford

Key to images in photospread, page 2 (clockwise from top, left) elaborate entrance sidewalk garden; spring daffodils in DeWitt Clinton Park, Manhattan's West Side; twin wall planters of annuals; cascading plants from SoHo fire escapes; fragrant roses and a Times Square view from roof garden; peach trees thrive in city gardens; terrace garden offers a roomy respite; (center page) tulips adorn a low brick sidewalk planter. Page 3 (top) hanging baskets on the street lamps in Harrogate, England provide function and beauty; (bottom, left) window boxes abound on Beacon Hill in Boston; (bottom, right) Hell's Kitchen, NYC roof garden thrives on recycled plastic deck. Page 4 (clockwise from top, left) brownstone steps in Greenwich Village in full bloom; an alfresco oasis offers organic herbs; Koi—a garden pond's pleasure; front steps showcase plants; layers of height, texture, color, and growing habit; color is chosen to blend, accent, or be bold; Maria's Perennial Garden bench design adapted from 1850s trellis; doorway surrounded by annuals

Published by Taylor Trade Publishing
An imprint of The Rowman & Littlefield Publishing Group, Inc.
4501 Forbes Boulevard, Suite 200
Lanham, Maryland 20706

Distributed by National Book Network

Library of Congress Cataloging-in-Publication Data
Feldt, Barbara Hobens.
  Garden your city / Barbara Hobens Feldt.—1st Taylor Trade Pub. ed.
    p. cm.
  Includes bibliographical references and index.
  ISBN 1-58979-169-X (cloth : alk. paper)
  1. Urban Gardening. 2. Gardening. 3. Container gardening. I. Title.
  SB453.F394 2005
  635'.09173'2—dc22   2004021661

I dedicate this book and my love to my husband, Fred, who brought me to this wonderful island in 1988 and shares the awe and joy of gardening and life.

These pages were written for all city dwellers who have questioned why their cities aren't greener and will now be able to answer by creating their own garden spaces.

contents

Part Three

places to grow

Part Four

city gardening resources

foreword

Craig Tufts, Chief Naturalist, National Wildlife Federation

Those of us who have chosen not to live in New York City characterize its inhabitants as hustling and bustling in the city that never sleeps. City gardeners, like author Barbara Feldt, have grown garden-wise through hard work, joy, sharing, fighting for their green spaces, and through years of experience. That's hustling and bustling with a healthier environment in mind, and so she may agree with that stereotype.

Her efforts and those of diverse thousands of other green-thumbed champions create—in brownstone front gardens, on apartment roofs and balconies, and in community gardens—a nurturing city life with flowers, fruit, vegetables, shade, and habitat for wildlife. They integrate the growing world, the natural world, into the cultural richness of city life with a requisite pace, resiliency, and intelligence from which all gardeners, urban, suburban, or rural, can learn much.

As a country gardener and naturalist who visits Manhattan sporadically, when I do visit, I easily find the life beyond—but almost always among—humankind that sparks my spirit and overcomes my uneasiness of glowering skyscrapers and seemingly no inch of the earth unpaved. I find it in places like Central Park, but equally and more clearly somehow in the community garden plots that dot the landscape and in the small yards and among container plantings by people like Barbara.

Anyone with a small quantity of soil, be it in a container or tiny postage-stamp-sized garden plot, can plant a seed or cover the roots of a flower or vegetable seedling. By exerting a little stewardship for that life, you may expect a burst of bloom, the luscious flavor of a fresh tomato, the zest of a pinched basil leaf, or that incredible visit from a multicolored butterfly.

My own path to the surprises and wonder of wildlife in the city received its jump start many years ago. I was detailed by a college professor to write about the life that had found its place in the basement of a burned-out upstate New York hotel. I didn't hold much hope that I would find anything but perhaps ants. I found the ants easily among an incredible variety of other living things. Even if neglected, the power of soil is its ability to sustain plants. The tendency of life is to never leave a niche unoccupied. That hotel basement held dozens of plants blooming, fruiting, and—with their vigorous growth—splitting apart the remnants of foundation and window wells. Insects and their eight-legged relatives (that's spiders!) abounded. Under old charred boards, salamanders pursued these wildlife species and birthed more of their own kind. From a shallow puddle in the corner of the basement, toads sang and mated.

For over thirty years, the National Wildlife Federation, my employer, has helped people grow habitat, that special combination of features which provides all the needs for wildlife, wherever they live. Barbara Feldt has grown, watched, mused over, and cares for one of the 45,000 certified properties meeting our program criteria of providing food, water, cover, and places where wildlife may raise their young. Gardening, especially when it is mindful of the needs of our nonhuman neighbors as well as our own, helps nurture an absolutely critical process of understanding and valuing the mystery and wonder of life, both our own and that of every other life with which we share the planet.

Barbara's book takes you on a journey of preparation and revelation. You'll come through the reading ready to grow and wonder on your own. Enjoy!

Craig Tufts
Chief Naturalist
National Wildlife Federation

preface

Why should we garden in our cities?

City gardening creates

 healthy food to eat and share,

 beauty in your life,

 excitement,

 vines to shade and provide privacy,

 increased oxygen,

 a sense of harmony,

 herbs for flavor and medicinal use,

 and flowers to gaze at, smell, and attract

  wildlife.

City gardening is

 relaxing,

 fun,

 a great hobby to develop with someone

  special,

 exercise,

 involving and evolving,

 a weekends-only or lifelong pastime,

 challenging,

 a lot of work,

 and rewarding.

A city garden arouses

 all five senses,

the sixth sense of intuition,

 love of learning,

 dormant spirituality,

 and memories.

A garden in the city brings

 smiles,

 beauty,

 enjoyment,

 peace to a troubled heart,

 birds and butterflies,

 realized goals,

 and respect of nature.

A garden in the city is a special place for

 contemplation,

 dining,

 sunning,

 reflecting,

 reading,

 a party,

 sketching,

 resting,

 and slowing down life.

Some positive repercussions of city gardening

 include

friendship,
more people gardening,
experimentation,
encouraging others,
and feeling productive.
City gardening inspires

daring,
imaginative recipes,
creative thought,
romance,
expanding public gardening efforts,
and even this book.

acknowledgments

With Thanks

This book would not be in your hands if not for the caring professionalism of my agents, Ann Tanenbaum, Jane Lahr, and Lyn DelliQuadri of LTD Editions LLC. Ann's insightful, supportive friendship will never be forgotten, nor will the calming voice of her assistant, Bill Mogan.

Acquisitions Editor Camille Cline, Taylor Trade Publishing, brought talent, knowledge, and support. Thanks to the vital support of "I need it today" Mandy Phillips; and my sincere gratitude for Stephen Driver's guidance and Christianne Thillen's smooth, focused, and oh-so-knowledgeable editing. The responsiveness and enthusiasm of Nancy Rothschild, Tracy Miracle, and Rick Rinehart of the Rowman & Littlefield Publishing Group continues, and Piper Furbush was a dream to work with. As a city gardener and artist, Paula Brinkman has created illustrations that capture both spirit and meaning. And, as a friend, I am so pleased and proud to have collaborated with her!

Heartfelt thanks to my brother, David Joseph Hobens Jr., and to dear friends, fellow gardeners, and all who have inspired, helped, and improved the earth while on it: Elke Fears, Aaron Fears, Jo Ann Macy, Diana Carulli, Alice Peterson, Fran Ellison, Pat Berger, Mallory Abramson, John Carney, Phil Tietz, Neil Schettler, Adam Honigman, Allegra Benveniste Honigman, Anne Hart, Fritz Mayer, J. P. Hughes, Mackenzie Hughes, the past and future Unsung Heroes of the Clinton Community Garden Steering Committee, Jean-Daniel Noland, Annie Chadwick, Faser Hardin, Jane Greenlaw, John Sheridan, Bruce Coleman, Debbie Mullins, Howard Maloney, Molly Padian, Andy Padian, Nancy Severance, Steve Roylance, Gerard Lordahl, Lenny Librizzi, John Doswell, Jean Preece, Guy Sliker, Mike Davis, Kathleen Garman, Betsy Wagner, Cynthia Hopkins, Wendy Casey, Robin Richardson-Clark, Friends of Pier 84, Fran Reiter, Rudy Giuliani, Connie Fishman, William Diamond, Noreen Doyle, Mike

Bradley, Mary Ann Monte, Marc Boddewyn, Lee White, Al Juba, John Williams, Ruth T. Kuhlmann, Jose Reyes, Signe Nielsen, R. D. Chin, Mark Davidoff, Joe Panetta, Chris Calhoon, Craig Tufts, Andy Stone, Carol Rinzler, Perry Luntz, Garrit Stryker, Jeff Hobbs, Anthony Vargas, Murphy Oshodi, Anthony Borelli, Wigens Lindor from Sitecraft planters, Jeff Sandberg and Victoria's Nursery crew (Jaime, Vicky, Kate, Victor, & John), David Protell's Chelsea Garden Center, The 461 Garden Club, "Compost King" Bill Galarno, David Schneider, Rev. Edmund Storer Janes, Rudi Paperi, Chuck Spence, Kevin Corbett, Lenore Rule, Gloria Rosen, Jim Seffens, Richard Kussmaul, Bill Huxley a.k.a. Tree Spirit, Skip Blumberg, Chris Laney, Cathy Drew, Diana Kline, Sandra Allen, J. A. and Geri Reynolds, L. Brandon Krall, J. Savona Bailey-McClain, Katherine Powis, Larry Ashmead, John Storey, Paul James, Adrian Benepe, Liam Kavanaugh, Bill Castro, Henry Stern, Margaret Asaro Peeler, John Mazza, Mary Price, Namshik Yoon, Jenny Hoffner, David Rivel, Dana Litvack Molina, Charlotte Kaiser, Anne LaFond, Bob Redmond, Michael Lytle, Bill Steyer, Christian Paro, Dawnette Roach, Tony Killeen, Arnold Williams, Mike Meli, Joe Bernardo, Chase and 411 volunteers, Danny Thompson, Midtown Precinct North, all MBG volunteers, Tom Duane, Christine Quinn, Dick Gottfried, Scott Stringer, Franz Leichter, Mike Bloomberg, Gerald Schoenfeld, Lee Silver, Heidi Endo, Tim Tompkins, Michele Vierno Ciganek, Ralph Vierno, Mary Jane Taylor Fellows, and to my home, Manhattan.

On September 11, 2001, after my husband, Fred, and I with disbelieving eyes watched the collapse of the World Trade Center towers, we joined thousands of New Yorkers in the need to be outside and to be together with others. Our parks and community gardens offered solace.

A month later, volunteers joined in the largest citywide planting project ever. Thanks to the friendship of public garden designer Lynden B. Miller, cochair of New Yorkers for Parks, with Hans van Waardenburg of B&K Flowerbulbs, over a million yellow daffodil bulbs were donated to the people of New York City by his company along with the Port of Rotterdam, in the Netherlands. Miller knew that New Yorkers needed something to do to unite and renew their spirit. She was right and thousands are thankful to her.

What an incredible gift to release stress, give purpose, work out grief, and plant a recurring living tribute to those who died. Each fall, 500,000 yellow daffodil bulbs are donated by B&K Flowerbulbs to the City of New York. There will never be a shortage of volunteers to plant these bulbs; we will never forget.

Because of The Daffodil Project, hundreds of gardens and parks pay homage to the memory of all those who simply went to work that morning and all the heroes who died trying to save them.

No matter where you garden, The Daffodil Project, cofounded by Lynden B. Miller and Parks & Recreation Commissioner Adrian Benepe, is an extraordinary example of camaraderie, meaning, comfort, and lasting joy that gardening brings. Learn more about park advocacy at www.ny4p.org. Your personal gardening efforts will produce not only flowers and vegetables, but peace and a deep personal appreciation of the beauty in the world around you.

introduction

Adrian Benepe, Commissioner of Parks and Recreation, City of New York

This book is a tool for everyone who cares about the health of his or her city. It is a gardening bible that smoothly organizes an impressive variety of approaches, resources, and insights. And it is the cumulative field notes (along with well-drawn conclusions) of a woman with decades of in-the-field volunteer work and environmental activism in New York City.

For as long as I've known her, Barbara Feldt has worked to get New Yorkers involved in greening the city. I first met Barbara when I was appointed the Manhattan Borough Parks Commissioner by my predecessor, Henry J. Stern. At that time, Barbara was volunteering as the park warden of Manhattan's Clinton Community Garden, a remarkable space that holds the unique distinction of being the first community garden to become remapped as parkland in New York. As a park warden of Clinton Community Garden (and Ramon Aponte Park before that), Barbara served as an invaluable link between her com-munity and the Parks Department by orchestrating ideas, resources, and community support. Thanks to Barbara and her fellow neighbors, the Clinton Community Garden has blossomed into a beautiful space featuring 108 individual garden plots and a park area including an extensive herb garden, tended lawn, flower beds, and over a hundred species of native trees, shrubs, and plants viewed by walking the serpentine path.

The Clinton Community Garden is also very special because it is one of forty-four Manhattan Botanical Garden satellite gardens. Realizing Manhattan's need for a botanical garden of its own, Barbara and other green thumbs collectively worked to secure space at various sites around the city for the planting of native plants and flowers. When the original botanical garden's home—Pier 84—was to be demolished, Barbara came to the Parks Department for help. We were happy to offer her an area of DeWitt Clinton Park for relocating the orphaned plants. The garden we created—nicknamed Maria's Perennial Garden (after Dewitt Clinton's first wife)—is one of several Parks properties established as a Manhattan Botanical Garden satellite while I served as borough commissioner.

Barbara's efforts have always complemented our goals at Parks. Through initiatives such as Partnerships for Parks, the Parks Department has sought to build strong relationships with residents in order to improve neighborhood parks. Barbara sets a model for citizen involvement. For years she has actively taken on great responsibilities and inspired others to follow her example. Barbara's right on the money in *Garden Your City* when she declares that the "surest way of reclaiming a park is using it." Following such plain and simple logic, her labors have helped reshape our city's greenscape. Our parks are lucky to have Barbara as a friend.

Around the world, every city faces the same crisis of struggling to protect its natural areas and living, green infrastructure from being lost forever. Public-private partnerships have thus become essential to keeping our cities verdant and alive. The growing number of volunteers who work in our parks each year makes me confident that together we will ultimately find ways to protect our cities and our planet.

The book you are holding in your hands is a small treasure. To establish its value, however, you must work to turn Barbara's words into action. I hope her enthusiasm and level-headed reasoning will inspire you to go outside and get your hands dirty, whether in your own garden or in the public gardens of your neighborhood. With this invaluable resource—along with a few tools and some elbow grease—you'll soon be greening your city's urban backyard.

Adrian Benepe
Commissioner
City of New York, Parks & Recreation

part one

Why Garden Your City?

I freeze. Passing beneath the rose arbor in full bloom, I see a yellow finch sipping water, then flipping it up onto its back from the spoon-shaped rock in the middle of the waterfall. I wait for the bird to finish and then wander through the whole garden, critically assessing the progress of each plant, seedling, shrub, and tree.

I peer behind the large planter bursting with bleeding hearts and primroses to see if one of the bronze frogs from last night's duet is still around. No such luck. Since they are usually in or under our planters, I make a mental note to find an unused terra-cotta pot to convert into a snug haven. Having seen toad houses, I think, "why not one for our frogs?" I feed four (hungry!) active koi and other pond fish, fill the bird feeder, water the garden, and pick some herbs for omelets.

This idyllic 1,175-square-foot garden grows behind a six-story cooperative apartment just three blocks west of Times Square in Manhattan.

City gardening can be challenging and, at times, downright frustrating. But, that's why it is incredibly rewarding. The spring after "marrying into Manhattan," I caught the gardening bug when I noticed window

boxes flowing with geraniums and fire escapes brimming with greenery nearby. Our fourth-floor walk-up apartment had a southern-exposure fire escape that soon held sun-loving tomato and pepper plants growing in coffee cans.

Referred to as "the last real neighborhood in Manhattan," this socioeconomically eclectic, ethnically diverse community known as both Hell's Kitchen and Clinton is a neighborhood that ranks as one of the most lacking in open space and parks in all of New York City's five boroughs.

Since 1989 I have gardened as a volunteer and as a paid gardener in conditions and sites as diverse as spectacular Park Avenue penthouses, West 40's street tree "pits," a public pier on the Hudson River, behind elegant brownstones, at entrances and courtyards of massive apartment buildings, and on alley walls.

Having a yard, no matter how small it may be, is not common for most would-be city gardeners. But it is true, as you will see, that if you want to grow flowers and even exotic vegetables you certainly can, even though you live on the sixteenth floor of an apartment building!

GARDENING YOUR CITY— THE BASICS

The "who, what, when, and why" of city gardening are covered right here in Part One. Part Two covers the "how." The obvious, the overlooked, and the underutilized places to grow—the "where" to garden in your city—are covered in Part Three. Photographs and illustrations will give you a sense of "Okay, I can do this, too" and show real examples to spark ideas.

Your interest in gardening led you to this book—or you have a great friend or relative who was thinking in your best interest. City gardeners face many obstacles. Since it is not often easy to secure places to plant, you'd think that growing things would be a breeze. But, that is just not the case. We have buildings that shade dear little patches to set containers on, strange microclimates we will discuss later, and weird wind tunnels that play havoc with our plants. But don't be discouraged.

Although magazine racks, bookstores, and libraries abound with gardening titles, the realities peculiar to city dwellers are rarely addressed. In Part Two, "The Elements of Success," chapters will inform and help you feel confident in creating successful gardening experiences for many seasons to come.

Like every avocation, field, or part-time hobby, gardening is as simple or as complex as you want it to become. The enthusiasm, time, and amount of money you contribute (or get donated or raise) all play a vital role in the success of your garden.

Who's the "who" in city gardening? You are. Maybe you live in an urban area and would love to plant, but feel you don't have anywhere to grow; or perhaps you're already gardening and have that irrepressible urge to expand. Would you love to add organic herbs to recipes? Do you imagine a rosebush for your local park fence, or do childhood memories of the scent of lilacs draw you to garden?

Since you are reading this, I assume that either you were born in, transferred to, married into, or simply moved yourself into your city home. If you have never grown a thing, and maybe a houseplant or two hasn't made it under your care, this is the right book for you. If you're a transplanted gardener who once enjoyed a spacious yard, or you have rented or purchased an apartment that has a terrace, backyard, or accessible roof and have decided to tackle the ultimate ever-changing decorating challenge—gardening—then you are also in the right place!

The "who" of city gardening can quickly grow from your individual efforts; soon it may include your spouse or significant other, children, friends, and neighbors. Gardening is contagious and guaranteed to have a magnetic effect. Enthusiasm and example draw others in. A little bit of organizational effort can involve fellow residents (building planters in the backyard), people living next door (matching window boxes), block or neighborhood associations (street tree gardening), and even your entire community (gardening in your local park, on school property, or converting a vacant lot into a community garden). No matter where or how simple, the act of growing plants results in the admiration of neighbors and passersby.

What you decide to grow is determined primarily by the particular needs of the plants themselves; will that species you have always admired grow in your partial sunny conditions or your city's climate/temperature zone?

If you always wanted to grow dramatic white alliums, but the catalog states they're only for full sun, try them anyway in your partial sunny area. Mother Nature has a strange way of being the ultimate decision maker. The rosebush you've been eyeing on the Internet may be 4 feet high and filled with blooms in full sun, but in your container, it may stretch 6 feet before it ultimately gives you only four perfect blooms.

Plant tag or stake information is provided with your plant purchase for a good reason. Depending on many growing factors, you can often grow that plant you adore. Many flowers and vegetables have numerous varieties and dwarf selections. For example, miniature sunflowers thrive in window boxes where giant varieties would collapse.

The "when" of physical gardening varies with your city's weather. But you'll also learn about extending the "when" to garden by tricking Mother Nature with raised beds or greenhouses, and by starting seeds indoors to get a jump on planting times.

The mental aspects of gardening never cease, but the brunt of physical work will be preparing your soil for the seeds and plants to come. The process of deciding which plants to add and reworking your design seems endless; but during times of dormant plant growth, you can sit back and assess your garden (hooray for the winter break to peruse catalogs!).

PSYCHOLOGICAL INSPIRATION

Why do we put our energy and time into anything? Often it's a "have to" or someone else's "should do" that motivates and dictates our energies. Even an inner-voice "supposed to" can drive us, usually via guilt, to action. These reasons can compel us; but they can also tax and drain our self-determination, mental and physical well-being, and our very being.

"Want to's" are totally different. When we enjoy what we're doing, we get wrapped up in total pleasure. Time and the world seem to melt away, and we feel satisfied. I'm not speaking about lovemaking, but about gardening, though the metaphor works for both.

City gardening involves work, painstaking strategy to overcome challenges, and considerable dedication. Yet, despite it all, it's still a "want to" activity.

Why is this? Maybe city gardeners just enjoy defying the odds. Or, maybe it's because gardens are somehow not "supposed" to be there—squeezed amongst all the brick, steel, and concrete. Since any space to garden is rare, it is cherished. Seeing flowers growing in the midst of the hustle and bustle is part of why we do it.

Adding beautiful flowers and growing vegetables where the public can watch them grow improves the quality of life for everyone. Gardens secluded behind buildings or on rooftops are very fulfilling, but seeing and hearing people react to the beauty and surprise of plantings in a window box, on a stoop, or in a tree bed gives the most satisfaction.

What a difference it would make for our cities if every resident decided to spend a little quality time on just one street tree bed! Just watering the bed would help it flourish, and cleaning and cultivating would really help, but adding flowers would make an astounding difference. The positive remarks you hear while watering and deadheading offer a rare feeling of accomplishment as people share a common bond—an appreciation of nature and transformation of the streetscape.

Attend flower shows and workshops, visit botanical and private gardens, and watch television gardening shows. Pick up a fancy garden design magazine, check the gardening sections in the bookstore, and look up a plant online or in the library.

Since you have limited gardening space, observe as much as you can to incorporate the absolute best. That towering hedge took your breath away, and now boxwoods frame your largest planter. Look for ideas to adapt to your space. To enhance or alter your design, add new plant varieties, and interesting combinations of color, shapes, and texture.

Once you start city gardening, it's a continual learning process that motivates you to plan for improvement, gauge future events based on the growing seasons, revel in the beauty you helped create, and talk about plants. It compels you to take more than a glance when walking past "good" garbage at the curb, your eye instinctively scouting for trellis possibilities.

There's truly a special bond connecting urban "plant people" who nurture growing things in demanding places. Overheard snippets of gardening conversation out in public can trigger an immediate bond between strangers as they freely share the best places for soil and perennials, chat about the size and sweetness of their tomatoes, and voice their concerns about the weather forecast.

Yes, you certainly can garden in your city. Finding a space and expanding your horticultural horizons is the key.

This book has been written with an "if I can do it, you certainly can" philosophy. You don't have to know the botanical name of a plant to grow it; you don't have to be an expert to garden. My gardening knowledge is based on the best teachers of all—desire, experience, mistakes, and success.

Continual learning, persistent attentiveness, and intense appreciation are the pleasurable "burdens" of gardening. When you love what you do, it is truly a pleasure. That is how my adopted city has affected my life and my love of gardening.

I couldn't find seat-of-the-pants answers to my city gardening questions. Tired of fruitless hours in the library and sick of hearing "someone should write a book" at seminars and workshops on community gardening, I decided to share my experiences, practical knowledge, and discoveries as a city gardener. I am confident that in gardening your city, you will get back much more than you will sow. Enjoy.

One touch of nature makes the whole world kin.
—William Shakespeare

part two

The Elements of Success

I

discovering your gardening spaces

Whether you live in a city of millions or a few thousand, an abundance of gardening opportunities are available. Your places to garden may literally be right outside your door.

YES, I HAVE MY OWN SPACE!

Congratulations! It is a rare apartment in any city that is blessed with a space of its own or one you can share with fellow residents! This could mean a windowsill, a fire escape, a balcony or terrace, or even luckier, your own backyard or roof. Does your apartment building share a "common garden" with neighboring backyards? Whether you searched for a new apartment because

of these features, or just found out that you happen to have gardening access, you are well on the way to growing.

Start at the beginning and take a total inventory of immediate gardening possibilities. Look out of every window of your apartment. What's out there? Are you blessed with a wide, roomy windowsill without a slant? A planter or a few terra-cotta pots, weighed down with at least two layers of rock, would certainly work.

APARTMENT FOR RENT
Common Garden
See Super in Apt. 1B

Open every window and look around. See any places a pot could possibly sit on? How about affixing a wrought iron flowerpot holder onto the wall on one, or both, sides of your window? What is the view from your favorite chair? Is there another building close by, or is a street tree in your view?

As you look out all of your windows, think about where you could possibly see plants growing. Of course, you must be able to tend them! But, you do not necessarily have to be able to reach them all the time. Our superintendent placed three sturdy plastic window boxes high up on a shelf he built on a northern wall. He chose plants that do not need pinching or deadheading, such as large periwinkle (*Vinca major*, 'Variegata'), with medium-green leaves edged in white with long-trailing runners; blue lobelia (*erinus*), which is compact yet trails over the box's edge with intense flowers; and leafy begonias (*Semperflorens cultorum*) in pink, white, and red. After adding a light layer of mulch to conserve water and deter weeds, he watered the plants with a variable-powered nozzle on the hose to properly reach them.

Where do you begin figuring out what to do with your growing space? Observe it. What kind of light do you have? Where is your water source? Is the space being viewed from just one side? What colors please you? Do you want to achieve a casual or formal look?

CITY GARDENERS ARE KINDRED SPIRITS

Your city is unique, yet it shares common influences that affect gardening efforts—regulations that determine weight limits of planters on roofs and open spaces, gardening supply availability, the challenge of multiple planting zones, and wind conditions caused by man-made structures. We city gardeners face many common obstacles, such as intense heat and wind on roofs, car and bus fumes, lead in vegetable garden soil, and dog owners who allow their pets to stroll in street tree gardens.

Odds are, no matter where you live, your city also has distinct gardening customs. Some may be based on historical or cultural experience. Some are dictated by sheer habit, or by the plants, shrubs, or trees that are native to your region. As you become more attuned to seeking out gardens and plantings, you will certainly be inspired with new ideas on how and what to grow.

I HAVE NO PLACE TO GARDEN!

No place to garden? Ridiculous! Of course you have; you just haven't found them yet! So, your apartment offers you no place whatsoever to garden, and the superintendent has totally nixed any thought of even one pot on the fire escape or a window box hanging over the sidewalk. Now what?

The first step is to go outside your front door and cross the street and really look at your building. Do you see any common or open space? Would containers on either side of the entrance door work? Does there appear to be space to add a brick planter to the front of the whole building? Do you have any street trees in front of your property? Is there room to add protective iron tree guards or a layer of brick or stone to plant flowers and safeguard your trees? Is there a garbage can enclosure that could hold a container for vines? How about securing hanging baskets to the fire escape or installing hanging brackets at one or both sides of the entrance door?

Now, look outside any back windows of your building and look down, and then go downstairs to the basement. Any space out there?

Finding Your Place to Grow

There are plenty of places to garden in your city if you keep your mind open to ideas before balking at viable possibilities. You may already be aware of local parks or a vacant lot in your community, but never thought of being able to garden there.

Proximity to where you live is a significant factor. The sure way not to miss discovering potential gardening space in your neighborhood is to comb it thoroughly. After I had lived in Manhattan for almost two years, sheer chance brought me past a thriving community garden just one block north and west of our first apartment!

When you are attempting to garden on anyone's property or on public land, there are two things to keep in mind: (1) You catch more flies with honey; and (2) it's not your property. Both may seem obvious, but to folk who have lovingly tended someone else's land for a decade or more, it's very hard to face an eviction notice.

Spread the Word

Whether you just moved in or have lived in the same apartment for twenty-five years, you should ask around. Your next-door neighbor or people you talk with down the block might know of a great opportunity or literally see something out their window. Spreading the word can help you get exactly what you want.

When a fellow community gardener "networked" his desire for more gardening space, he heard that someone across the street from his building had a huge (for Manhattan) untended yard outside of his rear apartment. He asked around for the man's name, called him up, and within four months he had transformed the garbage-strewn yard into a lovely garden. The gardener was given keys to the building and the back door after obtaining the landlord's permission. The renter of the rear apartment, who had no interest in physically gardening, was thrilled to be able to sit and read in his transformed yard. And, he even purchased a bird feeder! This arrangement suited both parties perfectly.

One neighbor's landlord flatly refused to allow her to put planters on the roof, but the adjoining roof contained a full garden. She buzzed one of the apartments to inquire about the gardener. They met. Soon after, just by stepping over the small raised wall between the rooftops, she was happily tending three of her own planters.

Securing Your Space to Grow

It doesn't matter if your garden is one window box, a wrap-around terrace, a street tree bed, or a penthouse; there are basic factors that will determine success for all of them. Wouldn't a few planters look great up on that wall in your garden? Sure, but do you own the wall? The first and foremost consideration to creating a garden is having the property owner's permission. No matter who owns the land and/or building—landlord, co-op, or condominium board; the city or state—the process is basically the same.

Make sure you are dealing with the actual legal owner of the property by checking your city's records or building department website online or in person. Verbal approval from your superintendent does not count. Try to arrange for a meeting, since negotiations are best handled in person and you can answer questions and counter any objections immediately. Have a written proposal of your garden design, and provide a sketch to make your ideas clear.

Gardens Entice!

Stress the benefits when meeting with the property owner. Having an attractive garden space adds increased value to a property. Creating a garden on your terrace or in a common area such as a courtyard, backyard, or roof, can easily add 15–20 percent to the selling price. Shareholders of a cooperative and condominium owners enjoy both the garden and the increased sales price.

But the dollar value isn't the prime consequence for residents; there is an improved quality of life for all who participate and/or enjoy the efforts and rewards of gardening. The very essence of public gardening is that your efforts will be admired and appreciated by people passing through as well as by residents on your block.

Responsibility

Whether you're meeting the owner face-to-face or through the mail, a common concern for any landlord will be liability issues. You can point out a similar project in the neighborhood or make a sketch for the owner to get a clear idea of your project. Most gardening efforts on residential property would already be covered by the building's insurance policy (i.e., tripping on a stair or the guard around a tree bed), but your project must include safety precautions.

Once you have the owner's blessing, ask if he or she could donate supplies or funds to purchase some plants. It never hurts to ask, and the owner's generosity may surprise you.

The only exception to gaining formal permission is planting seeds along the edges of fenced-in or open vacant lots. Keep in mind that your efforts can last for years or be destroyed at any moment. One caring neighborhood gardener, Paula, took time to plant morning glory and wildflower seeds along the fences of vacant lots each spring. The flowers offered stunning displays for years; her simple, admirable effort transformed eyesores.

EVALUATING YOUR SITE

Once you have secured permission, the next step is ensuring a reliable water source. Unless you are planting very hardy and drought-resistant plants, you and your plants will not be happy unless you have water nearby. Memories of hauling water down four flights of steps to save newly planted street tree flowers in a heat wave still haunt me.

When you're creating either a window box or roof garden, it is more than worth your time—if not crucial to success—to have a plan. Literally getting it down on paper is vital, and your initial design will be an indispensable practical tool for adding future plantings.

Armed with permission and secure with your access to water, your next concern is knowing your soil and preparing it for seeds and plants. Now it is time to look up to the sky. Sounds simple, but knowing how long your particular site actually receives direct and indirect sunlight is critical. If you literally monitor the progression of sunlight during your growing season, you will be far ahead of the game and prevent many costly mistakes. That scrawny scented geranium you planted would thrive if you would transplant it just three feet west to catch that extra hour of sun!

Spend the time during your growing season to watch when the sun shines in your garden. Listen to the weather forecast and pick two or three days forecasting sunny skies. The influence of sunlight and knowledge of prevailing winds and microclimates will have a major impact on gardening success.

How much time are you prepared to give your garden? If you are away on business or vacation, you will need to make arrangements for watering and maintenance. A garden takes commitment.

Once these basics are in place, the fun (yet sometimes equally agonizing) part begins—deciding what you're going to grow! The choices and decisions are vast: What kinds and colors? Do you choose seeds or get the plant? How many plants will fit in that planter? Which perennials bloom in August? Which vegetable variety will produce the highest yield? Where do you buy these plants? Keep reading to determine what is best suited for your garden.

Where are you going to store your gardening stuff? Although a section below your kitchen sink may suffice for your basics, if your garden space is growing, so will your need for storage. A place for a half-used bag of potting soil, trowel, and watering can isn't a problem; but add a pruner, cultivator, mulch, fish emulsion bottle, pots your plants outgrew but you can't throw away, shovel, and spade, and you have a predicament.

Since many city apartments are closet-space challenged, you have to be creative to find places that are easy to get to—yet not in the way. A cleaning bucket fits perfectly on the hall closet floor, and hand tools can tuck inside a canvas tote bag hanging on a hook behind the door. Maybe you can find space in your building's basement, or even outside in a watertight container or a plastic garbage can with fitted lid.

With all of these factors in mind, you're now set to garden.

Spend a day tending a garden—
experience real freedom.
Allow the soil to trickle between your fingers.
Feel life.
At the end of the day
stand back, smile,
and reap the rewards of tomorrow.
—Dorothy Sampson, rose gardener,
Watts Senior Citizen Center, Los Angeles

2

Your Garden's Sun, Zone, Wind, & Microclimates

Understanding the impact of nature around you is the key to being a successful gardener. Spending time in the space where you expect your seeds to grow and plants to thrive is the best way to discover your environment. What are your plants facing year-round?

Know your sun. After securing a reliable water source, knowing how much sun will actually reach your plants is your next major consideration.

Seeing exactly where the sun directly shines and for what length of time will save you unnecessary angst and failure. Many gardeners blame the store where they purchased plants, the soil, and even the weather when their plants don't thrive. Placing plants in the wrong amount of sunlight is often the reason.

Go out there and watch your backyard or sill. You may think your space is in shade most of the time; but you might see that around three o'clock, direct sun enters as it passes through the break in the two buildings across the street.

The sun we experience in our city gardens is very tricky. Though some roof gardens enjoy complete full sun, many roof gardeners have to deal with variations of direct and reflected sun and shade from their own building's structures and taller buildings.

Often, light bounces off windows of a building behind us, a tree in a neighbor's backyard creates dappled sunlight, and light reflects from a wall or two.

Placement of containers within your garden space is an important determination. If you want to grow sun-loving perennials or have an early show of crocus bulbs, plant them in sunnier spots. A planter or windowsill box facing north receives less light, and the soil will stay cooler. With the many shade and partial-shade choices available, you can have a bountiful garden!

HOW BRIGHT IS YOUR SHADE?

So, you tell friends that you have a shade garden. Are you sure? It is amazing how diverse the lighting can be in a shade garden. It sounds odd, but even roses and daffodils (which are known to be sun lovers) can thrive. Even rose catalogs indicate that certain varieties can be grown in partial shade.

Create Your Shade

Cast meaningful shadows. Plant some taller plants to create the shade for you to grow some favorite shade lovers underneath. Lily of the valley multiplies under a dogwood tree, and rings of primrose bloom profusely under forsythia.

Shady Ideas

In the suburbs, the most common plant choice for shade appears to be pachysandra, but hosta reigns in the city. A striking combination would include multicolored primrose and hosta; once the primrose flowers fade, the hosta leaves begin to unfold and will later send up long spikes of lavender-and-white flowers.

Joining these (literally) perennial favorites are astilbes. Red, white, coral, and pink plumes liven up the darkest shade gardens, and long before and after the colors fade, the astilbe offers delicate, full foliage.

Turn on the light in your shady area or entire garden by planting white and silver plants. Many plants that prefer shade have variegated varieties that offer splashes of white and yellow. Send away for catalogues special-izing in hosta and you will be amazed at the dramatic combinations. Some varieties are truly blue, or gold, and offer combinations that will add spark to your garden.

Colorful arrow- or elephant-ear-shaped caladiums are dramatic additions to any garden. In northern climates, you have to dig up the tubers in the fall and store them in a dry place for the winter months.

Partial Isn't Partisan

Plants need differing amounts of sunlight to exist. Learn from plant labels, knowledgeable personnel, and book or catalog descriptions how much sun your plants require to reach their fullest potential.

You may have marked up a catalog or two and found that some of your favorites include plants needing full sun, partial sun, partial shade, and shade. Yes, it is quite confusing. The interesting reality is that partial-sun plants can be grown right next to partial-shade plants. Hundreds of varieties of so many commonly grown plants are available—if not at the nearest garden shop, certainly through catalogs—to suit any spot in your garden.

Working within your zone, take some chances with "variable survivors" and plant a few "some sun" plants in your "bright shade" spots. Remember, plants aren't glued in; if you find the plant looks a bit stressed even though you have watered properly, then by all means, move it!

great to grow in your city's zone

Look around to see what bulbs, plants, shrubs and trees are flourishing. Odds are that they're ideal for the climate range of your city. Here are some "tried and true" selections for your planting zone. Most grow beautifully in zones nearest yours; look for new varieties and hardy choices in local nurseries, catalogs, and the Internet.

S = Sun; SH = Shade; PS = Partial Shade; B = bulb; H = herb

Zone	Perennials	Annuals
1	Pennsylvania Cinquefoil (*Potentialla pensylvanica*) S English Daisy (*Bellis perennis*) S Island Poppy (*Papaver nudicaule*) S	Pot Marigold (*Calendula officinalis*) S Lobelia (*Lobelia erinus*) SH-PS Snapdragon (*Antirrhinum majus*) S-PS
2	Squill (*Scilla*) S-PS, B American Cranberry Bush (*Viburnum trilobum*) S-PS Bellflower (*Campanula glomerata*) S	Jasmine Tobacco Flower (*Nicotiana alata*) S-PS Geranium (*Pelargonium*) S-PS Sage (*Salvia officinalis 'Berggarten'*) S, H
3	Common Snowdrop (*Galanthus nivalia*) S-SH, B Guacomole Hosta (*Hosta*) SH Columbines (*Aquilegia canadensis 'Corbett'*)	Sweet Potato Vine (*Ipomoea batatas 'Margarita'*) S-PS Rosemary (*Rosmarinus officinalis*) S, H Lantana (*Lantana montevidensis 'Lavender Swirl'*) S
4	Bluebell (*Hyacinthoides*) B, S-SH Tickseed (*Coreopsis verticillata 'Moonbeam'*) S	Nasturtiums (*Tropaeolum*) S Stock (*Matthiola incana*) S Sweet Basil (*Ocimum basilicum*) S, H
5	Tulips (*Tulipa*) S, B Phlox 'David' (*Phlox*) S Clematis (*Clemats 'Nelly Moser'*) S-PS	Petunia 'Wave' (*Petunia x hybrid*) S Lemon Thyme (*Thymus citriodorus*) S, H Bacopa 'Giant Snowflake' (*Sutera hydrid*) S
6	Daffodils (*Narcissus*) S-PS, B Stonecrop (*Sedum spectabile 'Autumn Joy'*) S Lavender (*Lavandula angustifolia*) S, H	Busy Lizzie (*Impatiens*) SH-PS Pineapple Sage (*Salvia elegans*) S, H Lemon Rose Geranium (*Pelargonium*) S, H

7	Lilies (Lilium) S-PS, B	Zinnia (Zinnia elegans) S
	Siberian Iris (Iris sibirica), S, PS, B	Dusty Miller (Senecio cineraria) S-PS
	Sweet Woodruff (Galium odoratum) S-SH	Wax Begonia (Begonia semperflorens) S-SH
8	Windflower (Amemone) B, S-PS	Pinks (Dianthus chinensis) S
	Japanese Painted Fern (Athyrium niponicu) PS-SH	Lemon Verbena (Aloysia triphylla) S, H
	Coral Honeysuckle (Lonicera sempervirens) S-PS	Coleus (Coleus blumei) PS-S
9	Trout Lily (Erythronium) B, PS	Greek Oregano (Origanum vulgare hirtum) S, H
	Passion Flower (Passiflora incarnate) PS-S	Sweet Alyssum (Lobularia maritime) S
	Calla Lily (Zantedeschia aethiopica) S-SH	Yellow Cosmos (C. sulphureus) S
10	Bougainvillea (Bougainvillea spectabilis) S	Black-eyed Susan (Rudbeckia hirta) S
	Royal palm (Roystonea regia) S	Ivy-leaf Geranium (Pelargonium peltatum) S
	Gardenia (Jasminoides 'August Beauty') S-PS	Baby's Breath (Gypsophila Muralis) S
11	Flamingo Flower (Anthurium) PS-SH	Larkspur (Consolida Orientalis) S-PS
	Lemon Grass (Cymbopogon citratus) S-PS	Rose Moss (Portulaca oleracea) S
		Ornamental Pepper (Capsicum annuum) S

general planting zones

Austin	8	Fort Worth	8	Oklahoma City	7
Baltimore	7	Houston	9	Philadelphia	6
Boston	6	Indianapolis	5	Phoenix	9
Chicago	5	Jacksonville	9	Portland	8
Cleveland	6	Los Angeles	10	San Antonio	8
Columbus	5	Milwaukee	5	San Diego	11
Dallas	7	Memphis	7	San Francisco	9
Denver	5	Nashville	6	San Jose	9
Detroit	5	New Orleans	9	Seattle	8
El Paso	7	New York	6	Washington, DC	7

YOUR OWN ZONE

Plant hardiness maps, climate maps, and temperature zones are tried-and-true guides to aid you in plant selection. They should be consulted, but should not determine what to grow.

Common sense tells you that palm trees will not survive a winter in Columbus, Ohio. Plant hardiness zone maps consider more than just the air temperature; they also take into account a plant's ability to survive frozen soils without root damage as well as its ability to survive the heat of an early spring.

Look up your city on these maps. Almost every seed, bulb, and plant catalog includes a zone map, since they don't want people to order things that won't survive. Some catalogs even include your planting zone next to your mailing label!

Crossing Zones

Zone maps are guides. If you are near a zone "borderline," you should be growing your favorites from the neighboring zone. Although Miami lies in zone 10, gardeners there grow plants recommended for zone 9 and cross their fingers and plant "higher" to zone 11.

Zones are odd; plants intended for zone 10 grow in the protected entrance yard of a brick apartment building located in zone 9, and zone 11 plants cover the roof deck. Experimentation pays off.

WEATHERING WIND

Before you place a planter or squeeze and tap a plant out of its container, give thought to the wind. If you never gave it a thought, there probably isn't a problem. Due to haphazard construction decisions, some city streets are true wind tunnels. You can be walking along and then take a left and find yourself fighting through the air! Think what these gusts could do to your plants on a consistent basis.

Slow It Down!

If you have identified a steady northern wind as part of your garden's environment, you need to protect your venture; plants are often both a financial and emotional investment.

It may be as simple as moving a few containers a few feet out of the way or securing a piece of plexiglass to the back of a planter for a windbreak. Trellis work and fencing also aid in dispersing wind flow. A good idea and great excuse to buy more plants is to plant a row of evergreens as a shield.

Added Elements

Unless you have a 16-pane, 20-foot custom greenhouse attached to your building, welcome to the reality of weather. Torrential rain, snow (Mother Nature's mulch), and hail happen. Other than trying to cover some plants up or frantically move some containers to a safer place, all that we gardeners can do is hold our breath and pray when ice storms, tornadoes, or floods are forecasted.

MICROMANAGING MICROCLIMATES

Something is happening, and you don't quite know why. You planted the same variety of crocus bulbs in four different places, but the ones over there are in full bloom and the others haven't even broken through the soil. What's going on here?

It's a microclimate. For an assortment of reasons, the soil heated up quicker in one spot. Something affected that area differently and altered the amount of heat or sunlight. It could be intense sunlight, shadows, soil depth, drainage, or a wind tunnel.

Spring bulbs are protected if planted in pockets of soil near exposed rocks, because the sun heats up the bulbs long before warming the open sections of soil. The earliest bulbs are likely to emerge from a spot with the most sun, in well-drained soil, and away from strong winds. With city gardening, the increase of soil temperature may not be "natural" but created by heat reflecting off or coming from a surrounding building. The sun heats up brick, stone, and concrete planters and radiates the heat back during the night.

Knowing the path of the sun and the length of time it stays in your planting area is crucial for planning what to grow. Since the sun is at its highest point in the sky on June 21st, the summer solstice, it is the ideal date to observe where the sun actually shines in your garden. Pick a clear, cloudless day near this time to record the most accurate hours of sunlight.

Once you have figured out your mystery areas, you can take advantage of this interesting phenomenon. Plant tomatoes earlier, grow a plant in the next highest planting zone, or just enjoy a longer show of your favorite spring flowers. Try the same variety of plant in different areas of your garden and see for yourself.

CHANGE YOUR CLIMATE

Many parts of a backyard, roof, or community garden can have different ecosystems, or you can create your own to take advantage of elevated or reduced temperatures. It just takes a few degrees difference to change the way plants perform.

A damp, shady corner may be the perfect spot to place a water feature such as a birdbath and to grow shade-loving marsh plants. Add stonework to heat up the soil, create a south-facing slope, and make use of walls that face south by planting against them to encourage earlier blooms. Cooler spots can make blooms and fragrant flowers last a week or more longer than the same plants growing in warmer areas.

TIME WELL SPENT

Spending time in your garden, rain and shine, is the best investment you can make to understand its unique environment. Experience what your plants are tolerating out there. Know exactly where the sun shines, and if there are any odd wind or rain patterns.

Do you see anything that would improve your space or help to create a special, beautiful retreat? A wind chime is just a decorative object until you move it to the corner of your building to catch the breeze. And, if not for an early morning observation of a stream of sunlight into a mostly shady garden, you might never plant that tub of morning glories.

When near hurricane-force winds head in, I use natural hemp, tall bamboo stakes, and bungie cords to secure my rubber and lemon trees to the ironwork balcony. I just take them off the bicycle rack and put them to work. The elasticity is a lot less stressful on the plant and you can link them together.
—Linn Tyrrell Champagne, balcony gardener,
New Orleans, Louisiana

3

plan—then plan again

Have you ever heard someone say this? "I garden by pure instinct." Rubbish. Accomplished gardeners plan. If not in detail on maps, plans are running through their heads.

There is much to decide on and organize: ordering, starting, and transplanting seeds, deciding on what plants to buy and their proper placement, and when to fertilize, deadhead, and harvest. What do you want to grow, and what style and design are you trying to attain?

Whew. The diverse aspects of gardening are quite complex. Take your time, grow what you enjoy seeing or eating, know that mistakes will happen, pay attention to the elements around you, and plant!

YOUR GARDEN DESIGN

No matter what size garden you are planning, it will surely be a process of evolution.

As a window box or penthouse gardener knows, it takes effort and care to choose the best flowers, herbs, or vegetables and grow healthy, full specimens throughout the growing season.

You planted it, but the following year it just doesn't belong. Dig it out and move it! A garden design is just that—a blueprint for your garden that is not set in stone. Yes, there are many design "rules"; but rules are made to be stretched, even broken, to adapt to your space and personality.

Visualize!

Before you start paging frantically through plant books and catalogs, or run to the nursery, think about what you want to accomplish. Have you always been attracted to a particular theme or color scheme?

Take a photograph of your garden space before you start. It can be a great reference for future design and a real shocker to see a few years down the road.

Get It on Paper!

No matter the size of the growing area, you must plan for what to grow. Begin with pencil and paper and draw out the spaces as much to scale as possible. Don't forget realities in your garden map. Mark down the areas that must stay clear; where are the drainage holes, electrical outlets, windows, downspouts, mechanicals such as air vents and air conditioners, walls, and exits?

Indicate sun and shade on your garden map, too. Add crisscrossed light lines where shade is always cast, leave the sunny areas clear, and make thin light lines where you have partial sun or light shade areas.

Once you have mapped a real representation of what you have in your garden, make at least twenty copies. You can now organize and reorganize plants, using this garden map as the basis for change and growth. For example, add dashes to indicate where you want another planter to go. If other gardeners in your building, community garden, or park are involved, distribute copies of the map well before the next meeting for people to copy and share their ideas.

Out of planning comes learning, and more ideas. Especially with gardening, as you learn more, your interest increases. Make a point of going to see local gardens, or visit the nearest botanical garden.

A pen can be mightier than the trowel. Have one handy whenever you visit a garden or nursery, so you can jot down the plants and design ideas you "ooh and ah" over. Gardening is physical doing and intellectual learning. This combination will allow you to grow along with your plants and create a spe-cial place for both the mind and body to enjoy.

DETAILS, DETAILS . . . WHAT'S IN A NAME?

"What is that?" they ask. You can't answer. You love that plant. You have been tending it and watching it grow for two years, and you just can't remember its name.

It's a bit embarrassing to be unable to tell someone the common name of a plant. But it's even more problematic when you want to buy more, or something is wrong with the plant and you can't even look it up!

Keep track of the seeds and plants you buy each season. Once the plant is in the ground, plastic plant labels are perfect if your memory is not. Metal labels are available—you press the name in with a sharp pencil—or use wood plant markers, or tongue depressors labeled with an indelible ink marker. But also write it down in your journal and on your garden map! Labels can fade, break, or get misplaced.

Make the best use of your garden map by writing in exactly what you planted, the date it was planted, and where it went. Since you should already know the common or botanical names and growing habits of every plant you bought, include how much room it will need and the color and length of bloom.

Especially with vegetables, keeping track of the varieties you planted, their taste, and harvest dates will help you plan for successional plantings. Keeping track also lessens your chances of making future seed purchase mistakes.

YOUR GARDENING RECORDS

Saving odd-shaped plastic labels and plant stakes in envelopes gets tedious very quickly. It can be an exhaustive search to locate the facts you want on a specific plant stake, only to find the text has rubbed off or faded.

Determining what you should hold onto is strictly a personal matter. Some people keep everything they get their hands on for possible future reference. Other gardeners keep a running journal of specific maintenance or pest control information on plants they have, along with a separate file of interesting plants to grow in the future.

The Journal

A journal consolidates everything related to your garden, holding all your notes in one place and in chronological order. The journal is your permanent record. When you learn something new, add it to your journal; or jot down a specific botanical name of a plant you saw in a magazine. Blooming times of your perennials, great foliage and color combinations of plants seen in other gardens, websites, rough sketches of arbor ideas, and mail-order nursery addresses will all be there.

Purchase a large notebook for exclusive use as a continuous journal of your garden. Head to a large stationery or bookstore, where you'll find a good selection of blank, hardcover notebooks with lined pages. Abundant choices of distinctive cover designs and sizes are available to grace your desk. If you need them, this is a great excuse to purchase a distinctive bookmark and fancy pen to use for your journal entries.

If you can't find a lined journal with page numbers, take time to number the pages in the upper or lower corner of the right-hand page. Say that on page 4, you wrote down three names of purple-flowering perennials for a particular planter from your trip to the botanical garden; and now, twenty pages later, you are adding notes on varieties of purple tulips for the same planter. It's easy to find your references for this planter by adding, "See pg. 4," instead of searching.

Keep an ongoing index. Leave the last dozen or so pages blank for your finished index. For your draft index, staple a few sheets of paper together, and then fasten them with a paper clip to the last page in your journal. Start the draft by writing each letter of the alphabet and leaving a few inches of spaces underneath. The skimpiest listings (e, i, j, k, n, o, u, x, y, and z) will not take much space. Once your journal has filled up, or you continue to another, transfer the draft index into the journal for a lasting reference.

To get started on your journal, use the "Garden Journal—Notes & Sketches" section at the end of this book.

The "Must-Save's"

What do you do with that great booklet on soil testing, the article on blueberries, and the garden design for the community garden plot? If you're thinking of just adding a file folder or two to your file cabinet, think again. Either clear out a drawer, or create space for a dedicated, accessible file for gardening. Alphabetical dividers with pocket holders make the most of spiral-bound notebooks.

Do you cut out magazine clips of plant names or sources? Tape them onto a journal page, or if the clip is short, write the information in your journal.

FORM FOLLOWS FUNCTION

Your garden's design will develop over time. You will think of new ideas, different plants will catch your interest, and even new uses may come to mind.

Magnificent border, herb, and wall plantings common in English gardens appear to be natural and effortless; yet they follow traditional design principles and require regular maintenance. You can achieve a flow of color with multiple plantings placed together. Gertrude Jekyll's (1843–1932) training as a painter certainly enhanced garden designs for her wealthy English clients, yet she employed centuries-old planting techniques used in simple cottage gardens.

You have a table and chairs in place for people to use for backyard dining, yet the space does not give the surrounded-by-plants effect you wanted. Push existing planters closer together; or set small, round containers in front of other planters. Choose plants that overflow toward the seating arrangement. Is there a wall where you can attach a bracket and hang a basket of annuals with trailing ivy? Vary the shapes of containers and plants, and add dramatic lighting or candles.

Sit in each chair and think of what you can add to improve the sight line. Place small pots on either side of the chairs, allowing room for movement. How about placing a plant on top of the table, and even underneath if it's a glass top?

LIGHTING

Lighting is a personal choice. It is both functional (reading, security, viewing plantings) and decorative. You have choices in brightness, depending on the wattage and type of bulbs you buy, as well as an abundant selection of fixtures. Try stringing up strands of little white lights on wire, to both surround an area and support an annual climbing vine. They supply subdued light and dance in the slightest summer breeze.

What exactly do you want to light up? Why? Go to the area at night to figure it out. Does light from the neighboring building already light up half the garden, or does the street light bathe the entrance to the garden in light?

Lighting is an important, permanent aspect of your garden design. Make your lighting decisions with a great deal of thought, and have the lights installed by an electrician or a very knowledgeable person.

PATHS

Path design often sets the design or "tone" of a garden. Even if you may see only one possible placement as you look at the physical layout of your terrace or yard, draw it out on paper and play with it. In general, straight lines are formal; winding paths are more casual and friendly.

DESIGN BY NATURE

Garden by following nature's cues. Stick with selections from your planting zone, mind light requirements, and be aware of rainfall and the different watering preferences of your plants. You can achieve a natural setting in your container garden.

When the community garden director asked me to volunteer as keeper of the rock garden, I knew I had a challenge. The 10-foot circle of rounded stones was placed on level ground, with one clump of orange marigolds growing in the center. I visited the New York Botanical Garden with a notebook and camera; then I went to the library and used-book store for design research. Within two months, the rock garden really looked like something; and by the next spring it was, well, gorgeous!

In nature, plants sprout up along the sides and in between crevices of small and huge boulders. If you really want realism in your mini-woodland or rock garden, grow some moss on the north side of your rocks!

LOOK TO THE PROS

Although most landscape designers and architects create plans for private country homes and expansive areas in botanical gardens, see what can translate to your city space. Which plants work beautifully together?

American landscape architect Ellen Biddle Shipman (1869–1950) planned more than 650 gardens, and her blueprints and herbaceous border plans are just as meaningful today. Sadly, her gardens disappeared with the demand for formal gardens. Only one restored garden is open to the public—the English Garden at the Stan Hywet Hall & Gardens in Akron, Ohio.

Shipman included with her plans instructions for planting, cultivating, and staking, and she advised clients on maintenance during her visits. She chose plants to soften the hard edges of cement walls and hedges. Good garden design has no age.

SPECIALIZATION

As the seasons pass, your tastes in plant species and color combinations will expand and change. Your fondness for a certain plant may even induce you to become a collector.

Even in small city spaces, you can grow exotic plants from tropical gardens. But keep in mind that hibiscus, oleander, and cactus will need indoor space—unless you live in a tropical climate! I have seen a small yard enclosed by a sidewalk gate overflowing with dozens of different colors and varieties of columbines, hydrangeas, and asters. In other words, if you like it, grow it!

Although orchids are considered highly sensitive, many can join your favorite houseplants outdoors when temperatures rise. Know which orchid variety you have, since many cannot tolerate an air temperature lower than 60 or 50 degrees.

READY, SET—GARDEN!

When heading out to your garden, be prepared. You should not only have a checklist of everything you are going to need—whether you'll be planting bulbs or transplanting—but you should be prepared to work.

If you are not ready, then you'll be bothered for days by sore neck muscles from using a bulb planter for hours, or by an aching back and shoulders from digging. Gardening is a great form of exercise and mentally invigorating. If you don't exercise regularly, take fifteen minutes to stretch before heading out.

A CITY VIEW

Whether they're planning a 12-foot-by-6-foot terrace or a street tree garden, city gardeners have a different view of, and a real respect for, the small amount of space they can garden.

Suburban backyard gardeners and rural landowners who carve out a small spot of their acreage for a flower or vegetable garden cannot understand how dear a bit of land for growing is to city gardeners.

No matter what size your city garden is, be very proud of what you have accomplished. There are many odds against you as a city gardener; but creating beauty is truly wonderful and special.

Whenever you find gardens you find culture—or should I say when you find culture, you usually find gardens, for they are the flowers of culture.
—Ellen Biddle Shipman

4

water, soil, & staying organic

It's pouring outside. But you're happy and relieved since you have just finished planting your new window box. You layered rocks over the drainage holes, and the soil you used is both suitably rich and lightweight. The storm ends, and you open the window—and the planter is dry as a bone! What?

Stick your head out the window and look up. The rain never watered your new plantings because there is a fire escape, terrace, or an eave right above; or the prevailing winds pushed the rain completely out of reach of your plants!

It happens. We just cannot count on Mother Nature to provide the correct amount of water for every plant we grow. Especially in the heat of summer, count on watering your small containers at least once a day.

A water source to supplement rainfall is the most important factor to consider before you begin to garden. Before you pick up one pot or a bag of soil, be secure in knowing how you are getting water to your gar-

den. Plants can fight and survive wind, poor soil, and adverse light conditions; but without water, your plants are guaranteed to die.

Watering cans are ideal for small garden areas. However, if you are planning to garden on the roof or in areas around your building on a large scale, it is likely that a water spigot is already in place. If not, it is time to get estimates for plumbers to install one, or to extend pipe and a spigot to where water is needed.

IT'S RAINING!

It's funny how you're now drawn to the stacks of almanacs at the supermarket checkout at the end of the year (and can't resist scanning the covers of magazines for meaningful gardening titles). Your interest in rainfall has certainly increased, and television weather forecasts are now a "must watch."

watering solutions for city gardening

- Run a hose out the window from your kitchen or bathroom faucet, or from a garden-friendly neighbor's faucet.
- Connect a hose from the sink in your building's basement and run it through an open window or air vent.
- Ask a local deli if you can bring in a bucket and fill up in their sink to water nearby street trees; or, ask them to donate two gallons of bottled water a week to keep their trees healthy.
- Contact your local fire department, or ask the parks department for permission and instructions to tap fire hydrants.
- Many commercial establishments wash down their sidewalks (so do building superintendents), so ask them to water their trees while they're at it! A small community garden struck a deal with the tourist bus company across the street to use their water spigot during off hours.
- Ask people living on the first floor to haul out a bucket of water for their street trees once a week.

- Is there a spigot or mechanism to attach a hose at the front of your building? Ask the superintendent for permission to use pliers to turn on the water. No spigot? Ask the landlord to install one in order to care for the building's street trees.
- Use any solid barrel or bucket to catch rainwater, and keep it covered to slow down evaporation. An old serving plate found at a flea market is a great cover for a plastic bucket. Empty any standing water into your garden soil twice a week during mosquito season.
- Tap into the city's water line! If you plan to be a viable community garden, ask for a direct hookup. Ask for free use of the water, or negotiate a reasonable monthly charge if metered.
- Off for the weekend and no rain forecasted? First, thoroughly water your plants; then insert cotton rags or handkerchiefs through the drainage holes of small empty clay pots, "plant" them in your planters so just the rims are above the soil, and fill with water.

You may even find yourself defending the pouring rain to people you run into. When they say: "Isn't this awful?" You say: "Oh no, this is great, we really needed a good deep rain."

How much water do you really need? What is the perfect balance between drowned and parched? You want to water long enough to give the roots a good long drink without saturating them.

Enough Is Enough

Before you water, stick your fingers into the soil and wiggle them around the soil. How does it feel? Can you easily move your fingers around, or is the soil compacted? Healthy soil and good drainage are vital to your plants. If you are having a tough time wiggling your fingers, think about what the roots are going through. Other than sticking a water meter into the soil near every plant (and wiping it down after each time you use it), your easiest gauge is to stick in your finger about 3 inches deep every couple of days to feel if the soil is dry.

To check that their plants are getting about an inch of water a week, some community gardeners have borrowed a trick from suburban sprinkler users. They "plant" an empty 5- or 6-ounce tuna or cat-food can into the soil concealed between plants. If the can's full, the gardener knows that last night's thunderstorm sufficiently watered the garden, so they won't overwater. Remember to remove any standing water if you have mosquitoes.

If the soil is in good condition—not a heavy clay, compacted, or loaded with thick topsoil—turn your nozzle to a steady-gentle rain setting for a full ten seconds over every section of exposed soil in your garden. This will give your plants a great soaking without using a can!

Obviously, a window box will take less water than a 3-foot-high container does. Be extra vigilant in hot weather. You can water,

Gardening in San Francisco immediately raises the issue of watershed protection, because much of the land is really former sand dunes. Here, the trees and flowers in many of our urban parks are a living example of water's unique ability to transform the landscape. Speaking directly, the eastern and southern United States' gardening model that is copied out here is wildly inappropriate. We Californians need to start appreciating and gardening with our own native drought-resistant plants and trees. We must preserve our watershed.

—Elizabeth Sullivan, Program Manager,
Neighborhood Parks Council, San Francisco

stop to weed or chat with others, then go back and check your soil with your finger and find that it's still dry, almost dusty, 2 inches down. Keep watering!

Wise Water Planting

A window box would sure look great there, but how the heck do you water it? Plan for watering before planting.

You needn't be a gardener living in a desert to be exposed to drought or water restrictions. But if you are faced with a water shortage, hold off on any fertilizing and pruning since doing either stimulates new growth. Unless you are watering vegetables, you will likely face a costly summons if caught watering. Water is one of our most precious resources, but we tend to take the availability of clean water for granted.

Watch your newly planted treasures carefully. Wilting is the strongest indicator that they need water, now. New trees and shrubs need special watering attention; never allow their soil to dry out.

Xeriscaping is catching on! It sounds complex, but it's simply planning your plantings for the most efficient use of water. Certain plants, and many regional native species, are "naturally" drought-tolerant. Selecting and grouping "like water need" plants can save you both money and time.

Contact your County Cooperative Extension agent for your city's recommended drought-tolerant plants. Great ground covers include liriope, periwinkle, and English ivy. Recommended vines for xeriscaping are wintercreeper, wisteria, trumpet honeysuckle, and clematis; and flowers such as Black-eyed

Susan, cornflower, cosmos, goldenrod, and sedum are hardy growers.

PONDER YOUR SOIL

After ensuring a water supply for your plants, you can concentrate on what they will grow in. Have you ever read the ingredients on a bag of soil, or wondered what exactly was in the soil you already have? If you're starting a new container planting, you know that only organic growing mediums are being used. But for existing soil, you'll need to add compost for nutrients and other organic amendments to improve soil texture and keep it healthy.

Although the offer of a load of "topsoil" to use in any public garden can get volunteers' hearts beating fast, be well aware of the quality before you accept it. Anything is not better than nothing—especially if you are left with a mound of inferior soil containing rocks and construction rubble.

Healthy soil provides plants with the proper support, air, water, and nutrients. It contains living organisms (such as bacteria, microorganisms, and earthworms), inorganic soil particles (worn-down rocks), organic matter (decomposing plant and animal life), water, and air. A proper combination of these ingredients will provide proper "food" and drainage for your plants.

Most city gardens are created in containers. When you create a garden from scratch, you have total control, and knowledge, of what has gone into your soil. But what if you move into an apartment that already has soil in a terrace, roof garden, or backyard?

Exactly what kind of soil do you have? There are many types, and all of them can be improved by altering the texture and ingredients. Since tender roots push through and grow between the spaces within the soil, you want to make sure they don't have to maneuver around rocks or be stunted by heavy, compacted soil.

Soil Sorts

Your soil type depends on how much sand, silt, and clay are present. Bring a 16-ounce glass jar to the garden, and fill it up a third of the way with some soil. Add water, tighten the lid, and shake it up. Leave the jar undisturbed overnight and see what you have. The sand settles to the bottom first, the silt settles next, and then comes the clay; the organic matter is on top, floating around in the water.

Clay soil is hard, yet finely textured, and it compacts when dry. It has great trouble with draining properly, and your plants' roots can easily rot. Sandy soil is coarse and easily falls apart. It drains easily, but it can't hold onto the nutrients needed for plants to survive. Loamy soils are classified as ranging from sandy to silt. A medium-textured loam is considered ideal since it has an even mixture of sand, silt, and clay; feels soft; and is rich in organic matter.

To keep great soil year after year, keep adding compost, peat moss (it has no nutrients but aerates the soil), and aged manure. After harvesting your vegetables, try planting fava beans before a winter freeze to improve the soil's structure and add organic matter.

Many organic commercial potting soils are available that you can "trowel in" or culti-vate into your existing soil. Compost is the best amendment for retaining nutrients and water. There is nothing harmful in adding a few handfuls of perlite or vermiculite (light-weight minerals) or coarse sand to a heavy soil during the growing season.

Perfect pH

No, not your hair, your soil! The soil sample you send for testing will determine what is needed to adjust your pH (a measure of your soil's acidity or alkalinity) for the most productive garden. As with any additives, it's much easier to adjust the pH of your soil before plants are established.

Depending on what you want to grow, you may desire soil that is more acidic, alkaline, or perfectly balanced. The pH scale runs from 1 to 14, with 1 the most acidic and over 10 extremely alkaline. Most vegetables, herbs, flowers, and fruit trees are happiest with a slightly acidic to neutral soil (between 6.2 and 7.0) since nutrients can easily reach the plants in this range.

Soil Tests Tell

You may find yourself with "real" soil in your local park, community garden, or backyard; but you can't predict what's in it by how it looks, feels, or smells. Before wasting growing time and money by merely guessing, get your soil tested to find out what you have. The test will also point out any deficiencies (low in magnesium, potassium, etc.) that you can augment before planting.

The sample you take must represent the soil conditions. No matter how small the garden area is, take samples from several different spots. Use a trowel to get your soil sample, at a depth of 4 to 6 inches. Remove any rocks from the soil sample you collected and mail it away.

Call your County Cooperative Extension agent for a soil-test mailer. It's a small price to pay, instead of staring in disgust at costly planting mistakes. If you're planning on growing herbs or vegetables, spend the extra fee for a lead test.

Continue Enriching Your Soil

Just because last year's test reported a perfect pH of 7 doesn't mean that your soil didn't change this year. If the soil is too acidic, work in some bonemeal and well-crushed eggshells. If you're adding some spring bulbs to your vegetable garden, bulbs love to be placed on a sprinkling of bonemeal at the bottom of their planting holes.

If your soil is very acidic, you may need to amend it through a simple, systematic, yet labor-intensive process called double-digging. Dig a trench a shovel's depth and width, and place the soil a few feet away or on a tarp or in a wheelbarrow. Loosen the soil at the bottom with the shovel and toss in some lime (ground-up limestone), peat moss, and compost. Once you finish with that line, dig another trench along side it, using the topsoil of the new trench to place inside the first trench. Keep digging, adding amendments, and topping until the whole garden bed is complete. If you are blessed to have a wood-burning fireplace, save the ashes from hardwood logs and cultivate them into your soil to neutralize its acidity.

The first soil test for our community garden vegetable plot noted that the sandy loam soil had an "acceptable range" of pH 6.8, but suggested we add more organic matter. The next year's test showed a pH of 6.2 and remarked that we should continue to add compost, peat moss, and well-rotted manure.

You can adjust soil that is a bit too alkaline (having a pH over 7.0) by adding topsoil, compost, and peat moss. Keep that compost coming to ensure a balanced soil. To decrease high alkalinity, add pine needles or garden sulfur.

Alkaline-loving plants include wild indigo, phlox, garden sage, petunias, asters, cosmos, and dahlias. Dogwoods, azaleas, hydrangeas, camellias, and Japanese maples thrive in acidic soil.

As a container gardener, you are the "master" of your own soil and can easily amend it to meet the specific needs of certain plants. But, once you start gardening and deplete the soil's nutrients during the gardening season, you must devote some time and energy to preserving a steady balance.

Worms certainly warrant mentioning every time healthy soil is described. What could be better than sticking your trowel into the soil to plant those healthy seedlings and seeing an earthworm squiggling up from the bottom and into the side of the hole you just dug? Every day, worms add over six times their body weight in nitrogen, calcium, and magnesium as they turn natural waste into soil. Earthworm cocoons and live red worms (great for the compost pile) are easily shipped to your door.

Warning: Lead!

Have your soil tested for lead if you plan to grow anything edible in the ground. The results will give you parts per million (ppm) levels of lead.

There were many dour faces when results of the community garden lead test were posted on the bulletin board. The report was not good. It recommended not eating—and to stop growing—root crops and all leafy vegetables that season. Ouch! Raised beds and bags of cow manure became a common sight.

Add compost, and stay away from gardening near painted structures and exhaust fumes. If your test results are at a really high level, you may need to remove the existing soil and add all new to a lined, raised bed. Since lead poisoning is a common city health problem for city children, have any young ones tested.

What's the Fuss?

Your garden must have healthy soil. Without it, you will be discouraged and disappointed with everything you try to grow.

If you want spectacular azaleas, you must have well-drained, acidic soil. Spread unflavored, cool coffee grounds around your hydrangeas to turn the pink flowers to blue. An acid soil, with pH of 4 to 5.5, is ideal for growing blueberries. If you don't want to share them with local or migrating birds,

cover the shrub with netting as the berries emerge.

MULCH

Mulch is placed to protect plants and soil. Organic mulches are made from shredded or chopped cedar nuggets, cedar mulch, pine needles, pine bark, hay, and leaves. Some areas of the country offer dyed mulches, and some areas top their winter garden beds with seaweed. Inorganic mulches such as gravel, marble chips, or plastic can do the job; but they can look messy, contribute nothing to the soil, and be a pain to maintain. "Native" stones or seashells placed between perennial plants look beautiful; and rain running off them adds minerals to your soil.

Some northern gardeners wait until the ground is totally frozen; others do this pre-winter chore the day after the first frost. But a goodly number mulch when they find the time to finish planting spring bulbs.

To ensure that water reaches down to the roots after you've just planted and mulched, push it back with your hand so that the nozzle can directly contact the soil. Use a gentle

The Multifaceted Merits of Mulch

- Conserves water by retaining moisture
- Regulates the soil temperature
- Lowers the temperature of the soil in summer and retains heat in the winter
- Reduces weed growth by blocking out

sunlight so weeds can't sprout
- Holds soil in place against wind and erosion caused by severe weather
- Provides an attractive, "finished" look to plantings

setting, or just let the water flow from the hose; don't blast!

ONCE IS JUST NOT ENOUGH

The seeds are happily planted in perfectly tested, properly balanced, and well-drained soil. So that's it for the growing season, right? No. Actually, once the initial soil preparation is done, it will be a pleasure to move the cultivator through the soil. Take care not to clip any roots.

Wait until all of your seeds have sprouted. The ideal is to aerate the soil to ensure that water and nutrients are reaching down to the base of the roots about once a week, to thwart compacting the soil, and to discourage weeds.

WHY FERTILIZE?

In a small space such as a foot-square planter, you can't expect an unending source of nutrients. Organic fertilizers can safely be applied to any type of soil.

Many gardeners make a major fuss out of feeding their plants. It's not precise or complicated. Read all labels before you buy. Whether you buy fertilizer in a powder, slow-release pellet, or water-soluble form, read the ingredients and directions carefully. In general, water the soil thoroughly before applying any fertilizer, and take care not to get any

on growing plant leaves or stems. Develop a schedule to fertilize every other Saturday, or track the slow-release pellets on your calendar.

Note that organic and all general fertilizers list a ratio consisting of three numbers. The first is nitrogen, the middle is phosphate, and the third is potassium. The closer in value the numbers are, the more "balanced" the fertilizer. You can add a 5-10-5 granular mix in early spring and follow with a time-release fertilizer to last the rest of the gardening season—but the benefits will not last from year to year.

For containers of flowers, you can add some 14-14-14 slow-release fertilizer to the surface when you plant. Add organic fertilizer to your annuals every two weeks with a water-soluble 14-14-14 or even higher numbers for incredible blooms. Always follow fertilizing with a deep watering; and never leave your garden unwatered for a few days right after fertilizing, since feeding stimulates plant growth and increases the need for water.

Organic Fertilizers & Amendments

Fish emulsion, commonly available in liquid form, is easily diluted with water in a clean gallon-sized milk jug or in a bucket. Warning: Pour with an extended arm, because fish emulsion has a powerful odor. Since the scent does linger a bit, wait a day or two for that party.

Read plant and garden supply catalogs for an amazing assortment of liquefied, concentrated, pelleted, composted, and granulated organic fertilizers and soil amendments. Some amazing natural, recycled ingredients available include kelp; cow and chicken manure; worm and cricket castings; ground crab, lobster, and crawfish shells; bat and seabird guano (manures); rock powders; and even dried blood, which is high in nitrogen and a great summer soil booster.

Composted rhinoceros and elephant manures are sold molded into adorable animal shapes that look great in the garden and slowly disintegrate while improving your soil. Since all the ingredients listed in this section are organic, you can add them to the soil around your plants.

Hot temperatures have done a real number on your tomato plants. You've watered well but the leaves are yellowing—just when so many of the tomatoes are starting to turn red. It could be a magnesium deficiency. Scratching some Epsom salts into the soil could do the job and give a natural boost to the roots.

It's Tea Time

Treat your plants to some compost tea! There are many recipe variations, but an easy "tea" is to scoop a few trowelfuls of finished compost or manure onto the middle of a piece of cheesecloth or into an old, clean cotton sock. Close the top with a rubber band, and add your "tea bag" to a bucket of water. Cover the bucket, let it sit for a week, and remove the bag before pouring your tea into a watering can to distribute.

PESTS!

While pruning your rosebush, you may see black dots attached to the stem (aphids); or notice that the full, pink phlox you planted last year looks like someone shook baby powder on the leaves and stems (powdery mildew). Don't run out for strong chemicals before trying less toxic remedies. It will be better for the plant, the health of the soil, and you.

One way to get rid of isolated aphids is to literally grab onto the affected area (such as the stem of a hosta flower), set your water nozzle at the strongest setting, then blast all the aphids off. You can spray on some organic insecticidal soap to kill harmful insects such as aphids, mealybugs, and whiteflies. Or try this organic homemade remedy right from the kitchen. Chop four whole garlic bulbs (don't bother peeling them), cover with vegetable oil in a quart jar, and tape on a sign marked "Bug Killer." Let sit for a day, then add 2 tablespoons of cayenne pepper, 10 shakes of Tabasco sauce, and 2 tablespoons of grease-cutting dishwashing liquid and shake. After it settles, pour the mixture into a rinsed 32-ounce plastic spray bottle and fill to the top with water. Spray away—on and under leaves and on stems! Label the bottle and refrigerate the rest for future use.

Control garden pests organically by spraying on a multipurpose pest killer, horticultural oil, concentrated liquid garlic, fungicide, and gardener-created recipes. All are readily available through sources on the Internet and through catalogs.

One of the most disgusting of all God's creatures is the slug. If you don't have slugs, you're blessed. If you do, join the party. Here are some things to try: buying special anti-slug pellets or mothballs, pouring salt on them, ringing every plant with crushed seashells or eggshells (ants don't like this either), picking them off the soil with a trowel and crushing them, encircling your garden by pushing copper flashing tape into the soil, putting out nonalcoholic beer in sunken cat-food cans, and trying again. Slipping dryer sheets just under the soil is the latest "hot" deterrent to slugs and black ants.

Bring in Beneficials!

Order up some bugs! No matter which region of the country your city is in, there are beneficial insects just a call or a click of the mouse away. Once you have identified the pests, you can figure out the natural remedy. Numerous catalogs offer live delivery of insects that will eat aphids and scale (a pint of ladybugs); aphids and mealybugs (black ladybugs); aphids, mites, thrips, and white flies (green lacewing larvae); fleas and flies (spiders); and thrips and spider mites (predatory mites).

Plan a backyard party or local park event around your beneficial "bug release day." What a great opportunity to educate others in organic, healthy gardening practices. Kids of all ages love to look for praying mantises and are in awe of their ability to "disappear" on foliage. Shipped in cases, mantises hatch and eat every insect in sight. They have a special appetite for tomato hornworms and flies.

WEEDS

Unless you grew edible weeds on purpose, pick your weeds by hand as soon as you see them. Make sure you get out the whole root, or it will return and probably spread.

If you want to garden organically and grow healthy plants, never, under any circumstance, use a chemical weed-killing spray or product. You could never plant an herb or vegetable in that soil again with a clear conscience. Weeding is part of the gardening experience, and your city garden is small enough to tend.

ladybug

spider

green lacewing larvae

tomato hornworm

ant

STAYING ORGANIC

Temptations to stray to chemical warfare may emerge when pests attack. Don't. There are many organic products and homemade cures that can be just as effective. Pyrethrum spray and insecticidal soap can work wonders.

For powdery mildew, try this: Get a bucket or a gallon milk jug, and add a heaping tablespoon of baking soda and three level tablespoons of horticultural oil. Then fill the jug with water. Fancy sprayers that attach to your hose work great, but so do well-cleaned household sprayer bottles (remember to label them!).

EAT ORGANIC!

Ever bite into a stalk of organically grown celery? What a treat—and undoubtedly, a surprise—to actually taste real flavor. Grow your own favorite vegetables organically, and taste the difference; you'll never go back to chemical additives. You can grow delicious organic vegetables in your city garden. Yes, even in the window box!

To supplement the vegetables you grow, especially after your harvesting is over, look into organic food co-ops or services for great variety.

Organic agriculture maintains biological diversity and replenishes the soil's fertility. When you choose organic produce, you care about the earth in the most fundamental way. You eliminate the need for using chemicals and pesticides.
—Moe Moalawi, General Manager, Urban Organic

5

basic supplies for you & your plants

As with any other product or service, you generally get what you pay for. But "buyer extra beware," since the gardening industry is flooded with the cutest things that may not do the best job. The most expensive item in that popular catalog can be junk. Be sure to check on the terms, and save the return policy! One of the national supermarket checkout-line magazines regularly offers readers garden plants by mail that cost at least five times more than any other place!

Buy the best quality you can afford. Many tools are now designed to be "ergonomically correct" for your hand and to reduce back strain. Plastic trowels and cultivators are best saved for toddlers to use in a sandbox.

NOZZLE

Invest in an adjustable spray nozzle that gives you options from a fine mist spray to a powerful jet stream. Look for a stable, comfortable grip and a nozzle that easily and securely attaches to the hose. Adjustable-spray brass nozzles last a long time (you twist them to adjust the spray), but even their lowest setting can be too strong and will flatten tender seedlings.

NON-KINKING HOSE

Cast embarrassment aside and unravel and twist that hose in the store aisle to make sure its "nonkink" claim holds up! Although a hose is not as easy to judge without water pulsing through it, you can see instantly if it overlaps in a knot. Get a good one and spare yourself endless headaches and backaches from bending over and undoing kinks.

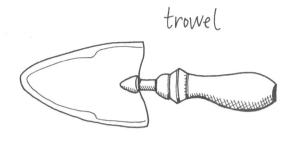

trowel

TROWEL

A trowel with a sturdy, comfortable handle made of wood, plastic, or metal is imperative for ease of use. Hold it in your hand, curved metal toward you, and feel the grip before you purchase. Solid cast aluminum will never break, rust, or corrode, and it is surprisingly lightweight. The inside curve of trowels is often marked in inches to indicate the varied planting depths of bulbs.

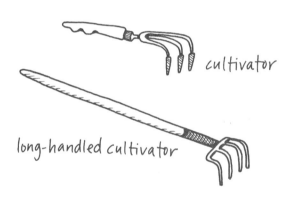

cultivator

long-handled cultivator

CULTIVATOR

A handheld, three-prong cultivator is a soil "care and air" staple. Make sure the wood or plastic handle fits your hand, to avoid blisters. You can get handheld and long-handled weeders with a spring in the middle of the prongs that sort of bounces when the tool hits the soil. The long handle helps you to reach farther; and the thinner, longer tines dig deeper and aerate the soil without as much effort.

PRUNER

Keep your plants healthy and growing with proper pruning. To do the job right and without harming the plant, shrub, or tree or before undertaking any topiary, you'll need a good pair of pruners.

Pruners have different grips, so try before you buy. Quality pruners are not inexpensive, but they're well worth the investment. Even petunias and pansies are easily deadheaded with clean-cut snips! When trimming shrubs and trees, feel confident in using a pruner to safely remove crisscrossed branches up to the thickness of your index finger.

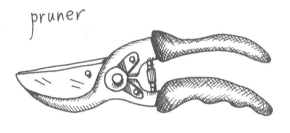

pruner

TOOL CARE

Keep your tools in good shape, never leave them outside, and you'll be rewarded with years of use. No matter how tired you are, remove any residue soil, sponge off with some dishwashing detergent, and dry completely. At the end of the season, rub a steel-wool pad in a circular motion over the rusty areas and buff to a shine. For trowels, you may want to use a flat sharpener (drag the back edge of the trowel across it in one direction) to give them more of an edge. Add a dab of petroleum jelly and rub it all over the metal before you stow it away.

KNEELING PAD

Don't leave home without it. Cement is not a "giving" surface. Shifting around on your knees as you cultivate and plant a tree bed downright hurts. Pliable inch-thick kneeling mats are just long enough to maneuver around and slide over as you shift. Available in discount stores, all garden centers, and most catalogs, knee pads often have silly, fun gardening comments on them. Knee pads that strap onto each knee are another option for those who spend a lot of time crawling around.

GLOVES

Yes, digging your bare hands down into gorgeous soil is fantastic; but what about dealing with rocky muck, cement chunks, and fresh manure? Although they are pricey, washable leather gloves are long lasting. Goatskin gloves feel great but are best for lighter chores if you want them to last; fleece-lined work gloves are also available.

Pliable (thicker than dishwashing type) plastic gloves can be thrown in the washing machine. They allow you to pick up little radish seeds and immerse your hands deep in muck, and they'll last a few gardening seasons.

Glove sizes do vary, so try them on to be sure you can return them before heading to the cash register or placing a phone order! If you see a great deal on cotton or canvas gloves, pick up a few, but know they won't withstand the rigors of gardening.

A note to women who want to keep long, manicured nails: Wear gloves for all chores, not just the obvious tough ones; and use a nail hardener and polish, even if clear, throughout the gardening season.

CONES & CAGES

Cones and cages are a necessity for tomato-loving gardeners. Although many gardeners swear by wood dowels or bamboo stakes, cones and cages need only a firm push into the soil to hold up and contain robust plants.

RULER

A metal ruler will last forever and is ideal to use for creating shallow furrows for your

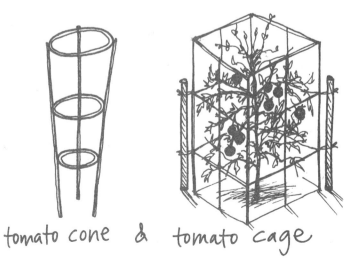

tomato cone & tomato cage

seeds. Although you can certainly eyeball 3 inches apart, it's so much easier to have the ruler handy when planting seeds with different recommended spacing distances.

CAMERA

See how you started, see what needs filling in next year, gauge your progress, and send copies showing off your gardening efforts! It's a riot to e-mail pictures of your successes, especially vegetables, to relatives in the suburbs!

Every year in early spring, even though the barren, unworked soil in our community garden plots looks exactly the same, we take "before" shots. Through the years, the borders have changed from rocks to bricks and recently to raised beds. But each year's late-

spring, midsummer, and harvest photographs are totally different and reflect our changing tastes and new challenges.

ACCESSORIES

Candlelight is a perfect evening accent for your focal points. Personalize your space with drama and laughter with well-chosen accessories. A wooden black-and-white cow has been grazing on a nearby terrace and making passersby smile for years. Choices include sun dials, birdbaths, sculptures, fountains, gazing globes, weather vanes, gnomes, dreamcatchers, gargoyles, wind chimes, wind socks, mirrors (reflecting a spectacular section or plant), pinwheels, and whirligigs that catch the wind.

There always seems to be something to cut or tie up in the garden. I carry a pair of scissors and some string in my back pocket for deadheading, cutting suckers, and snipping herbs and flowers to take home, and, since I do a lot of vertical growing, the string secures pole beans and cucumber vines that go berserk.
—Jean-Daniel Noland, gardener, Hell's Kitchen, New York

6

what to plant—
local hunting & mail order

How do you begin choosing what plants to grow? Start with listing the plants you really like. Have you always loved the scent of sweet peas, the grace of hollyhocks, or the beauty of yellow snapdragons? Are you drawn to a particular color combination, want a succession of flowers in full bloom throughout the entire growing season, or want to bring what you grow to your dinner plate? Write down your wish list and start planning.

Look at the space you have to grow in, for a reality check. Besides the actual measurements of the physical surface area and the depth of the soil, also consider the air space available on any or all sides and any height limitations. Specific plant names may not come instantly to mind, but certain plant shapes and structure will be apparent.

You may always have adored lilacs, but have four window boxes. You can capture many of lilac's desired assets, such as the gentle branches and scent, with lantana and the subdued color of lavender. Your goal here is to find plants that are perfect for your space, planting zone, and available sunlight. Some considerations are plant height, width, maintenance, life span, time and duration of bloom, and color. Check the growing habit if you need a plant to climb, drape, wrap, or spread. You may choose a plant not only for how it looks, or for its particular scent, but purely for its culinary or medicinal use.

When thinking of what you want to plant, your best sources of ideas are your memory, plant and seed catalogs, and the Internet. As you turn a page, a corner, or scroll down and see a plant that makes you say "Ooh" out loud, stop. Even though that plant can be grown only in the tropics, what was it that initially attracted you?

When you see a plant you really like, look for the zone. If not obvious, ask an employee, call the toll-free number, or e-mail the company to find out. Never consider purchasing a "zone unknown" plant.

Knowing the botanical name of a plant you were drawn to is essential if you want to end up with the same plant in your garden!

There are around nine hundred species of the *Salvia* genus (sage) of the plant you saw last August at the botanical garden, but only a few *officinalis* (garden sage) species have scented leaves; and one cultivar, *purpurea,* with purple-tinged leaves, has survived many snowy winters.

Botanical nomenclature is fascinating; Latin adjectives inform you about the plants' genus, species, fragrance (*odorata*), color (*alba* is white), and even the size of its flowers. But you needn't get bogged down with knowing Latin; just be sure to write down the plant's botanical name and put it in your journal for future reference.

PLANT LOCATION, LOCATION, LOCATION

Where you are planting is very important, whether it's directly into the ground or a container. This determination depends, of course, on what plants you have selected. If you've read this book in sequence, you already "know your sun" and have wonderful soil!

You don't want to make the mistake of planting dwarf varieties behind tall ones. Once you know their growing habits, you can imagine how plants will look and can plan groupings that will grow great together.

LOCAL HUNTING

Finding plants to grow on the fire escape, on the roof, or in the park can be very interesting in the city. Oddly enough, bodegas, delicatessens, and discount stores wheel out carts filled with spring flowers, roses, and flats of annuals. They know that city gardeners are out there, or they wouldn't stock so many!

Look for discounted flower and vegetable seeds and bulbs, but check the "packed for" year stamped on the seed packet. If the packet has last year's date, it means that you shouldn't expect every seed to germinate. When you are counting on those dwarf zinnias to fill in your window box, make sure the odds are with you by purchasing this year's fresh seeds.

Pick a nice weekend to visit some community gardens and chat with the gardeners about their seed sources. Call your Parks Department and ask where they purchase plants and seeds. Who knows, maybe you could piggyback on a truck order of azaleas at a great price.

SAVING SEEDS

Grow your own, harvest, and plant them next year! It is not as difficult as you may think. Year after year, we pick the plumpest, longest scarlet runner beans for saving. Small glass jars that once held spices and fancy mustards are now home to seeds. Come fall, the rear of the bottom shelf of the refrigerator is jammed with an assortment of seed jars.

Since we want the smallest but brightest yellow marigolds for the community garden plots, we choose the ten tiniest blooms for saving. Once home, we gently peel the flowers open from the bottom over an open business-size envelope. The envelope is marked and filed under "Plant in May."

Four o'clocks are another pick-and-file flower; they are fun to harvest since their seeds look like huge peppercorns. For vegetables, save from the biggest and best of open-pollinated or heirloom vegetables like butternut squash and string beans. Don't bother trying to save any hybrid varieties, since they just don't grow like the parent plant.

LET 'EM BE

Grow more plants by just leaving them in the soil! Many plants die down but reseed themselves without any intervention from you; the seeds develop and fall. Impatiens plants have comeback. And look for sunflowers, nicotiana (flowering tobacco), marigolds, and snapdragons to surface again.

CUTTINGS TO CULTIVATE

Make more of your favorite plants! Pick out the healthiest and prune with a purpose. Make sure you take a clean cutting, at least 3 inches long, with your pruner or sharp scissors. Certain plants such as coleus and

spearmint will easily root in water, or use a well-drained pot. Mix together one part vermiculite to two of sand, and water completely. After pushing down on the mixture with a paper towel to remove excess water, insert a third of the cutting into it. Make sure you've removed any lower leaves, and keep the cutting well watered. Wait about a month and a half for the roots to establish themselves before transplanting into 2-inch pots with potting soil. Keep the plant moist and shaded until you notice roots coming out of the drainage holes.

WHERE GARDEN SUPPLIES HIDE

Half the battle for city gardeners is finding all the necessary materials, such as drainage material and soil.

Many local and chain hardware stores and florists carry small and pricey 5- to 10-pound bags of all-purpose potting soil. If there are no obvious gardening supply places in your neighborhood, head to the hardware store or florist to speak with the manager or owners. Ask them to order 40-pound bags of potting soil from one of their suppliers for you; and negotiate a price, since larger sizes cost appreciably less. National drug store and discount store chains also carry gardening gloves and other supplies.

Keep ever vigilant for "street finds" such as decorative iron for vines to climb. Demolition sites are ideal for finding bricks to pave garden paths and to raise planters off the ground.

PHONE, INTERNET, & MAIL ORDERS

You know you're really into gardening when you don't mind having a mailbox packed with catalogs. Head to the best magazine rack and spend a few dollars on the thickest, glossiest gardening magazines. National bookstore chains have fantastic selections! Read the articles some other time, since you are on a hunt for seed and plant catalogs. Armed with postcards and paper for listing toll-free numbers and websites, you can comb through the display and classified advertisements and find a varied selection.

When placing an order, feel free to ask more questions concerning color selection,

growing habits, special requirements, and guarantees. Keep track of all your orders. Don't be nervous about getting plants through the mail or delivery service. The nurseries know how to pack the plants properly, and will not ship them during a heat wave.

GARDEN CENTERS & NURSERIES

Where are they? Yes, some gardening stores have found their way inside of city limits since discovering that city gardeners are alive, well, and spend money. But, garden centers and nurseries that offer acres of selections in plants and supplies are out in the suburbs.

If you don't know the names of the best nurseries outside your city, ask other gardeners, neighbors, and local florists. Turn over labels where plants are sold to check their

Almost 500 rosebushes adorn our garden. Since we are accredited as an All-American Rose Selection garden, care is taken to select from quality catalogs specializing in roses. I love roses and always find the room for a donated rosebush.
—Dorothy Sampson, gardener-caretaker, Watts Senior Citizen Center and Rose Garden, Los Angeles, California

sources. Head back to the Internet or library for the yellow pages of the nearest county outside your city.

Give the nursery a call and ask about transportation. What would the delivery charge be? Maybe a bus stops right at the entrance, or you can get other people together and hire a van service to take you to the nursery. Post a notice in your building or neighborhood bulletin board "Seeking fellow gardening fanatics for nursery buying trips." Fellow gardeners understand the desire to find new, and even better, plant sources. Think about people you know who have a car and would enjoy a day trip (offer gas, pay any tolls, and bribe with lunch).

Picking Brains

At the nursery, ask any employee to tell you whom you should speak with about their selection of perennials. Write down names, and don't leave without getting business cards. Develop a friendly relationship with the most knowledgeable expert on staff, since they know their inventory and can suggest new varieties, point out what's best for your growing conditions, and even steer you to some bargains.

When your growing season is winding down, you should not only find lower prices, but maybe some perennials pushed off to the side that look destined for the compost pile. They'll be back next year, so it never hurts to ask nicely if they are free.

Knowledge Is Vital

Save yourself aggravation and research time, and check that your plants have labels or stakes. They should include the common name, in English, and botanical name, in Latin. If the plant has no label, find it out and write it down before heading home. Some labels may also include the plants' family, origin, and native habitat. Water requirements, sunlight conditions, growing habits, and place of origin are usually included.

From the school of "it never hurts to ask," don't hesitate to question any aspect of care for the plants you purchase. Ask about trellis height requirements for a cup-and-saucer vine (*Cobaea scandens*), recommended spacing for the flat of ajuga (*Ajuga reptans,* also known as bugleweed), or dividing a peony. This goes for Internet and mail orders, too!

Narrowing Your Selection

So many choices, such little space! You may be tempted to just get one of those, and one of those—but where are they all going to go? Overbuying is a definite negative in gardening and a common affliction. Jamming six plants into a space meant for two will result in stunted growth or death as their roots fight for space to grow, nutrients, and water.

Desired Impact

What do you want to achieve with the plants you are buying? Hunting for beautiful flowers is different from selecting delicious vegetables, or choosing plants for their incredible foliage. Yes, it's hard, but keep your gardening goals in mind as you select.

A big aspect of choosing a desirable flowering plant is, of course, its flowers. You need to know their color, when they will be in full bloom, and if they bloom all season or all at once. You also need to know if the plant is an annual or hardy perennial for your zone, and how long its blooming period will last.

Two plants with distinctive leaves and branch structure are lupines and bleeding hearts; their leaves are interesting long after the flowers fade. You may not even care so much for the flower the plant produces, but love the foliage. Or you may be attracted to texture, such as the soft feel of lamb's ears.

The Nose Knows

People respond positively to scents they enjoy; but don't obscure sweet odors by planting them too close together. Growing summer-flowering sweet autumn clematis in the same container as night-scented stock is overkill, but they're perfect when planted ten feet apart.

Perfume the air with a sun-loving honeysuckle vine, phlox, and roses; and sow some evening primrose and moonflower seeds. Lily of the valley and fragrant varieties of hosta are delightful in shadier areas.

Scrutinize Now

The biggest, fullest plant in the whole bunch may not be all it seems. Before buying, check for some warning signs. Turn the plant over and lift it out of the container if possible to inspect the bottom. Is it totally covered with roots coming out of every drainage hole? Roots that poke through are normal; but reject the plant if the bottom is covered with them. If the plant has been growing in that pot for all that time, it probably has not got-

ten the nutrients needed for the best growth. No sense starting out with problems, so look for another plant.

While you're checking the plant's container, don't ignore the soil. Stick a finger in on the side. The medium should feel moist (not hard and dusty). Also look for any sign of flying movement (pests) or slugs on the surface or under the pot.

Lift the underside of a few top and bottom leaves to check for bugs. See any little white specks, or what looks like finely ground pepper (aphids)? But, if you see an earthworm wriggling around, all the better. Bring it home to aerate your outdoor soil!

Other than safeguarding the health of the plants you purchase, you don't want to bring an infestation home with you from the garden center. This prepurchase checkup can result in unexpected bonuses: While all the other containers held one plant per 4-inch plastic pot, two healthy seedlings are now heading for the cashier's line.

Beware of Hostile Takeovers

Some plants want it all. And, they will hog the whole area if given an eighth of a chance. One of the most notorious invasives is mint! If you love growing mint to add to a refreshing cocktail, iced tea, or to a tabouli recipe, make sure you insert a tall metal coffee can in the soil first, or grow them in their own containers. Bamboo also needs its own large container.

Some plants sneak over into other areas at a slower rate; but they can be lifted out, separated, and planted elsewhere. Give the lemon rose roots a haircut or the plant will take over.

Ajuga, with striking gradations of purple in its leaves, sends up delicate blue flowers and fills in rapidly.

Out of Your Zone = Out of Your Mind

Just know right off that if you choose to buy a plant that is three or more zones away from yours, then you will just have to pay the consequences. This translates into either driving yourself crazy with lifesaving efforts, or just hurting your wallet a bit by buying a new one on an annual basis.

Although valiant efforts were made to save a gorgeous gardenia by wrapping burlap in layers around propped-up stakes, it did not survive a light snow.

If you have a plant or particular flowers that you can't do without, then by all means, buy it, plant it, and enjoy it for that season! Having a passionflower and oleander in zone 6 is certainly not sane, but that sweet "Bermuda-is-calling-me" scent inspires the extra effort to move them just inside the building's stairwell to keep them watered and alive for the next season.

Wintering over a delicate warm-climate plant involves scrambling for indoor space as soon as night temperatures take a dive. Find room to capture waning sunlight by a window—not always feasible in a city apartment. Somehow the scented geraniums make it through.

OTHER SOURCES

If your city has "green markets," you will be able to find tons of plants to choose from throughout the gardening season, and you may be able to find some soil and compost sources. If you don't find what you need, ask around for the name of the market's organizer and contact them; it never hurts to ask.

Keep your eyes peeled for moving sale notices. Someone with a backyard or roof garden may have a great sale or giveaway! Make up a wish list and ask your local florist to carry flats of annuals. Street fairs may also have plant vendors.

Share. Networking with other gardeners is the surest way to expand your garden. Perennials must be divided, a whole flat of lobelia may be too much, and that garlic chive plant is taking too much room.

WHAT TO PLANT
Annuals

There are three guarantees in growing annuals: color, consistency, and easy care. Plunk them in the soil in the spring, and enjoy them until the first frost. Annuals are great for filling in gaps or replacing other plants that didn't quite take.

There are always places to tuck in some silver dusty-miller, marigolds, impatience, and pink and white begonias to fill out and brighten up your garden. A 9-inch clay pot looks great packed with all marigolds, next to another pot of marigolds combined with deep purple petunias.

Bring in the outdoors by planting a cutting garden. Grow snapdragons, cosmos, dwarf sunflowers, or zinnias. Go wild at the seed packet display, or order seeds from a catalog. Many packets and plant descriptions specify that they are perfect for cutting.

For lasting beauty for vases, pitchers, and baskets in your home, grow flowers that air-dry well. Try some statice, marigolds, bachelor buttons, strawflower, bells-of-Ireland, salvia, cockscomb, or globe amaranth. Pick just when they're in full bloom and there's been little rain. Remove the bottom leaves, use a rubber band to hold the stems together, and hang the flowers upside down in a dark place with good air circulation. Loop string, or use paper clips to attach the rubber bands to a length of string or wire; or hook onto nails. Once the flowers are dry to the touch, arrange them in a favorite vase and preserve with a touch of hairspray.

High Maintenance

The two most demanding annuals you could impose on yourself are petunias and pansies, the "terrible two's." Yes, petunias are beautiful and popular, but so demanding of your time! To keep them looking great and growing full, you must deadhead them daily. Popular cultivars also have sticky flower heads. You have to love them! Do look for new cultivars that offer full, bushy plants that need absolutely no maintenance.

Pansies are also a top-selling annual, although they are also perennial. They bloom from spring and long into the fall in the north and from fall through spring where winters are mild. To keep the flowers bloom-ing, you need to deadhead them weekly. As you see the petals all folded in against an individual stem, slide your fingers down and snap off against the base, or use your pruner.

Perennials

Choose and plant with care, since perennials come back year after year. They will grace your garden for at least two years, or for generations to come. Perennial flowers don't last as long as those of annuals, but you can stagger the blooming times of your perennials to last the whole season. Daylilies are a city gardener's friend since they grow very well in all types of light, save dense shade, and are easy to cultivate. Plant and transplant in the spring, and divide these hardy clumps every four years or so.

As the growing season wanes, the cost of purchasing perennials from your local sources decreases. As mentioned, buy them at better prices in early fall and enjoy for years to come! Although it's understood that nurseries and garden centers stock plants in their full-bloom glory to attract customers, it doesn't make sense to most gardeners. Yes, you see the "actual color," but wouldn't you rather plant it in your own garden and watch it come into bloom?

What would a shade garden be without some standard perennials like bleeding hearts, primrose, hellebores, and hosta?

Great perennials for air-drying include English lavender, lamb's ears, yarrow, thrift, and ornamental grasses. Just tie them upside down, let dry, and decorate. Or, you can use drying mediums and protectant sprays, sold in craft stores, that claim a longer and truer-to-harvest appearance.

Dividing Tricks

Don't panic; dividing plants really isn't as traumatic as it sounds. Whether your established perennial plant is taking over a space, just not looking great, or you want another one, then divide!

Perennials can be separated into halves; but to be really safe, take only a third to transplant. There are two ways to do this. Ideally, in the early spring just as the new growth is breaking ground, take a trowel or shovel and push the blade smack through a third of the plant. Work it down until you get most of the root system for that section. Lift up with your trowel, and holding as much soil as possible intact with your other hand, place it right down into the hole you have already prepared.

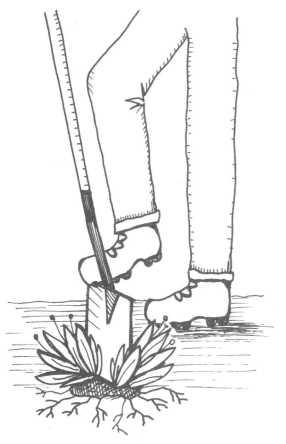

Dividing Perennials

Or, insert your trowel and dig a circle around the entire plant's root system, and lay it on its side on top of the soil. Gently wiggle and pull the roots apart, yanking as carefully as you can.

IN-BETWEEN PLANTS

Biennials bear foliage the first year, flower the next year, and then die. Mulleins, which grow happily in cracks in asphalt, produce copious amounts of seed and create lovely flowers along the entire top of a 4- to 8-foot stalk that bends with the prevailing winds.

There are many plants that, despite being marked as an annual, may come back to surprise you. Don't be too quick to cultivate the soil in spring. If you have a protected, warm microclimate, don't be shocked if impatiens, pansies, and trailing vinca come back.

SEEDS

Yes, growing vegetables and flowers from seed may take longer, but planting and watching their progress is a whole different—and very worthwhile—gardening experience. You will find varieties in seed catalogs that you'll never find in local nurseries.

Purchase what you need; or, in other words, think about where you have space to grow the seeds into full plants. Who ever thought bush cucumbers could have such different qualities! Do you really have the space for all three types of red leaf lettuce. See chapter 8 for information on how to choose seeds.

Seed packets often offer a wealth of information. Along with suggested planting guidelines, germination time, and harvesting dates, many growers add important advice on spacing and tending as well as harvesting tips. To save this information, use a scissors to cut, not tear, the seed packet open. Before discarding your seed packets (and catalogs), save yourself confusion and frustration by transferring the information to your journal.

BULBS

Myriads of spring-flowering bulbs are available in all but the southernmost states. Dutch bulbs need a cold winter, or you can duplicate those conditions in the refrigerator. Many summer- and fall-flowering bulbs—such as autumn crocus, lilies, and colchicums—are available in catalogs and online, especially for southern gardeners.

Unless you already have rich loam, for best results add peat moss, sand, and compost to the soil and a handful of bonemeal at the bottom of the planting hole. Plant before a heavy frost or until December in the north, and wait for cooler temperatures in the south.

Bulbs are easy to grow, as long as you plant them to the recommended depth—or a tad lower in colder climes. They are perennials; but some varieties last longer than others, so read the descriptions. Bulbs enjoy being mulched in the fall, but be sure to push mulch aside on warm days in early spring to aid the plant as the shoots break the soil. Choices include early-blooming snowdrops, then crocus, daffodils, hyacinth, tulips, anemone, allium, and July's iris. Summer-flowering bulbs include lilies, dahlias, gladioli, and shade-loving begonias.

Bulbs work great in any container. Northern gardeners should steer clear of using terra-cotta and other clay, since all the soil must be removed before frost hits. Layer late-blooming tulips on the bottom, add soil, then narcissus, more soil, and top with crocuses and snowdrops. Make note of the varying heights of the flowers you are buying before you plant them. For instance, a dwarf daffodil would be lost behind a grouping of 21-inch tulips. Plan your arrangement in groups of three or more for a nice effect.

The only negative with tulips and daffodils is that once the bloom has faded and you've pinched them off, you need to deal with the yellowing leaves. The nutrients need to go from the leaves back into the bulbs, so you don't want to break or cut the foliage. Wrap, tie, or braid them together and grow other plants that will hide the fading leaves; annuals come in very handy here!

Tubers & Rhizomes & Corms, Oh My!

If you adore showy dahlias (tubers), the pink, red, and white leaves of caladiums (they grow from tubers), and the stately, tropical, bold colors of cannas (rhizomes), then be prepared to dig them up for winter and find a place to store them. If you live in zone 8 or higher, then ignore this, smile, and enjoy these plants year round.

Dahlias grown in zones 9 and above spend winter in the ground; those grown in zone 8 and below spend winter in storage. After the first frost, cut off plants 5 inches above the ground, dig out, and brush away the soil. The easiest method is to wrap each whole clump in newspaper; then drop the bundles into a paper shopping bag, staple it shut, and put it in the hall closet. Come spring, throw out any rotten bulbs and cut the clumps up. Pot up the tuberous roots that have shoots at the top for an early start. If your clump doesn't have any shoots at all, stick it into some moist potting soil for a few weeks.

Few city dwellers have the space to keep caladium tubers stored in a box of vermiculite, or canna rhizomes in moist peat moss. One space-saving and successful (for two years running) solution is to dig them up once the frost hits. Shake off excess dirt and slip a tuber or rhizome inside old panty hose, tie a knot approximately 2 inches above it, then add the next bulb and continue on. Fold up the panty hose and put into a paper bag or tote, and hang the bag inside the hall closet. A month before the last frost date, pot up the tubers and rhizomes to establish roots. Plant them once night temperatures climb above 50 degrees.

Crocuses and gladiolus are not really bulbs; they grow from corms. The original ones you planted actually die off, and new ones rise to the occasion. Lilies propagate by scaling, like a large clove of garlic. In the fall, gently separate the outer layers and plant in some peat moss and sand to grow into healthy new bulbs. Come spring, plant where you want them to grow.

Yes, tender perennials can be tricky, but they are well worth it. The ideal storage environment is an unheated area or a basement, but how many city apartments have it? Try saving some; but know that the other, much easier, solution is to buy new ones each year!

Bulbs for Indoor Display

Forcing bulbs sounds more complicated than it is. You just have to fake them out with a false winter. Measure the lower shelves of your refrigerator, and find a pot or even a cereal bowl that fits. If you use a container with drainage holes, place a saucer underneath.

Wherever bulbs are sold, there is information indicating what varieties of iris, crocuses, tulips, and so forth are best for forcing. Bulbs need between thirteen and fifteen weeks of chilling. Remember to add a bit of water to keep the soil lightly moist, but don't overwater during this dormant period.

First put a thin layer of potting soil in the bottom of the container; then add the tulip and narcissus bulbs, cover them with soil, and water lightly until moist throughout. Stick in four toothpicks (spaced evenly), stretch a piece of cellophane across the container, and secure.

All paperwhite bulbs need is a bowl with rocks or seashells covering the bottom; just add water and sunlight. No chilling, no fuss. The idea is to have the water just touching the base of the bulbs. As with all forced bulbs, check the water daily and turn the container each day for uniform growth.

VINES & OTHER CLIMBERS

Although vines are difficult to grow in a window box, a thin, 6-foot-tall plant stake placed diagonally and leaning against the inside sill can support incredible cascading annuals, like sweet peas or morning glories. There always seems to be room for adding a climbing plant, as long as full sun or partial shade is available.

No matter what your climate, you can choose from many annual and perennial vines, which offer a variety of colors, flower shapes, fragrances, and growing habits. Be careful to read labels to match your sun and temperature requirements.

If you decide to grow a perennial vine, make sure that it's not going to grow against a fence or wall that's only temporary. If you share a wall, or you want to cover up a neighbor's wall, check with them prior to planting or risk having it removed in the future.

Climbing roses are not complicated to grow; figuring out what they should climb on is often the challenge! They don't attach on their own, but need training and securing. Search the catalogs and think creatively for a sturdy brace. Being alert while passing construction sites can pay off handsomely. Thin metal poles used to reinforce cement were bent into an arch and took only two years to be covered with roses coming from plants on either side.

Perennial Vines

Depending on the variety, many vines that are labeled as perennials are grown as annuals in northern cities. Some trumpet creepers and honeysuckles flourish as perennials only in zones 8–10, and others thrive in zones 5–10.

Once you have one clematis, you'll grow more for their beauty and—with the right variety—fragrance. Clematis vines like to have their bottoms in the shade and the rest in sun. This does not mean having the bottom leaves at soil level, but shaded at least a foot or two up. Adding mulch helps to shade and cool the base of the plant, but growing other plants around these vines works wonders.

Be sure to provide a sturdy trellis with thin rungs for the vines to grasp. For maximum impact, choose early- and late-flowering clematis vines to share the trellis. Many varieties are delighted with partial sun and shade (such as the hybrid 'Nelly Moser').

Know which clematis is an early bloomer, since you'll need to prune the weak and dead stems just after blooming. The late-flowering vines bloom only on new growth, so you'll need to prune away the top growth to ensure next year's blooms.

Two hardy partial-shade to full-sun vines are Dutchman's-pipe (reaching over 20 feet in zones 5–8) and climbing hydrangea (commonly reaching over 50 feet in zones 5–10).

Annual Vines

When it's time to plant tomato seedlings, you can also think about planting moonflower seeds to add nighttime beauty and fragrance. After they flower, keep removing the spent pods to encourage more blooms.

Morning glories and scarlet runner beans are easy and lovely, and they climb up anything you give them. The foliage is impressive and the flowers are pleasant.

Annual sweet peas, not perennial varieties, are the fragrant ones. They grow 6 feet tall up a trellis, or they'll grab onto string suspended between decorative, sturdy branches. Nick the seeds with a knife and soak overnight to speed germination. In the north, plant seeds in full sun in the early spring; in the south, plant seeds in the fall.

The Supporting Cast

There are many styles of trellis to consider for your garden. Do you want a gateway arch, an ornamental or fan trellis, a metal rose tower, wooden slats that open like an accordion, an arbor, or your own grapevine creation to secure to the wall? Know the mature height of the vine or climber you are considering before placing your order or building your own trellis.

Although touted as maintenance-free and lasting forever, plastic trellises are roundly rejected by the very vines they were meant to support. When the vines reach out to grab, or even when you try training the tender shoots to wrap, even morning glories (*Ipomoea purpurea*) literally pull away from the smooth plastic. Attach vines loosely for growth with green twist ties or thin wire.

All vines like to grow, and before they cover your upstairs neighbors' window, you may even need to prune them. Trellises made of wood or bamboo slats provide support for all kinds of twiners and for those that send out aerial rootlets, tendrils, or physically latch onto the slats.

Grow your own plant supports for other vines. Great supports include those made of grapevines and bamboo; or just plant tall sunflowers, dahlias, and pole beans for morning glories and sweet peas to wrap around and cucumber vines to climb.

GO NATIVE!

Since they grow on their own, native plants will thrive in your garden without fertilizer, muss, or fuss. Botanists are rightfully concerned about the survival of some 20 percent (over 4,000) of our nations' 20,000 native species. Never take plants from the wild, but look for nursery-propagated species. The plants in the Manhattan Botanical Garden were ordered by mail from nurseries in Kentucky and Tennessee that offered a wide selection of northeastern species.

Do a little catalog reading to find native plants to your region that are also drought-resistant, have great flowers for drying, or attract butterflies. Get more for your garden by learning more about specific plants.

HERBS ARE PLANTS TOO!

Herbs are great not only for adding flavor and nutrition to your favorite meals but also for soothing your skin and soul in the bath, and for adding beauty and fragrance to your garden. Vast choices of herbs are available. Herbs are perfect to tuck in and around flowers or to grow alongside vegetables. They are ideal for grouping together in containers or in individual pots.

Whether annual or perennial, herbs love well-drained soil and have better flavor with less fertilizer.

Annual herbs that can be transplanted into the soil or directly planted include basil, cilantro, dill, and fennel. Though parsley is a biennial, ensure a full harvest by planting it every year. Read catalog descriptions and seed packets, and ask questions in order to know what you're growing.

Eat Up

Herbs also have great nutritional and healing benefits. Our favorite eating herbs include basil (top a just-picked tomato with fresh mozzarella, and drizzle with some extra-virgin olive oil), parsley (on just about everything and in butter), chives and garlic chives (on all types of potatoes, soups, and stews), cilantro (salads, chicken, salsa), dill (fish and salads), nasturtium (salads), oregano (pasta and vegetables), and sage (crumble some in stuffing for turkey and roasted chicken; also insert whole leaves underneath the turkey's skin).

The culinary uses of herbs are limited only by your imagination and taste buds. Born and raised in England, my dear grandmother, Nanny, loved sandwiches made with watercress and added it to her salads. Check through your general cookbooks for charts describing which herbs are suggested for varied dishes. Experiment with your favorites to enhance, not overpower, flavors.

Eating particular herbs can also be beneficial to your health. It is said that garlic protects against infection and lowers blood pressure, hyssop tea aids with colds and bronchitis, sage tea soothes sore throats, and St.-John's-wort aids in calming nerves and improving circulation. Self-prescribing combinations of herbs for medicinal purposes is not advised; it is best left to a qualified herbalist. The saying "Don't mess with Mother Nature" should be taken very seriously.

Another multiuse herb is catnip. It is relaxing in the bath and as tea. We throw some on the living room rug for our cat before vacuuming; the only herb our dog takes bites of is pineapple sage.

Add Flavor!

Flavored vinegars add zest to any salad. All you need is a handful of fresh herbs, vinegar, a bottle with a tight seal, and a month's time for the flavors to be totally absorbed. Add an assortment of herbs for your salad dressing; and try single-herb vinegars such as lemon thyme, salad burnet, and French tarragon.

Hunt for glass bottles, decorative jars, decanters, and beer bottles with porcelain tops and wire clamps on the side to seal in the flavors. The key is a tight seal. If the cap's made of metal, just overlap the lid with a piece of waxed paper before sealing it to avoid a negative chemical reaction. Cork stoppers can be a hassle since they can dry out, don't hold the seal well with use, and can drop into the bottle.

Depending on your taste, use cider or white vinegar; but the herbs can be seen best if you use the white, and they look so nice! Some recipes call for bringing the vinegar almost to a boil, but it's not necessary. Ever open a bottle of wine and it just wasn't any good? Save it for your next flavored vinegar.

Wash the glass containers first, then gently place in boiling water for ten minutes and let dry. Rinse off your fresh herbs and add assorted kinds of peppercorns, peeled cloves of garlic, and whole hot peppers to the vinegar-filled jars. Cut whole sprigs of rosemary, oregano, or thyme. Leave in a sunny window or out in full sun (if not freezing out) for a few days; then store the herb vinegar in a cool, dark place or cabinet for a month.

Some herb-flavored vinegars take a month to "ripen," and hot-pepper vinegars can sit for years and get even hotter. Tie a ribbon around the top of the bottle or jar, add a label, and you have a great gift to give from your garden! Are the herbs looking a bit tired to give as a gift? Pour the vinegar into another glass bottle and add some fresh and dried herbs to it.

Herb-flavored oils are very popular and available in many stores, but it's fun to make your own. Take some olive oil and try adding some thickly sliced, peeled garlic cloves on a wood skewer along with your favorite dried herbs. Experiment with flavors by adding

herbal holiday fragrance

It just wouldn't be Christmas without the fragrance of the tree—and this delicious herbal concoction, simmering on the stovetop. Feel free to add other favorite herbs from your garden.

Christmas Scent

3 sticks of cinnamon
2 bay leaves
1/4 up whole cloves
1/2 lemon, halved
1/2 orange, halved
2 scented geranium leaves (optional)
1 quart of water

Combine all ingredients in a saucepan and bring to a boil. Simmer. The scent will waft throughout your home; but check the water often and add more as it burns down. Store in the refrigerator for a few days and reuse, or just keep adding to it throughout the holidays.

Reprinted with permission, *The Clinton Community Garden Cookbook*, by Patricia Berger and Barbara Feldt (New York: LarkOwl Publications, 1992).

different oils and herbs in a couple of small jars. A combination of dried cilantro and garlic works nicely.

Make sure you remember to write down which herbs you have used in each bottle, and put labels on each one. You want to know not only what you are using, but what was a great success—or what not to repeat.

Ah, the Scent of It!

As visitors slowly walk through your garden, it's great to suggest that they gently rub different leaves to smell the incredible fragrances of rosemary, pineapple sage, oregano, lavender, lemon balm, and thyme.

Don't bury fragrant plants where noses and fingers have to struggle to reach. Place the most fragrant flowers and herbs near your sitting areas, along the path, and directly outside your window. Growing vanilla-scented heliotrope and an assortment of scented geraniums will be well worth the effort.

Relax in a bath of chamomile, violets, jasmine, mullein, and catnip; or take a stimulating bath with basil, lemon verbena or thyme, rosemary, fennel, peppermint, and sage. Don't just toss them in, since they'll clog the drain and stick to you. You can put the herbs in the middle of a handkerchief or cheesecloth, tie with a string or ribbon, and place in the bathtub or bring the herbs to a boil in a pot of water, reduce to low for 15 minutes, and add to your bath.

NASTY BUGS BEGONE

What could be more natural to keep mosquitoes at bay than growing some special plants next to your dining area? Try the full, attractive 'Citrosa' geranium; and grow a pot of peppermint. Feverfew keeps the bees away. Drop some lemon peels where you see ants. Pick a bunch of lemon thyme leaves and rub them on your bare arms to dissuade bugs.

Decorative Outdoors & In

Surprise! The herbs you love also add beautiful flowers to your garden. Grow some nasturtiums, chives, bee balm, calendula, fennel, and yarrow.

Some herbs have such distinctive foliage that it's reason enough to include in your garden. Try some rue, assorted basil and sage varieties, scented geraniums, rosemary, eucalyptus, lovage (prefers partial shade), tansy, and santolina.

You can keep them growing through the cold months, if you have a sunny window. Get out the trowel and transplant your favorite annual herbs into pots, and bring them inside before the frost.

A simple basket or vase becomes a striking centerpiece when filled with sprigs of lavender, sage, yarrow, bee balm, and lamb's ears from the garden. Either add water or let them dry where they are.

Go all out and make an everlasting herbal wreath using twisted grapevines if available or purchase a readymade vine from a florist supply store. Stick in dried and fresh herbs, securing bunches with thin florist's wire.

Add dried herbs to a box of writing paper to scent them, or make your own special stationery. Press sprigs of herbs (dill, violet flowers, and sage look nice) between your thickest books for a week, then get out some nice stationery. Water down some white glue, dab it onto the herbs with a toothpick, and arrange on the stationery. Put a clean piece of white paper on top, and press for another week. You can also preserve dried herbs and flowers in matching little frames.

Drying Herbs

Bunches of drying herbs look so good tied upside down in the kitchen that we pick extra to keep there as decoration through the winter months. A brass-colored tension rod above the door holds a dozen bunches tied with green yarn.

Branches of sage, scented geranium, basil, lemon balm, and parsley emit lingering scents and look wonderful. Pull out the entire plant, roots and all, if you are harvesting an annual herb. For perennials, cut the stems low enough so that you can tie them together.

When harvesting, bring a large plastic or shopping bag for carrying the herbs. At home, shake or wash the dirt off the roots; the herb leaves should be fine. Wrap rubber bands or tie string around bunches, and hang them out of direct sunlight until they're completely dry.

Depending on air circulation and damp weather, herbs can take from four days to three weeks to dry. To crumble herbs into storage jars, place a colander on top of a dinner plate and fill with the herb branches. Crush the leaves between your fingers and remove any stems. Large pieces are fine, since you can crumble them when using herbs for cooking.

Store the herbs in tightly covered jars and enjoy in all your dishes until the next crop is ready to pick. Use peel-and-stick labels (file-folder labels work fine) to mark the jars, since many herbs—like dried oregano and basil—look similar.

Basil and parsley hold their flavor when frozen inside a plastic freezer bag. Wash the leaves, pat dry with a paper towel, and place in the bag. You can also tear up leaves into small pieces, or blend with some water, and freeze them in ice-cube trays. The cubes take longer to freeze, but then you can pop them out and store in freezer bags. These cubes are nice to plop into soups and stews.

Herbs are also used in cosmetics and lotions, and for dyeing fabric and yarn. You may find that herbs are important not only for cooking, but for complementing many aspects of your life. Herb seeds with growing instructions or plants are a welcome gift at any time of year.

The Allure of Scent

Aromatherapy is a current rage, but it's also an ancient holistic practice. The oils (known as essential oils) are extracted from plants and used to improve both mental and physical health and soothe the soul. Single scents or blended combinations are used to relieve stress (chamomile, lavender, marjoram), energize your mood (orange, ylang-ylang, eucalyptus), and make your home smell terrific.

Don't forget potpourri for adding the scent of nature to your home, especially when it's too cold to open windows. Pick fragrant herbs and flowers, and dry on paper towels overnight. Slice a few strips of lemon or orange peel as a fixative, and place with the dried mixture into a glass jar with a tight lid. Add your favorite spices, like cinnamon, and let sit for a month or more. Pour the potpourri into a dish, or use a potpourri container with holes to release the scent.

Get creative and sew up some sachets, combining flower petals and herbs, to tuck into drawers and tie on your closet rods. Make an herb pillow or a pomander (put on your garden gloves and stick whole cloves into the skin of a lemon or orange) to bring the scent of nature indoors. To extend the life of

the fragrance, you'll need to find a source (check the Internet, phone book, and catalogs) that sells botanical fixatives such as dried orris root and essential oils.

NOT TO BE OVERLOOKED

If you have the space, don't ignore the beauty of shrubs, evergreens, and trees. Dwarf cultivars are ideal for containers, rock gardens, and as focal points. Add some ferns and moss to the shade garden, or create a cactus display to add interest in a full-sun garden.

Variegated ivy trails from window boxes, hanging baskets, and from the corners of planters. Spreading ground covers like vinca, lady's mantle, sedum, lamb's ears, and creeping varieties of thyme and phlox are attractive.

Centuries ago, "city gardeners" in China had a great desire to be near the trees of the forest. They dug up old but dwarfed trees and brought them home. These small specimens were planted in containers and placed in their courtyards. Today's bonsai can serve the same purpose. Before you bring part of the forest to your garden, find out which tree will do best in your environment and what it will take to keep it alive.

—Mary C. Miller, editor, *Bonsai with Tropicals*, Miami, Florida

garden your city

Ornamental grasses make a graceful statement year-round. They can be space hogs; so instead of making an impulse purchase, know the habits of the variety you are buying. They are carefree, rustle in the gentlest breezes, and add beauty to any indoor flower arrangement. Check to see which color foliages and native grasses are ideal for your zone. Enjoy their beauty throughout the winter, and cut them back in early spring.

Birdhouse gourds, loofahs, and pumpkins are interesting and useful. They're also a lot of fun since they're quite strange to see growing in a city.

Weeds—yes, weeds—for edible and medicinal use include dandelion, violet, burdock, red clover, dock, sweet Annie, mugwort, and pokeweed. Please, don't go pulling and munching unless you can identify the edible weeds in your region.

HOW CAN YOUR GARDEN GROW?

Start with your most immediate sources and favorites, and then expand your horizons. Be selective from the beginning, and you'll be rewarded for years after. An offer of extra daylilies or an orange rosebush isn't great if you don't like them. There is so much to choose from, so take your time and plan.

Aside from the one or two new introductions that immediately make it to my "must have" list, it is indeed difficult to decide which new daylily cultivars I will add to my garden each year. During winter, the catalogs start coming in—filled with colorful pictures of each hybridizer's latest introductions. I make a list of those I want, carefully noting why each entry was selected for the list. As more catalogs come in, the list gets longer and longer. Of course in the end, I am only able to buy a few from the list. But the thrill of the hunt is part of the fun of collecting daylilies.
—Bill Jarvis, daylily grower and hybridizer, Houston, Texas

7

growing vegetables—
a.k.a. urban farming

It's hard to explain the thrill of leaning over to pick a vegetable that you grew. Yes, it did grow on its own, but you readied the soil, picked out the seed or chose the plant, worried over the weather and eyeballed for pests, worked in compost and added fish emulsion, deeply watered, and stared at every stage of progress throughout the growing season. Now it's time to take the ultimate reward—a beautiful, delicious, chemical-free vegetable.

Is it worth all the time, effort, and suspense to grow your own vegetables? Absolutely! After one season, you'll be hooked. You may find that you have saved on the food budget. But there's a warning involved: You'll forever notice the difference in taste compared to nonorganically grown vegetables. You'll find yourself saying, "It's not as good as ours!"

Make the most out of your growing space by giving careful thought to your absolute favorite vegetables. This is not as easy as it sounds. As you page through a vegetable seed catalog, your list may grow out of control. Your heart is racing as you check off the plants that will be delivered right to your apartment, but WHERE ARE YOU GOING TO PLANT THEM? More is not better. Overbuying results in overcrowding and a poor or nonexistent harvest.

SPACING'S KEY TO GROWTH

You can't begin to plan how many seeds to order, or what variety of plants to purchase, until you accurately measure your whole gardening space. Now, try to visualize your plants at maturity in that space. You have sketched five tomato plants for a particular planter; but now, after actually measuring the planter outside, you clearly see that only three of the wire tomato cages will comfortably fit into that space. Zucchini are fascinating plants, and delicious; but they are "space hogs," so you'd better really love them. As a perennial, asparagus also takes up a lot of space. If you are hoping to eat more than a couple of spears, buying them will be much cheaper and less time consuming than growing your own.

Vegetables can be grown in various sizes of containers. Lettuce does great in window boxes, pepper plants thrive in terra-cotta pots, and tomatoes happily wrap around their cages when grown in large plastic containers.

PLANTS OR SEEDS

Most vegetables are grown by planting the seed directly into the soil where they are going to grow. But tomatoes, peppers, and eggplants must be started indoors or purchased as transplants. If you just don't have the space, sun, or desire to set up lights at home, then purchasing six-packs of seedlings of your favorite vegetables works out very well. They are also ideal for unexpected late frosts that have obliterated your own tomato seedlings.

There are exceptions. Asparagus and rhubarb are perennials that are commonly grown from roots; garlic bulbs grow from planting individual cloves; and onion sets (small bulbs) are shipped ready to plant, although onions

grown from seed are larger and tend to taste better.

Seeds offer variety, the thrill of "creation," and bragging rights: "Those bush cucumbers came from a wonderful specialty catalog." Plants give you a real jump start on the season, more certainty of success, and earlier harvests.

WHAT TO GROW

Try anything you want and be adventurous! Meeting challenges, adapting to conditions,

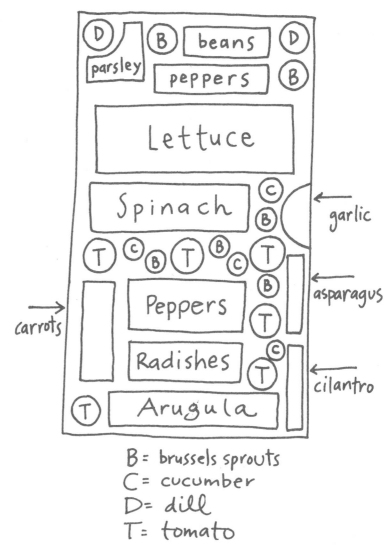

B = brussels sprouts
C = cucumber
D = dill
T = tomato

vegetables—what grows when

EARLY CROPS

Cooler temperatures and spring rains are perfect for many crops. Hold off until the soil feels dry, then go ahead and plant away. Pests are rare at this time, and weeds are easy to spot.

arugula

beets

cabbage

carrots

cilantro

collards

cress

endive

kale

kohlrabi

leek

lettuce—crisphead, butterhead, loose-leaf, romaine (cos)

mesclun

mustard

Chinese cabbage

peas and snap peas

radish

spinach

swiss chard

turnips

MAIN-SEASON VEGETABLES

broccoli

bush beans—green, wax
   (yellow), lima

cauliflower

celery

cucumbers—slicing and pickling

eggplant

melons

muskmelons—cantaloupe

okra

peppers—bell, hot, and sweet

pole beans—snap, pole, lima

potatoes and sweet potatoes

rutabaga

summer squash

winter squash—butternut, acorn, and giant

tomatoes—early, main crop, paste,
   and cherry

snow peas

watermelon

yellow wax beans

zucchini

PERENNIALS

asparagus

rhubarb (harvest the stems; the leaves are poisonous but can be added
   to the compost)

SAVE SPACE FOR SLOW GROWERS

garlic (Elephant garlic has a milder flavor.)

onions

lettuce

brussels sprouts

mustard greens

kale

turnips

and sheer determination are crucial to successful gardening. Your geographical location may offer only short seasons (such as growing tomatoes in Fairbanks, Alaska) and opting for container-grown carrots where the soil is poor or rocky, but you really can grow vegetables anywhere.

As you read through lists of vegetables to consider growing in your garden, some may trigger different responses, such as: "Absolutely," "Yuck," or "Wow, I never thought of it." Bolster your confidence by growing radishes. They're ready to eat in less than thirty days and are almost always successful! Remember to save some room for annual and perennial herbs such as parsley and sage.

Although yes, lettuce is traditionally a cool-weather crop, some varieties are truly heat-resistant and slow to bolt (go to seed). You can grow them with confidence all summer long!

JUST FOR THE FUN OF IT!

Hollow, ornamental gourds aren't edible, but they make fabulous birdhouses and decorative bowls. The long, thin bottleneck gourds are eerily enchanting when dangling off an arbor. To dry them, cut them off the vine with the stem attached; wash off in soapy, warm water; rinse; and let dry completely. Keep them out of sunlight in a large basket or bag, turning it once a week until, in a few months, you'll be able to shake the gourds and hear the seeds rattle around.

For the birdhouse, use a sharp knife to cut a hole at least $1\frac{1}{4}$-inches in diameter (drill two holes through the top to attach wire, and poke a small one in the bottom for water drainage). You can fashion gourds into a scoop for birdseed, or a dipper for reaching down into a rain barrel; or, cut one in half and coat with polyurethane for a bowl. Sandpaper softens the edges, and you can use a paste wax to preserve and paint to decorate.

Grow some small ornamental gourds or dwarf orange-and-white pumpkin vines up a trellis in a sunny spot for a great Halloween display or to add a nice autumn touch to a centerpiece for the dining table.

Grow great gifts! Warm-weather-loving luffas climb up and hang off a trellis, sparking many comments as they grow. Once the luffas turn brown on the vine, pick them and let dry for a month. Soak them overnight in the bathtub and peel off the tough rind. Keep soaking until it's all off, and dry the luffas in a sunny window. Cut your new sponges into whatever sizes you want. Add a scented soap and tie together with ribbon and a sprig of lavender!

HARVEST FUN

Whether you are trying to grow larger roses than those you see on your neighbor's rooftop, to produce the sweetest tomatoes in your community garden, or to get the reddest geranium blooms in your fire escape window box, there's always room for some healthy, friendly gardening competition.

Have contests for the earliest, most abundant, largest, and weirdest-looking vegetables. The categories are as limited as your imagination and the judges' patience. Some city gardeners even try to grow giant vegetables (buying seeds with the genetic predisposition certainly helps!). We all see the news each fall about the fattest pumpkin; but how about your city's biggest radish, longest carrot, or heaviest pepper?

Set a date to correspond with your city's peak harvest times (hold two contests for midsummer and fall harvests), ask some people who aren't competing to judge, and have refreshments and gardening-related prizes at the ready. As mentioned previously, a camera is a must.

TRIED-AND-TRUE TIPS & UNIQUE PECCADILLOES

Don't forget to rotate your crops! This is where your journal really pays off. Make sure you plant your year-to-year favorites in a different spot or container each growing season, to ensure healthy vegetables.

Before planting your cucumber seedlings or seeds, lean over the soil and push it into a mini raised bed, just a foot-wide mound about 4 inches high, to increase your surface planting area.

When you plant tomato seedlings, plant them all the way up to the bottom leaves, or trench the plant. To trench, first figure out

Tomato Trench Planting

where you want the plant to grow up, and then dig a trench off to the side, making it deep enough (around 3 inches) to hold the stem and roots. Keeping the top leaves aboveground, lay the tomato plant in sideways and remove the leaves. Cover the stem, pat the soil down, and water well. Mark the trench with a chopstick or rock, so you don't plant into it! It may look a bit odd for awhile, but roots will develop along the buried stem to create a very strong root system. No matter which way it grows, you may notice an added stem, or sucker, growing right out of the joints formed by the main stem and branches. Either snap them right off or prune them.

Don't touch bean plants when they are wet! They hate it. Pole beans love air circulation, so tie four or six 6-foot-tall bamboo poles in the middle and spread them out in an hourglass, teepee-fashion; or put up a net for beans to climb. Plant the seeds, with the "eye" side down for quicker germination, half an inch from the base of each pole and with two more in the middle for good measure. Sow where you want them to grow, and on the north end of your gardening space so you don't shade out everything else. Pole beans also adore wrapping up (and over) chain-link fences. Water the plants deeply, and keep picking tender pole and bush beans to encourage more growth! Hold back on planting all of the seeds for your green and yellow bush snap beans (don't forget to leave space!), and plant some every two weeks for a summer of harvest. Give bush bean plants room to spread. Crowding doesn't work here, so pay attention to the recommended spacing on your seed packet. If overwhelmed with growing pods, support them by tying the stems to chopsticks.

Two 4-foot-tall, tight-meshed wire cages will keep the birds from devouring sweet, tender snow peas growing on bamboo poles with netting in between.

Dig deep and add some sand and peat moss to your fertile, neutral pH soil for the best carrots. They like aged compost, love to be planted where lettuce or peas last grew, and appreciate a light mulch around—not on top of—them. To sow, grab as few as possible of the minuscule seeds between your thumb and middle finger. Thin to 2 inches apart when the tops are over an inch high; and to discourage pests, don't disturb the carrots' leaves. To harvest, dig around the emerging top with your fingers and grasp underneath the soil line on the very first date of maturity and for the next week or so. If harvesting is difficult, carefully use your trowel. Fall harvest time can stretch well past three weeks.

For maximum flavor, pick arugula when it's young, between 3 and 5 inches high.

Seeing your first green bell pepper starting to turn red is akin to seeing unexpected fireworks. Once they start, the colors expand daily to white, yellow, orange, red, lavender, purple, and even chocolate within three weeks! Stuffed, chopped, fried, grilled, or eaten raw, peppers are versatile vegetables that are easy to grow; taste mild, sweet, or fire hot; and are decorative in the garden and on the table. You can't sow seed directly in the soil, but they're easy to start indoors. Use a scissors or pruner to harvest (yanking can pull the whole plant out), and leave about a half-inch or less stem on the pepper.

For earlier and heavier cucumber yields, use some black plastic to mulch around bush and pole cucumber vines. Whether you choose slicers or those grown for pickling, wait for temperatures nearing 80 degrees before planting, and keep evenly watered. When flowers form, spray a mixture of water and sugar on the leaves to attract pollinating bees. Keep picking to keep them coming, but never refrigerate! Keep in the coolest spot before slicing to chill and eat or pickling.

Reminder: Gardeners who smoke must wash their hands before tending tobacco-sensitive vegetables, such as tomato, bean, and pepper plants.

Carrots, lettuce, and bush beans are perfect for successive plantings. Mark out the space you want for growing each vegetable, and then divide the seeds into three separate envelopes. Plant only the seeds from the first envelope, leaving space free for the rest. Two weeks later, plant the seeds from the second envelope. Plant seeds from the third envelope two weeks after that, and your harvest will be more spread out.

Thinning lettuce can be a pleasure since it makes a savory, early tender salad. Fresh lettuce is so easy to grow, yet people are terribly impressed by the colorful combinations and the remarkable tastes. Pick just the outer leaves, instead of the whole plant, to extend your harvests. Unless you doubt birds will visit, cover up the lettuce as soon as you sow. Build a lettuce cage that will last for years by bending chicken wire to create the sides and by figuring out the mature height of the plants and adding at least 4 inches.

Round, red radishes are a favorite; but also try white, French breakfast varieties, and Easter egg mixes for fun and flavor! Buy enough to plant every week, all season long.

Plant the radishes between rows of carrots to mark rows and reduce thinning. Make sure they get enough water! Store in the refrigerator in sealed plastic bags or containers, but don't pick all your radishes. Let a few keep growing and go to seed. The tall, white-flowered plants develop light-green pods to pick and chew, or to chop for topping a mixed green or potato salad.

Remember to check everything before adding it to your soil to make sure it's organic. Stick with natural. It's worth it.

There's always room for delicious, easy-growing garlic! Poke holes in the soil 4 inches apart, then pull a clove from the bulb and push it, root side down, so the top rests an inch or less deep in the soil. Plant garlic in mid-October in the north and in December in the south; use well-drained soil, then add mulch. When most of the stalk has yellowed and the tips are brown (mid-July; later in the south), slip a trowel deep underneath the bulb and lift one out. You don't need to harvest the garlic all at once. To store, brush off the dirt, but wait until bulbs are totally dry before cutting the tops or roots an inch away from the bulbs. Or you can braid or tie the tops together and hang in a cool place out of sunlight; or store in a cool, dry place to make the garlic last up to a year. The larger, outer cloves have the most flavor.

It's such a pleasure to see a ripe strawberry or two peeking out from the leaves. Grown in all zones and native to America, this fruit coexists between other full-sun crops very well if you keep them in control. Plant virus-free spring-planted everbearing (a crop in summer, more in the fall) and a standard June-bearing variety (plant now and pick off the flowers for next year's big harvest). Strawberries easily transplant into their own container or to a friend's garden if you plant the crown—where you see the roots start to come out—right at the soil line. The plants will produce fruit for three and more years if the soil is well drained and composted. And they'll taste so sweet, you'll swear someone threw sugar on them. Harvest with the caps on and store (unwashed) for a day in the refrigerator (if they make it that far).

YOU GREW THIS WHERE?

The irony was lost on no one when we brought luscious, organic, Manhattan-grown tomatoes to my father's party in New Jersey. Were we proud? Absolutely!

As city gardeners, we have every right to be totally thrilled over every single thing we grow. Every aspect of gardening in a city poses its unique challenges, and as such, makes the whole experience all the more special, rewarding, and dear!

Since the mid-1970s, the Pennsylvania Horticultural Society has helped people start community gardens in low and moderate income neighborhoods through its outreach program called Philadelphia Green. In our Garden Tenders classes, people learn how to start their own community gardens and start by planting over half the space with vegetables. Over 400 community vegetable gardens, and many hundreds of ornamental gardens, street tree blocks, and community parks are thriving throughout the city. Through the City Gardens Contest and the Harvest Show, two annual events sponsored by the Society, gardeners receive recognition and rewards for their enthusiasm and hard work. Gardening brings people together and empowers them to improve their neighborhood in other ways, like graffiti removal and town watch. Community gardens are also a great way for kids to learn how to care for their surroundings. The power of community gardening is that it turns the liability of a vacant lot into a beautiful positive statement about the people who live there.
—Patricia Schrieber, Philadelphia Green Outreach Manager, The Pennsylvania Horticultural Society, Philadelphia, Pennsylvania

8

seeds—choosing, starting, sowing, & planting

Sure, of course you know that vegetables grow from seeds. So? Well, when you see the sprouts you carefully planted breaking through the soil, whether indoors or out in the garden, this simple fact turns to excitement and wonder. Even the most reserved adults in the community garden have been heard shouting, "Look, look, the lettuce and radishes are up!"

There's nothing like taking the first bite into the season's first tomato. The one that you just picked from the plant that you carefully selected, planted, staked or caged, nurtured, and tended.

Starting your own seeds indoors is a must for tomatoes, peppers, eggplants, and other vegetables. These warm-weather crops won't germinate in cold soil and they will need warm temperatures and soil to develop. Starting seeds indoors also gives you a jump start for early harvests of many other plants, including lettuce and warm-weather cucumbers, herbs, and your favorite flowers.

Your local garden center's seed rack can be pretty good, but nothing compares with sorting through ten or more catalogs and surfing websites. Once you get on the mailing lists, the catalogs will start arriving at your door in December.

CHOOSING VARIETIES TO SOW & GROW

The easiest way not to go completely overboard with seed buying is to plan ahead. Have your garden plan in front of you to check how much space you have allocated for different vegetables and varieties. Not only do you have to narrow down the choices of what vegetables you want to grow, but just one slim catalog can easily carry twelve varieties of string beans and twenty-two kinds of tomatoes!

The names and descriptions of the varieties sound so tempting, but you need to be tough with yourself. Compare the text carefully for harvest dates, needs for growing space, ideal conditions, pest and virus resistance, and height. Are the tomatoes determinate (roughly 3-foot tall plants that ripen around the same time) or indeterminate (long vines that produce the largest tomatoes over a longer period of time)?

Read the catalogs carefully to see how many seeds come in each packet; the amount can vary greatly. Why pay more if you have room for only ten tomato plants? Sometimes, the ultimate decision between two ideal varieties finally comes down to the catchiest name!

Those little seeds grow into mature plants! If you're planning to start seeds indoors, make sure you buy more than one seed per pot. Some may not germinate, and you'll need to thin out the weakest seedlings. You must be tough and realistic with yourself. Where are all the seeds going to be planted? Those little seeds grow into mature plants.

PLACING ORDERS

Check the box on the seed company's order form to indicate that you'll accept substitutions if they're out of your choice. Avoid disappointment by placing your orders early.

Before the pictures and descriptions dazzle your mind, look at the shipping and handling charges. Narrowing down orders to a select few can save serious money. Yes, seeds are much cheaper than purchasing whole plants, but many gardeners order too many. Copy your orders and keep with your plan and planting records.

STARTING SEEDS INDOORS

Starting your garden inside is a promise of warmer days. Before planting the seeds, you need to count back from the ideal planting

I always use all natural, untreated, non-hybrid seeds. Seek out seed houses that that specialize in heirloom varieties. They are quicker to sprout and are always healthier plants with bigger yields.

—Jimmy Carlton, backyard gardener,
San Francisco, California

time for each vegetable you want to grow. Get started at least eight weeks before you plan to transplant young plants into the ground.

Your dual concerns are providing adequate lighting once the seeds have sprouted and having the space to put the growing seedlings. If you don't have a sunny window with at least eight hours of sunlight, but are determined to grow your own tomatoes, peppers, or eggplant, you'll need to set up artificial lights.

Lighting systems can be simple or elaborate and expensive. The Internet and gardening catalogs offer a range of systems to meet your needs.

The ideal height is an inch or less above the tops of the seedlings. Check with your hand and adjust as needed. Seedlings need both a simulated full day of light (between 12 and 15 hours of light) and darkness to fully develop. The more light the seedlings get, the better, or they will be too thin and weak.

The top of the refrigerator fits all of our seed-starting trays, and the bottom warmth is ideal for germination. A radiator's heat is the worst idea; investing in warming mats is the best.

WHAT TO GROW IN

Bags of lightweight seed-starting or sowing mix are available through most seed catalogs, websites, and garden centers. Make sure the mix is marked as sterilized. Regular potting soil will just not do. Buy double the amount you will need to fill the initial seedling containers, since they will have to be transplanted into more pots with some potting soil. Seeds prefer this soilless mix that is usually composed of peat moss, vermiculite, fertilizer, and ground limestone. If you want to create your own mix of soil, be sure to place it in a baking pan at 325 degrees for 45 minutes to make sure the seedlings won't catch any disease.

One of the most confusing purchases can be choosing the kind of pots or packs in which to grow your seeds. Two-inch-square pots and larger are great. Round, biodegradable peat pots are often used. You can plant them right into the ground (the roots push through), but their shape can take up a lot of room. You can also poke holes in the bottoms of cutoff milk cartons or paper cups; then fill with 3 inches of starting mix.

Plastic, individual "cells" designed for growing seeds come in four- and six-packs and will last over a decade. If the surface areas are too narrow, however, the mixture will dry out too quickly and the seeds will suffer. Drainage holes are a must for any container you use. The starter trays with long, narrow plugs make it difficult to remove seedlings. You can also sow seeds in rows in wide rectangular peat flats, but the seedlings will still need to be transplanted into their own pots.

Make sure your seed-starter trays come with covers (to use until you see the first sprouts break through) and bottom trays so water doesn't flow all over the place. If water is still sitting at the bottom 10 minutes later, lift the containers out and dump the water, or use paper towels to sop it up. Rimmed baking sheets and shallow roasting pans come in handy for holding soggy peat pots.

There's more. You'll also need more pots, because once the seedlings grow their second set of leaves (known as "true" leaves), they'll need to be transplanted. Plastic square pots or six-pack planters take up the least amount of room. The ideal, if you can create the space and provide adequate light, is to sow the seed directly into individual pots where the plants will spend all their growing time.

PREPARE FOR GROWING

Before you add the seed-starting mix, wash all the containers (not peat pots!) in soapy water, then rinse and dry completely. You will also need tweezers, a spray bottle, and a small-spouted watering can for reaching the bottom trays. Clear off the top of your refrigerator, or set up the warming mats before getting out the seed-starting mix.

Put the starting mix into the largest bowl or pot you have, place it in the kitchen sink, and mix in some lukewarm water. Work slowly so the mixture doesn't fly everywhere. Keep adding water, and work it through the starting mix with your hands or a spoon so it is completely and uniformly moist, not dripping wet. Fill your seed starters or peat pots all the way to the top for good air circulation; but don't pack the mix in too tightly, or you'll thwart root growth. Once your container is filled, shake or tap it against the sink to make sure the starting mix settles in without gaps.

THE ART OF SOWING

It's not hard, just tricky. Although fingers do just fine for larger seeds, getting smaller seeds just where you want them is a lot easier with tweezers. You can also try folding a piece of paper in half, placing seeds along the inside fold, and tapping them into place. Read your packets carefully, since some seeds aren't covered up at all. Practice over a dinner plate first to get the feel of it. If too many seeds come out, use tweezers to move them.

Since most seeds are planted a quarter-inch down, just fill up each cell or pot most of the way. Place the seeds on top of the starting mix, then sprinkle more mix on top and mist well. Plant at least two seeds to ensure that at least one will germinate and survive.

Another neat technique is to place the seeds where you want to plant them. Then use a toothpick or tweezer to push them down into the mix. Add a pinch of mix and pat down.

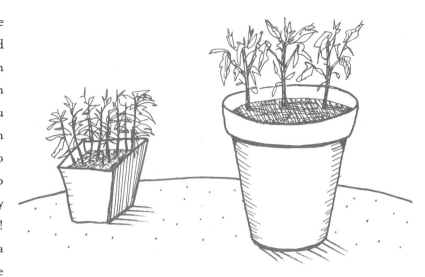

Once the seeds are in place and patted down, mist the top with the sprayer filled with lukewarm water. As you finish planting each kind of seed, be sure to mark the containers so you'll know exactly which seeds they are! Tape a slip of paper to a toothpick, or tape the paper onto the side of the container; cover the name with tape to protect it from water. Jot down the sowing date in your journal, and track germination dates and seedling progress.

Cover all the containers and place them on top of the refrigerator, in indirect light, until they sprout. If you don't have covers for all the containers, use cellophane wrap; or place the containers inside a cellophane bag with some holes poked in for ventilation. The ideal temperature for germination ranges from 65 to 80 degrees. Check daily to make sure the starting mix is moist, and use the sprayer. Once the first sprouts appear, remove the covers and move the containers to the light. Even if you see sprouts in only half of the containers, take off the cover.

Never let the mix dry out completely. To keep the seedlings evenly moist, to protect them against overwatering, and to promote strong root growth, water the containers from the bottom. If the bottom trays are just too difficult to water correctly, fill the kitchen sink with a half-inch or less of lukewarm water; then set each container in the water to

soak for about 5 minutes. The top of the seed-starting mix should change to a darker shade when moist.

THE FIRST TRANSPLANTING

Remember, the little cells or peat pots are small, so to give seedlings the proper space to grow, you'll need to thin them to the strongest one or two. Never just pull out the seedlings, since it could disturb the others. Use a scissors to snip the weakest ones right at soil level. Or, if a strong seedling is close to an edge, try using a toothpick to lift it up and out to transplant to another container.

Once the seedlings have several sets of leaves and are an inch high, it's time to give them more space to grow.

Combine more moistened starting mix with potting soil, and fill up the new pots. Make sure there are drainage holes. Bring the seedling containers to the kitchen sink, and tip them over a bowl to catch falling starter mix for reuse. Sliding a butter knife down the inside edges of containers may help loosen the soil as you catch the seedlings. You want to disturb the roots as little as possible; a teaspoon or salad fork makes a nice trowel.

Since stems are so fragile, lightly hold them by the leaves to transplant one at a time into the center of a readymade hole in the mix. Very gently, push the mix in around the seedling to firm it in place. As long as the original container is 2 inches wide, you can keep one seedling growing there. Plant seedlings at their original growing depth; or, if tomato stems and roots are strong and firm, plant them a bit deeper.

This all sounds very complicated, but it really isn't. Take your time, and know that after you've gone through the steps once, it will be much easier next time.

Add a weak, water-soluble organic plant fertilizer to the top of the soil. To prevent transplant shock, give them only 4 hours of light a day for the first 2 days, and then put them back on their schedule of 12–15 hours of light. You may see the transplants leaning toward the light, so be sure to turn them so they don't permanently lean to one side. Add some organic fertilizer solution every two weeks until the transplants are ready to go outside.

Once they have their leaves, pepper seedlings enjoy being misted; and tomato seedlings love to be shaken! To toughen up your tomatoes, just grab onto the container and shake it about 10 seconds once or twice a day. It won't hurt the leaves!

DETERRENTS TO DAMPING OFF

The condition known as *damping off* is caused by a fungus that kills seedlings. Make sure you use sterilized soil, clean containers and pots, and proper drainage. If all your seedlings have just toppled over, throw them out—along with the soil mix. Add a touch of bleach to warm water and wash the containers thoroughly before using again.

Once you have moved your seedlings under the light, take care to avoid overwatering, and ensure proper ventilation. The ideal is to set a fan on low and position it across the room. Now that they have sprouted, the plants like a cooler room temperature of 65 to 75 degrees. It isn't easy to tell when the medium is dry, so stick in your finger on the side of the pot daily to make sure it's moist.

ACCLIMATE YOUR SEEDLINGS

Your seedlings are growing into real plants! *Hardening off* is the gardening term for preparing your plants for the rigors of the real world. Open the window to get them used to breezes and cooler air. Check the weather forecast to make sure a cold snap or torrential rains aren't heading your way, and get the plants used to the great outdoors.

Place all your plants on a serving tray or in a baking pan, and carry them out to the nearest, secure outdoor spot. Take them to the fire escape, backyard or side alley, or up to the roof. Leave them outside for 2 hours—in a calm spot out of direct sunlight—for 2 days, then start leaving them out

wisely takes thought, but it will reward you with the fullest, healthiest plants.

Save yourself from thinning hell by not jamming fifty seeds where only ten will properly grow. Properly planting each seed takes less time than thinning out all the wasted seedlings. Save extra seeds to sow in two weeks, swap for other seeds with other gardeners, or save them for next year.

for longer periods of time. Move them into the sunlight, and then leave them out overnight for a few days before transplanting. Slide them under a table if rain is forecasted. The gradual process of toughening up your seedlings should take between 7 and 10 days.

It is best to transplant your seedlings into the garden on a cloudy afternoon, to reduce plant stress. Gently water the soil after planting.

DIRECT SEEDING

Direct seeding is the practice of planting seeds outdoors in the soil exactly where you want them to grow to maturity. You want the best placement for optimum growth and full use of the soil. Bush bean leaves barely touch when planted in a well-spaced, crisscross pattern. Plant one seed in the center, and four more in each "corner," 4 inches away. Using your space

HAVE ON HAND

To make sowing seeds a breeze, gather your supplies: knee pad, trowel, ruler, garden plan, and seed packets. If you plan on planting more than a few packets a year, then purchase a dibble. It's a cone-shaped hand tool that is ideal for making uniform holes.

Stick to your plan. When you are bending over the soil, that is not the time to be deciding where everything is going. If you extend your carrots just another three rows, you'll mess up spacing for the lettuce cage and the bush beans!

Once your city's frost date has passed and the soil can be worked, seeds for early crops can be put right into the soil as long as it is dry.

Seeds must be in contact with the soil, so make sure you pat down soil gently once the seeds are in place. For really small seeds, you can empty your salt shaker or a spice shaker and tap out seeds as you move down the prepared row.

ROWS & HOLES

Stick with the recommended planting depths. A rule of thumb is to plant the seed at a depth that would allow three more seeds of the same size to be placed on top of it. But, you can reduce the amount of space between seeds that the seed packet demands. Experiment, as long as you envision the plant fully grown.

Use your trowel or a finger to create a row. Don't worry about making mistakes; you can always fill in and start again. A ruler comes in very handy to measure the correct planting depth.

When planning successive plantings of lettuce, carrots, and beans, you must remember to save space to plant them between the first plants that you are going to harvest.

TAKING RISKS

Buy enough seeds to risk planting some in the soil before you really should. If they take, you'll have a head start. Take a chance and plant the hardiest transplant you have a week early; cover it at night with a cutoff 2-liter plastic soda bottle. A serrated knife works great for cutting off the bottle tops.

Placing a cold frame over the soil in a full-sun spot warms up the soil (and extends your growing season). If you have a raised bed, you can place a glass window over it and open it during the day; shut it at night to keep out the cold. Or, if you're handy with a hammer, build a cold frame with solid sides and hinges, and use a board to prop it open. Prefabricated frames are also available in garden supply catalogs.

PLANTING THE PLANTS

Here you are. You are surrounded by your hardened-off tomato and pepper seedlings, carefully selected perennials in nursery pots, and flats (those egg-carton-like six-packs of thin black plastic) of selected annual flowers and vegetables. You watered all of them a few hours ago on this perfect, overcast afternoon.

Prepare the soil, and have the plant hole ready before removing the seedling from its container. Hold your trowel against the outside of the container to gauge the depth of the roots. Then insert the trowel (the top is facing you) into the soil to the same depth. Pull the trowel toward you through the soil to leave just enough room for inserting the plant.

Grasp one six-pack out of the flat, and jiggle it as you pull it away from the others. Squeeze the sides of the bottom cells gently to loosen the plants. As they pop out a bit, grasp the top of the soil and gently remove. Tickle the base of the roots to loosen them up so they will grow out and get strong. Roll large, round pots back and forth on the

ground with your hand or foot; squeeze small, square plastic ones at the edges to loosen them, and then tap the bottom if needed to get plants out.

You want to create the least amount of disturbance to the roots, so, as you plant, carefully push the soil in toward the plant.

TIPS FOR CONTAINER PLANTING

Just like when they're planted in the ground, vegetable seeds and plants in containers need a certain amount of space around them in which to flourish. Window boxes are great for pepper plants, lettuce, and bush beans. Push a tomato

cage into any shape container, and plant the strongest tomato seedling in the middle; edge with parsley or white alyssum.

Go wild with flats of annual flowers for filling your containers and surrounding your perennial flowers and herbs. The roots of annuals, such as lobelia, alyssum, marigolds, and impatiens, can be planted directly up against the inside edges of containers. Cram them in to your heart's content to enjoy overflowing flowers. When so many flowers are competing in such little soil, be sure to use an organic fertilizer every week to keep them all nourished. A watering can filled with a weak solution of fish emulsion or compost tea is a wonderful boost. As long as you have hardened them off, your seedlings should not go into shock; but they may look a bit forlorn for a week or two.

Whether you use labels in the soil or have the garden plan detailed and sketched in your journal, remember to mark what is planted where.

YOUR GARDENING CALENDAR

So much of the skill and artistry involved in gardening has to do with timing. The optimum date to sow varied indoor seeds and ready them for planting is dependent on your city's last frost date. Learn as much as you can about past weather patterns in your

a simple, successful strawberry planter

strawberries

herbs

They complement any garden and look quite complicated, but strawberry planters are easy to do. After you've filled your planter with strawberries, fill another with an assortment of herbs.

Wash the strawberry planter, and add some rocks at the bottom for drainage. Pour in potting soil an inch below the first opening, and insert your first plant through the outer opening on the diagonal, squeezing in the sides of the roots to fit inside. Water lightly, and push down the soil into a curved shape around the opening. Dirt will be pushing out. Keep adding soil up to the next opening and placing each of the plants until you reach the final side opening. After you insert the last side plant, position the top plant and add soil on all sides, using your fingers to ensure that roots are in position. Scoop out a bit of soil from each opening to form each plant's growing bed.

city. Planting calendars are culled from years of gardeners' experience, so expand your knowledge by asking your county extension agent to mail you everything about growing vegetables—a list of recommended varieties, approximate days to germinate, and suggested planting dates for your region.

As you keep your journal for the first full gardening season, certain "to do's" will become evident for each season. You can mark your gardening activities in a twelve-month calendar: list the chores, along with dates you should order seeds, start seeds, and plan to harvest.

Choosing what varieties of seeds to order has gotten much easier since fragrance is now key to my selection. Planting seeds each season shows me the newness of life. Gardening is like pallet painting with live plants, and having mountains as a backdrop is glorious! Seeds replenish the earth and reward me with the bounty of God's gifts.

—Jeanette Irwin, gardener at the
Honey House Bed and Breakfast, Phoenix, Arizona

9

weeding, deadheading, & avoiding thinning trauma

Spacing is everything when you want healthy seedlings. It may be a pain to do, but without thinning, growth is impaired if not impossible. Take time to plan, and resist planting more seeds just to use up the packet. Ensuring proper growing space for your vegetables and flowers will pay off with bountiful and healthy harvests.

Thinning is vital. Repeat this thought like a mantra as you snip the extras away! With forethought and proper placement, you can avoid the trauma involved with thinning.

THINNING TECHNIQUES

The idea is to keep the strongest seedlings in the group and remove those around them. Sounds simple, but it's not. The seedling that looked so good aboveground may come right out as you pull out its neighbor. Why? Because seedling roots have already wrapped around each other.

Make it easier on yourself and wait until after it has rained, or water the plants a few hours before thinning. Using your fingertips, grasp onto some of the seedling's leaves at the soil level and slowly pull straight up. Pat down the soil on either side of the strongest seedlings you're going to keep. If there is resistance, use scissors to cut off seedlings right at the soil level.

The earlier you recognize that seedlings are coming up too close to each other—since you planted the seeds too densely—the easier it will be to thin them out.

IDENTIFY VISITORS

These "visitors" are not strangers admiring your garden, but plants that are growing in your soil that you know you never planted! They're also known as volunteers, and you can immediately remove them at first glance (such as 2-inch silver maple saplings that fly in from your neighbor's backyard) or wait awhile until the plant grows a bit so you can identify what you may have.

Volunteers can be blown into fortieth-floor planters by the wind, or dropped into the soil by a bird in flight. Or, they may have snuck in with that basil plant you just bought and planted. In a community garden environment, the volunteer may be a strawberry plant, mint that has migrated under a raised bed to yours, a foxglove, or just a nasty weed.

THE ART OF WEEDING

Catch 'em young, before they take over. Weeds zap nutrients and take precious space from plants you want to grow. If you are not sure if an alien plant is a weed, a volunteer, or something that a friend might have planted, then pot it up until the mystery is solved.

Many gardeners, like me, really enjoy getting out there to weed. With kneeling pad in place, you are getting your hands down in the soil, feeling its texture, and ensuring that whatever you're growing has the best chance to survive. Weeding, like any "art," needs dedication.

Yanking weeds from their stems can do more harm than good. If a weed breaks as you are pulling it out, use your trowel to go underneath it to remove the whole root. Some gardeners churn up all the exposed soil with a hoe or cultivator and remove what's left of the weeds; but unless you got the roots, they'll be back! Taking time to remove weeds as they

emerge is the best use of your time, and the best practice for a successful garden.

DEADHEAD!

Deadheading has nothing to do with the rock-and-roll group, and it's certainly a miserable term for promoting your plants' health and extending their beauty! But deadheading, which means to take off fading or dead blooms, allows new flowers to grow. Removing the spent flowers instantly improves the appearance and directs the plant's energy into new growth.

As the marigold's perfect bloom starts to droop and petunia and pansy flowers fold up, it's time to move into action. Not all blooms like to be treated the same way. Many "solid" blooms, like marigolds, are the easiest. If you don't have pruners in hand, place your thumb underneath the dead bloom, grasp onto it, and flip your wrist to lift it off. The term *deadheading* refers to removing dying blooms to direct the plants' energy into producing new ones. A rule of thumb is to snip the "nonproductive" bloom where the stem meets the main "trunk." Pansy flowers literally fold, so feel where the thin stem ends, then snip using a diagonal cut with your pruners or scissors. Keep an eye out for, and remove, any dead or dying leaves.

If you are not sure how to get rid of a certain dead (or dying) part of a plant, then go with your instinct and eyesight. Prune for a clean cut just under the base of the fading bloom, and then observe how it was getting its energy. If other blooms share the same stem, prune down to that flower. Benefits from deadheading the first cluster of phlox blooms are bushier plants with more flower plants and fewer attacks of powdery mildew.

PINCHING: NOT FOR GOOD LUCK

Grow fuller, fatter annuals and perennials by pinching them. Don't be nervous. Although at first it's psychologically difficult to remove any part of a growing plant, it will pay off! Consider pinching as a gentle, very meaningful pruning.

What you're actually doing is taking off the growing tip of a stem to force it to branch out. As long as the plant naturally branches—so don't pinch one that blooms at the top of a single stem—it should benefit from timely pinching. It may take the plant a bit longer to bloom, but you may easily double the amount of flowers! Once seedlings have been acclimated to their growing environment, and well before they bloom, pay attention to pinching opportunities.

When you see a new set of leaves coming up out of a basil plant, use your fingers to pinch just above the stems of other mature leaves. The plant will look really silly and unbalanced for awhile; but before you know it, two stems will spring up with tons of leaves. Keep pinching for a nice plump plant and to keep it from flowering. If you're trying to grow the biggest zinnia on the block, hold off on pinching since it causes more, but smaller, flowers.

But luck is with us, since most plant labels, catalog descriptions, websites, and friendly people on toll-free numbers will often give pinching suggestions and specific instruction.

NIP IN THE BUD?

Peonies are one of those perennials that you can pass down to future generations. To produce enormous single flower heads, the technique of disbudding is used. Leave the center bud growing, but pinch off every side bud early with your finger. All the nutrients will go to the one bloom.

Used with roses, dahlias, and chrysanthe-

mums, disbudding also works in reverse. Pinch out the main bud for great multiple blooms.

SEASONAL HAIRCUTS

Many plants can benefit from a good haircut once they've bloomed, as a perk for a repeat performance or to encourage compact growth. Reviving summer-wilted or leggy plants by "cutting back" doesn't mean selective pruning, but cutting straight across halfway down, or even sheering them right down to the soil.

Four-season gardeners have winter choices in the garden. Unless a plant adds a decorative look or has seeds or berries for the birds to enjoy, you may want to groom your perennials and uproot the annuals. I leave ornamental grasses in place throughout the winter, but cut them with a pruning saw in February—well before new growth begins. The 6-inch tall, rounded clumps left behind develop green shoots in early spring.

REDUCE CHORES & ESCAPE MISTAKES

Know before you sow, and avert mistakes with planning. Observing your garden and tending to its needs will reward you with pleasure.

We knew that the string beans would climb up the trellis purchased just for them, but we had no clue how thick the leaves would be. They were fantastic, but they blocked out all of the late afternoon sunlight intended for other plants. And we were thrilled when the cucumbers grew so well; but then they crawled through and over everything else! They certainly weren't the bush variety we thought we

had planted, and the seed packet confirmed it. Oops.

Garden and learn; learn by gardening. Talk to as many other gardeners as possible; and read catalogs, labels, and seed packets carefully. Post questions to a gardening topic folder, or enter a chat room on the Internet for answers to your most pressing and mundane questions. Ask if anyone from your city or zone is in the room. Surf the net for websites dedicated to specific plants to anticipate or ward off problems with knowledge.

When you're weeding, be careful not to remove a prize! I have found, lifted, and potted-up or transplanted many an unexpected treasure. Had I been a less judicious gardener, I would have tossed out an extremely shiny-foliaged Oregon Grape Holly, a light powder blue balloon flower, a clematis with mottled foliage, and many others who seem to seed themselves in harm's way.

—Dean B. Scott, American cottage gardener, Detroit, Michigan

10

nature's way—compost & wildlife

After you bend over to examine your plants critically, step back and take a moment to admire them. Now, consider what little you actually had to do with creating the beauty before you. It really is amazing. Just when you're sure you pruned a shrub back too hard, or fearful that a midwinter thaw has destroyed the spring bulb display, or that you have completely killed something, back it comes! That's the wonder of nature.

Many plant species that grow in the wild can also be enjoyed in our city gardens. Collecting nonendangered plants from the wild is not restricted; but read plant labels or ask about their origins when purchasing. If plants were not propagated in a nursery, they are required to be labeled "wild collected." Nursery propagation, legislation, and consumer education are working to protect endangered species.

We have learned how to bend Mother Nature's rules to force blooms, increase harvests, and extend growing seasons. But for plants to survive in your garden, you must duplicate the environment in which they have naturally grown. Before you decide to make a purchase, pay close attention to the required soil, light, and water conditions.

Gardeners learn through experience, example, research, and the aid of technology to alter the natural order to make the most of their planting spaces or suit their desires. But we can learn meaningful lessons by taking time to observe what happens naturally in our own gardening spaces.

What a fantastic classroom to spend time in! Make notations in your journal; observe the daily progress, and notice the manner in which different plants are growing. Record when and how long a plant blooms, and what you want to change or add. Be on the lookout for pests and disease.

What an odd, but absolutely marvelous, sight to see a butterfly flapping its wings up on a tenth-story terrace. What fun to point out darting bats to an evening visitor to the community garden. Although some wildlife will naturally gravitate to your plantings, there are many ways to attract more insects and animals, especially those that are beneficial to your sensibilities and plants.

COMPOST FOR ENRICHING BENEFITS

Nothing is more beneficial to your garden than compost. It's well worth the effort (and actually very rewarding in and of itself) to recycle nature. Even a coffee can on the fire escape or window sill can hold spent blooms, unflavored coffee grounds, kitchen scraps, and crushed eggshells.

Compost improves your soil naturally by returning organic matter to the soil. There is no need to hold your nose if you've added the right ingredients; and compost isn't complicated or expensive, either! It will save you money on buying soil, it's environmentally correct, and it will improve everything you grow.

Benefits of adding organic matter include improving soil structure, adding oxygen, improving drainage, preventing erosion, and increasing both water retention and heat absorption. Compost is a great source of nutrients and minerals that are released slowly to surrounding plants. Compost reduces weeds and harmful insects, and it aids your plants in fighting against pests and disease. Compost produces healthier plants without adding any artificial, dangerous additives to your soil. In other words, compost is phenomenal!

Moistness, mixing, air circulation, and small pieces are the fundamentals for pro-

ducing handfuls of fluffy, rich compost in a short time. You want to achieve the best combination of ingredients that will heat up and literally "cook" itself into compost.

Gathering & Temporary Storage

Despite living in a city, you'll find there are plenty of compost ingredients right on hand, and others that you can scout out with a little extra effort. Until you get into the habit of composting, you'll be surprised at how often you automatically throw "good stuff" into the trash can. As you prepare meals, chop up vegetable scraps. The smaller the pieces, the quicker they will compost.

Before you start chopping, you need to find something to keep compost ingredients in until you can bring them to the compost pile. If you are composting in a plastic or terra-cotta pot out on the sill or fire escape, all you need to do is chop your ingredients into small pieces, toss into a bowl, and walk them to your pot. Add some soil and keep moist. If this is a temporary holding spot, find a sealed container for storing your partially finished compost until you can add it to the compost pile in the park, community garden, backyard, or on the roof.

Designate a place in the refrigerator to keep a covered container for storing compost ingredients. No matter what you use, make sure the seal is secure to eliminate any seeping or smell. Use the same plastic, metal, or glass container all the time; or make sure you label new ones so you don't alarm others who are searching for food! Just wash the container each time it's emptied, to keep odors away.

At-Home Fuel for Compost

Use a knife or scissors to chop up any vegetable parts you don't eat. Use the top stems and root of celery stalks, rip apart eggshells, cut up overripe fruit (but toss the pits), or go all out and use your food processor. Anything that grew from the ground can go back in.

Newsprint is great to add and readily available—grab a section of your newspaper, tear it from the top down into long shreds, and cut it into confetti. Don't use any of the slick inserts or any pages printed with colored ink. Make it really easy on yourself and shred a batch of newsprint at the office, or buy a low-cost paper shredder for your home.

In the summer, head to a park with a lawn and pick up—or ask the maintenance crew for—some grass clippings. In the fall, bring a shopping bag and gather up leaves.

If you're growing a lot of acid-loving plants, start a separate compost pile just for them. Load it up with coffee grounds, crushed eggshells, and finely chopped needles from evergreen trees.

As long as they're not artificially flavored, throw coffee grounds in your compost instead of the garbage. Cut used tea bags in half, rip unprinted paper towels into tiny pieces, and pour some ashes from a hardwood-burning fireplace (absolutely not from fake, packaged logs) into your compost.

Recycle Your Garden!

As you deadhead, prune, pick off dead leaves, or pull whole plants at the end of the season, add them all to your compost pile.

Cut up thin green stems and branches into pieces no more than 1 inch long to speed up the composting process. If the branches are brown, or thicker than a pencil, they should go into a long-term compost pile to decompose.

Anything that once grew in the garden can be composted. Fold up those dead, thin morning glory vines and prune them right into the pile.

Outside Sources

Does your health food store have grass growing in the window, and do they serve assorted vegetable juices? You're in luck, because their pulp waste is wonderful to add to your compost.

If a friend with a paper shredder brings you a huge bagful of newsprint, the balance that you have established would be thrown off if you put it all into the pile. Thank your friend, add two handfuls to the compost, and stir. Store the rest so it doesn't blow away.

Do you have horseback riding in your city, or does your police force have a mounted unit? We proudly credit our rich compost and healthy gardens to the addition of NYPD horse manure. On to the stable! Double up some large shopping bags, lined with a plastic trash liner draping out on either end. The stable will have shovels for filling your bags (half full—they get heavy); but avoid getting much hay mixed in, or you'll soon have sprouts growing. Unlike me, most people find the scent offensive, so be sure to seal up the liner before hopping on mass transit! Since fresh manure will burn and kill roots, it's best to bury it deep into your containers when the plants are dormant and use the rest for compost.

You may also want to contact the city zoo, or find out when the circus is heading back to town, and ask where and when manure will be made available to community gardeners. If your zoo is not already providing manure, make arrangements! The animals are there, so you should be able to take it "off their hands" without much fuss. One trip reaps enduring benefits.

My friend Pat and I still laugh about our trip to Madison Square Garden when the circus came. They provided shovels and we brought heavy-duty garbage bags and filled them to the brim with fresh elephant-doo. We hailed a taxi and packed the trunk with our bags of minutes-fresh manure. We placed the last bag on the backseat between us and chatted as if nothing was amiss. The driver moaned and groaned the whole fifteen blocks home—until we tipped him well. We spread out our bounty on top of our dormant garden beds and our building's roof until the sun baked it dry. Once it had cured, we stuffed it in sealable sandwich bags and sold them to benefit the community garden at the annual 9th Avenue International Food Festival in May. We attribute the largest tomatoes we have ever grown to that elephant manure!

Do you know people who commute into the city? Ask them for a bagful of cut grass (it is quite pungent, so it should be tightly sealed up) and have them ask an employee at the lumberyard to sweep up some carbon-rich sawdust.

Hold It There: Pile Ideas

Your choice of compost container correlates to the materials you have available and how much money you want to spend. The idea is to contain the pile in one tidy area.

If you have a wide windowsill, a small clay pot can heat up some compost in no time. Place a couple of 6-inch terra-cotta pots throughout the backyard and roof garden to collect handfuls of deadheaded flowers. Once the pots are full, their contents can go into the main compost pile.

The term *pile* is used loosely. Whether city gardeners are cooking their compost in a sealed plastic bag out on a sunny windowsill, in a large plastic garbage can with dozens of nail holes in the sides, or in a coffee can on the fire escape, they refer to that collection of fresh scraps as "the pile."

Create an easy compost pile by forming some thick-gauge chicken wire or snow fencing into a circle. You can also scout out scrap lumber or wood pallets to build a two-bin system, or stack concrete blocks in a U-shape with the holes directed into the pile. It's not as neat as an enclosed bin; but you really don't need much to build an active compost pile as long as you have a level, well-drained space.

The scope of your composting effort depends on the space you have, how much compost you plan to make, the effort you want to give it, and the money you want to spend. Your compost pile must be at least 3 feet high, wide, and deep for it to really heat up and decompose quickly. Your pile should also be within easy reach of the garden hose or the watering can, to help you to keep it moist.

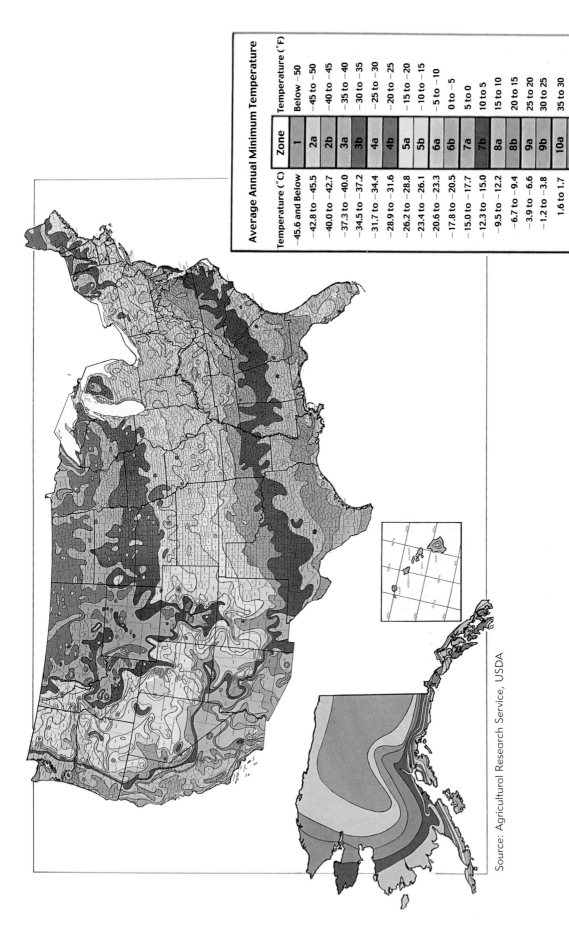

Average Annual Minimum Temperature

Temperature (°C)	Zone	Temperature (°F)
−45.6 and Below	1	Below −50
−42.8 to −45.5	2a	−45 to −50
−40.0 to −42.7	2b	−40 to −45
−37.3 to −40.0	3a	−35 to −40
−34.5 to −37.2	3b	−30 to −35
−31.7 to −34.4	4a	−25 to −30
−28.9 to −31.6	4b	−20 to −25
−26.2 to −28.8	5a	−15 to −20
−23.4 to −26.1	5b	−10 to −15
−20.6 to −23.3	6a	−5 to −10
−17.8 to −20.5	6b	0 to −5
−15.0 to −17.7	7a	5 to 0
−12.3 to −15.0	7b	10 to 5
−9.5 to −12.2	8a	15 to 10
−6.7 to −9.4	8b	20 to 15
−3.9 to −6.6	9a	25 to 20
−1.2 to −3.8	9b	30 to 25
1.6 to 1.7	10a	35 to 30
4.4 to 1.7	10b	40 to 35
4.5 and Above	11	40 and Above

Source: Agricultural Research Service, USDA

superb compost ingredients

This is a basic list to pick and choose from; do not think you have to add all these! A combination of vegetable scraps, green and brown plant parts, coffee grounds, and shredded newspaper will compost just beautifully.

Fresh clippings, deadheaded blooms
Thinned sprouts, dead plants
Vegetable peels and scraps
Finely chopped fruit peels, pieces, and cores
Coffee grounds and filters and tea bags
Human and pet hair and nail clippings
Crushed eggshells
Manure—horse, cow, bat, poultry, zoo, and circus animals
Food—soiled undecorated napkins and paper towels
Burlap bags—torn or cut up
Leftover bread, cereal, plain pasta, and rice
Grass clippings
Hosed-down seaweed
Shredded newsprint (black and white ink only, no slick paper)
Dead leaves
Straw (horse stable, nursery)
Sawdust (lumber yard)
Red wigglers (worms)

Citrus rinds, fruit pits, twigs, nutshells, wood chips, mussel and clam shells, or corncobs are slow to decompose. Save them for a long-term compost pile only.

Or, you can bury partially composted compost! If there is any open soil available between vegetable rows or plants, and you're not planning to plant there in the next six months, just dig out a trench or make holes at least 10 inches deep, add your compost, and cover it up.

A passive "cold" compost pile, ideal for fall-to-spring composting, can be constructed by placing four bricks under the corners of a plastic milk crate obtained from a delicatessen or supermarket. Pile in the ingredients, and slide an unused dinner plate beneath the crate to catch the liquid seeping through. Simply pull out the plate and pour the juice into a watering can for instant compost tea any time of year!

You can add new ingredients and mix them in to build up your compost pile

never put these in your compost

Weed seeds

Plants with disease or pests

Meat, chicken, or fish scraps

Dairy products, fats or oils, or greasy food scraps

Pasta or rice

Dog or cat feces and litter

Rose branches, sticks, coal

Ashes from a charcoal fire

Rocks or glass

Anything that isn't organic

throughout the growing season; or, you can just leave it alone. Remember, to be rewarded with rich, decaying matter, take the time to cut or tear everything into small pieces. Water when it doesn't rain, add some fresh manure to the harvest's remains, and then let nature take its course as the pile slows down in cold temperatures.

Two- & Three-Bin Systems

If you are all gung ho, have the space, and can hammer a nail, then a two- or three-bin open-front system will certainly speed up the composting process. Using untreated lumber (never buy arsenic-laden, pressure-treated wood), you can vary the bins' dimensions. Build your system right

over soil, throw a few inches of soil on the existing brick or cement, or build a solid bottom to raise the bins off the ground to keep the wood from rotting. To be practical, make each bin at least 3 feet high and 2 feet wide.

This is how it works. With a two-bin system, you add the ingredients in the first bin and, as it decays, transfer it to the second. Turning your compost pile moves the process along and lends a hand in its creation. When it starts looking and feeling like thick, crum-

Three-Bin Compost System

garden your city

bly, dark, chunky soil, it's ready! If you have three bins, use the third for more time to decompose and for storing compost until you're ready to use.

If you want to get more high-tech or are impatient for finished compost, rotating compost bins raised up on legs are available from garden supply companies. Pack the bin loosely, like you would a clothes dryer, and turn the crank daily to tumble everything. Many space-saving, recycled plastic compost bins have flaps you can raise when rain is forecast. There are compost turners designed to effectively turn these top-loading containers, and organic "starters" and "activators" speed up the process with combinations of microorganisms and materials high in nitrogen.

Striking a Balance

Creating rich compost depends not only on gathering the right materials and providing air and water, but combining them in the right proportions. Yes, things will eventually rot if you just throw them together and forget about them. But to produce timely results, you need to add equal amounts of green and brown matter and then, literally, toss things up a bit to become a compost chef!

Anything brown—leaves, newsprint, and straw—is rich in carbon, the food that gives decay-eating microorganisms their energy. The nitrogen in green materials (plant prunings, weed stems, vegetable scraps) produces protein for the microbes to be able to break down the carbons. Weeds are never added to the pile, as mentioned, because you certainly don't want to risk spreading weed seeds throughout your soil!

Since the proportions of carbon and nitrogen are matched, a pile composed of just horse manure with straw mixed in, and a combination of green and brown plant materials, will efficiently create great compost without your having to add another thing.

Get Cooking

Compost piles can be very efficient and effective! One winter after a blizzard, my husband Fred and I trudged four blocks to the community garden with a week's collection of compostables. The pile was smoking! We pulled open the gate and tried to keep to the path that was under 10 inches of snow. It really looked like the compost pile in the back was on fire, but it was actually steam rising up in the second bin. Talk about cooking!

To build a pile that will heat up quickly and produce compost within a few weeks, you'll need all the ingredients handy and ready to add. You never want to add a ton of one ingredient; be patient so you can build the pile correctly. Hold a pile of vegetable scraps or clippings (green), pruned into small pieces, off to the side until you have shredded newspaper (brown) ready to add with it.

Moisten the ingredients a few days before putting the pile together. If you are composting right on cement, put 2 inches of soil on it, and then place equal amounts of green and brown layers, 4 to 5 inches thick, on top of one another. A meal of steamers and oysters will provide a sturdy organic "floor" for a compost bin. Cover each green and brown layer with an inch of beneficial bacteria-containing soil and moisten with more water. The pile should end up looking like a sloppy pyramid.

You can also toss in some beneficial organic toppings, such as bloodmeal, ground limestone, and bonemeal. In a week, turn the pile by moving the outermost materials inside and shifting the bottom to the top. If you don't have a compost fork or turner yet, a broom handle or golf iron will work! Don't be bothered by a bunch of pill bugs (the ones that curl up) or the grey, oval, sow bugs that feast on compost; they'll die off as the pile heats up.

Your goal is to get plenty of air down into the layers to speed up decomposition by aerobic (oxygen-eating) bacteria. Be happy, not alarmed, to see the pile shrinking to a third or half of its original size. It's just doing what comes naturally. The temperature will lower as the process slows. You can hold fresh compost in your fist and actually feel the warmth.

Compost Tomato Well

It can take some work, but the more often you turn the pile, the quicker you'll have compost!

Some gardeners turn their compost pile only when they think about it, others turn it every week when they weed the garden, and some turn it every day.

Too many green ingredients can cause an odor, so bury them deep in the pile and cover the top lightly with soil. A waterlogged pile is just as ineffective as a dry one, so turn it over to get air inside and add some dry ingredients like shredded newsprint. Poke some holes in the pile, and form a bowl shape at the top for rainwater. Keeping the compost pile consistently moist is just as important as getting oxygen in to keep the good bacteria cooking!

It's Done!

Congratulations on your first "harvest" of rich, dark compost—referred to among gardeners as "black gold." Depending on the size, type, ingredients, temperature, and time that you put into your compost pile, it may have taken one month to a year or more to finish. Doesn't it look and smell great? Composting gets easier; use the "unfinished" twigs or eggshells for the bottom of your next pile.

You may want to invest in a compost sifter, or return what didn't sift through back to activate the new pile. Use a cultivator or trowel to work compost a few inches down into your soil before you plant. In a process known as top dressing, add finished compost about an inch away from established vegetables, flowers, and herbs; but keep it away from germinating seeds. Play it safe with seedlings and place compost on the soil's surface a few inches away.

Save some compost to spread on the soil throughout the growing season. Use compost in the bottom of planting holes for an extra boost, and use it to build little walls a few inches around tomato plants and roses to form compost-filled moats to conserve water, add nutrients, and ward off disease.

Keep it coming. Composting is an easy, constructive habit to get into since it's a natural process that is only hastened by your assistance. Not only are you recycling organic waste that would have gone out with the garbage, but your soil and future plants are reaping nutritional benefits. You also save money on buying fertilizers, bags of compost and manure, and more soil!

ATTRACTING BIRDS— NATURE'S PEST CONTROL

As I stretched between the hydrangeas to pluck out a stray weed, I sensed that someone was watching. I was right. Two bright red male house finches were perched on the brick wall, staring at me. They were out of the thistle in their tiny feeder.

Birds are nature's most worthwhile insect eaters. Attract them by providing food, water, places for cover, plants and surfaces to perch on, and houses for them to nest and raise

their young. Consider shrubs or trees that produce berries or cover from the rain or snow.

It's for the Birds

Birds that eat seeds would love you to grow sunflowers, perennial black-eyed Susan, and purple coneflowers. Like other wildlife, they gravitate to free-flowing gardens. Consider plants that supply sap, berries, fruits, and nuts. Grow a nectar-rich honeysuckle vine, a wild rose, winterberry or bayberry shrub, a pagoda dogwood tree, and ornamental grasses—for their beauty, for food, and for providing cover and nesting sites.

Feeders

Place the bird feeder not only where you can view it but also where it's convenient to fill. Be sure it's located where cats or other predators can't reach it. Never hang bird feeders directly over plants, since most birdseed will sprout.

Whether they're made of plastic, copper, or redwood—or shaped like a globe, tube, or beach cabana—hanging feeders must have a sturdy perch for the birds. There are even weight-controlled perches designed for small songbirds; if heavier birds or squirrels sit on them, the perches automatically close the seed supply.

Platform feeders, trays, or cereal bowls of seed attract ground-feeding birds such as sparrows, cardinals, and mourning doves. Such feeders are great for windy terraces and roof gardens. The seed must be protected from the elements.

Seed

If you are storing birdseed outdoors, invest in a tightly sealed plastic or metal can with a lid that has clasps on either side to keep moistness out. A scoop or a plastic cup is ideal to hold a good amount of seed that can be easily poured into the feeder.

Wild birdseed is widely available. A quick search of the Internet provides custom-blended mixes to attract particular species. Cardinals adore sunflower seeds, and sparrows love the mix with millet.

Feeding birds is a commitment. Their high body temperatures demand a constant supply of energy. Once the birds rely on your feeder, it's up to you to keep it filled when their natural supply ends.

Some species also enjoy suet cakes, slices of oranges, apple, cranberries, grapes, and raisins. For a cold-weather energy treat, slip string at the top of a pinecone (available at craft shops) to hang and roll in peanut butter and seed. Keep extra cones refrigerated on wax paper. Since these treats have no perch, place them within easy "pecking range." You can "reseed" the pinecones and use them again.

Baths

Water is essential for birds, and providing a birdbath is a rewarding and decorative element for any city garden. If freezing temperatures are forecasted, replenish the birdbath with lukewarm water and refill daily. Or, if an outdoor outlet is available, hook up a heater (sold through catalogs) that will shut off once the water warms.

Dripping water attracts birds. Solar-operated fountains and baths that plug into an outdoor outlet provide mini-waterfalls that also adjust to a mist for hummingbirds! For birdbaths that do not have moving water, change the water daily or add an anti-mosquito product.

Houses

Despite the name, birds don't live in birdhouses. They use them for shelter and to raise their young, and then they move out. If you ever see that a chick has fallen from its nest, it is fine to put it back in.

Position the entrance of your weatherproof birdhouse away from the prevailing winds. Make sure to get a collar with a bell for any cat heading out into the garden.

The size of the entrance hole and birdhouse dimensions are dictated by the species you want to attract. Over fifty types of birds will make their nests in a birdhouse, but they prefer different entrances. Bluebird houses have $1\frac{1}{2}$-inch holes, while a $1\frac{1}{4}$-inch entrance hole is ideal for a chickadee, nuthatch, titmouse, wren, or downy woodpecker. To keep predators out, most houses do not have perches; robins and song sparrows prefer covered houses with open fronts.

Before moving into a colony, purple martins demand $2\frac{1}{2}$-inch entrance holes, guard rails so the kids don't fall out, and door stoppers to keep other birds out. These specially designed houses, known as condos and high-rises, are sold to accommodate from twelve to twenty-four martins! Now, that's spoiled!

INVITING & INTRODUCING DIVERSE WILDLIFE

This year, on the Fourth of July weekend, the true sign of summer silently returned. My husband and I had just finished barbecuing in the backyard with neighbors. Just before we all headed to the roof garden to see the fireworks show near the Statue of Liberty, the first one was spotted, and then another—the lightning bugs were back! Talk turned to summer childhood memories as we all watched the lightning bugs dance through the garden.

In North America there are over 140 species of fireflies that communicate with luminous signals to attract their mates. Adult females flock to plantings to sit back and watch the males flash their yellow light as they fly past. A chemical reaction in the insects produces this light; and once the female is attracted by a male, she answers by flashing back at him. Ah, what a concept!

Butterflies

They don't call the *Buddleia davidii* the butterfly bush or *Asclepias tuberosa* the butterfly weed for nothing! One summer day, five monarch butterflies sat on the butterfly bush on our roof overlooking the Hudson River. Flying only in daylight, they travel for miles to suck nectar with their tongues from these favorite flowers. Lucky for city gardeners, they also carry pollen with them!

Monarch butterflies are drawn to bunches of nectar-producing, colorful, sun-loving plants: yellow marigolds, goldenrod, and black-eyed Susans; orange nasturtiums, pink summer phlox, and purple coneflowers; easy-to-land-on cosmos and late-blooming asters. They are also attracted to multicolored lantana, easy-to-sip lupines, impatiens, zinnias, snapdragons, and hollyhocks. Monarchs have been seen enjoying mint, among other herbs.

Monarchs (*Danaus plexippus*) can live up to six months throughout most of North America. They migrate thousands of miles (between Canada and Mexico), but most adults don't live for even two months. Keep them in your garden by providing the right plants—such as milkweed, nectar-bearing flowers, and butterfly bushes—for laying eggs and obtaining nourishment. Place a few smooth, dark-colored rocks in the sunlight for monarchs to warm themselves and dry off their wings. Place a butterfly house into the soil at plant height. Create a fake puddle by submerging a shallow saucer with small stones, and add soil or sand to the bottom to capture some drinking water for them.

As with humans, with wildlife—especially butterflies, birds, and frogs—there is absolutely no reason to use any kind of pesticide. Attract wildlife to eat pests instead of introducing poison to kill wildlife.

Don't forget to add visits from wildlife in your journal. This will not only help in monitoring your progress, but aid you in evaluating what plants to add to extend the stay of wildlife. For great photographs, observe the rhythm of a butterfly's wings to capture them fully open. Purchase a field guide to identify your visitors, and use binoculars to reveal a whole new dimension.

A Hummer!

Grow red, nectar-producing plants to coax "hummers" to hover over your flowers to lick up the nectar. Add some bee balm, geranium, cardinal flower, coral bells, trumpet honeysuckle, or aloe and some red varieties of morning glories, petunias, and salvia. Hummingbirds are attracted to the color red, and they're tempted by butterfly bushes, azaleas, and flowering crab trees.

If you live in eastern North America, you can fill red-colored hummingbird feeders with nectar to attract the ruby-throated hummingbird. A week prior to the hummingbirds' migration arrival—January in Jacksonville, Florida, and by May in Detroit, Michigan—hang the feeder with a bright red bow near some flowers they enjoy.

Fish, Turtles, Frogs, & Toads

Watching colorful fish swim around—or a turtle on a rock, craning his neck at the sound of your voice—adds much to the gardening experience. Deal with a reputable pet store or mail order concern that is forthcoming with answers to your questions.

Caring for any animal takes care, money, and commitment. You are obliged to provide them a proper habitat and ensure against any predators. If you don't plan to keep the pond

clean, safe, or healthy, don't buy goldfish or koi just to throw them out at the end of the season.

Attracting Bats?

If you could invite a valuable pollinator to your garden, and they promised to get rid of most of your pests—and do it without chemicals, quietly at night, and for free—wouldn't you welcome them? Although they give many people the creeps, bats eat insects such as mosquitoes, flies, gnats, and ants. Unlike birds, bats are endangered; and they will live in slender houses you can provide.

Paint the top half of the house black to raise the inside temperature, and install it 15 feet high up on a pole or wall where it's blocked from rainfall. Position the bat house to face southeast or east, and make sure that nothing is blocking the bats' flight path for at least 20 feet.

I've had the experience of bats divebombing the pool as I swam at night, so I know they're attracted to splashing water! They like standing water nearby, so provide a birdbath. Right before sunset, the bats come out and get to work; watching them in flight is mesmerizing.

URBAN BEEKEEPING

Many city gardeners are keeping productive hives on their roofs, terraces, and in community gardens. Bees are needed to pollinate flowering plants, their hives are fascinating to observe, and they make delicious honey.

Honeybees just love city life. Sidney Glaser, who works the hive at the Clinton Community Garden, stopped in to check on the bees in the middle of a very cold, snowy February. He was astonished to see them bringing back pollen to the hive. He couldn't figure out where they were getting it until he passed a corner grocery store two blocks away. There, on the sidewalk, he noticed dozens of bunches of flowers behind a protective wall of plastic, where the bees were happily feasting.

"Bee people" are passionate; you can't tend a hive by knowing just a tad about it! Before Lorenzo Langstroth invented the modern beehive in the mid-1800s, bees built permanent combs to store honey. To harvest honey, the beekeeper had to destroy the combs and kill the bees. Now, thin sheets of honeycomb-imprinted beeswax are held in place by removable frames with spaces between them for honeybees to move around.

Langstroth imported and developed the often-used strain of *Apis mellifera*, the Italian sweet bee. He wrote *The Hive and the Honeybee*, first published in 1853 and still a definitive text.

Swarms often occur in late spring if the hive is too crowded; or, if the hive raised a second queen, some fly off with the old queen. Though the bees seldom sting since there is no home to defend, a swarm is a startling sight to witness. Once they leave the hive, the honeybees lose all memory of where it was, and scout bees start searching for a new

The hive sits on the ground and shares the Clinton Community Garden with children of all ages. Yet, I've never heard one negative comment! It says so much about the total picture—the connection with nature and each other. I'm fortunate to be able to work with honeybees and to share this experience with interested people in fantastic garden settings!
—Sidney Glaser, beekeeper and teacher, Clinton Community Garden and Wave Hill, New York City

home. In the height of summer, a normal hive has around 600,000 bees.

Fascinating Honeybee Facts

When two queens meet, they'll fight to the death; the queen's sole function is to lay eggs. Male drones can't collect pollen or nectar. Once the queen has mated, the female workers bar the remaining drones from entering the hive, and they all die. Bees fly up to six miles away in their search for nectar. Female workers carry out the dead and place them away from the hive.

To observe bees, place a small saucer of sugar-flavored water on the soil. Put a very small drop of honey on your forearm to watch the bee's tongue suck it up.

Bee Balm—A Perennial Favorite

Bees depend on color and ultraviolet vision to locate flowers, and they don't see the color red! Keep that in mind, and buy seeds and plants in the bees' favorite shades of blue and violet.

Two species of monarda grow in the wild in eastern North America and flourish from zones 4–9. *Monarda fistulosa* (wild bergamot) enjoys dry, sandy soil; minty *Monarda didyma* (known as bee balm and Oswego tea) favors highly organic, moist soil. *Monarda fistulosa*'s light-purple-colored flowers bloom in the summer on 1- to 4-foot-high, square-shaped stems; but it's the bright red bee balm that city gardeners choose because it also attracts bees, butterflies, and hummingbirds. Keep deadheading your bee balm to keep the blooms coming.

WORMS & THEIR BINS

Invite worms to dine on your compost pile! Since they're 90 percent water, red wigglers survive in temperature ranging from 40 to 80 degrees. If you don't have outdoor space, but really want to recycle and compost, then vermicomposting may be the solution.

There's no special "worm food" to buy, since worms will eat up your kitchen scraps. Redworm or red wiggler worms (*Eisenia foetia*) digest food into nutrient-rich feces known as worm castings. Indoor worm bins are enclosed but have holes for air and drainage (and are even available with a sliding viewer). As finished "compost," the castings can be cultivated directly into soil to slowly release their benefits. Add them as you plant, and spread them on top of your soil.

MOTHER NATURE KNOWS BEST

Skilled gardeners have a healthy respect for nature. If you ignore nature's lessons, you might as well call yourself a "person who pushes around soil and sticks in plants" instead of a gardener, who strives to achieve what he or she envisions.

Watching, touching, listening, feeling, tasting, and smelling will all assist you in understanding changes in your garden. Being in tune with the weather, the condition of your soil, the sun, the scientific facts about your plants, and welcoming wildlife are all

Don't worry, a healthy worm bin smells of good fresh earth! With a little super-vision, even a five-year-old child can manage a productive bin and appreciate the recycling process. If you feed the worms, they'll feed the soil that, in turn, will provide you with healthy food!
—Frances Mastrota, expert vermicomposter and horticulture educator, director of Pleasant Village Community Gardens, Inc., East Harlem, New York

components of becoming an accomplished city gardener.

LEARN & GROW

Providing an ecologically balanced garden makes sense for you, your plants, and visiting wildlife. Consider participating in the Backyard Wildlife Habitat program. Over 45,000 certificates have been issued in all fifty states, six Canadian provinces, and several other countries. Most habitats are located in urban and suburban locations where volunteerism, gardening activities, and the need for habitats are at peak levels.

The Backyard Wildlife Habitat program was developed and is run by the National Wildlife Federation, America's largest member-supported conservation organization (see Appendices). The organization provides both inspiration and education for welcoming wildlife to your garden.

The National Wildlife Federation through its Backyard Wildlife Habitat Program awards this Certificate of Achievement to

BACKYARD WILDLIFE HABITAT™
NATIONAL WILDLIFE FEDERATION®

Manhattan Botanical Garden on Pier 84

This Certificate recognizes the establishment and maintenance of Backyard Wildlife Habitat

no. 20895

This habitat is certified in the National Wildlife Federation's worldwide network of mini-refuges where, because of the owner's conscientious planning, landscaping, and gardening, wildlife may find quality habitat–food, water, cover, and places to raise their young.

President

printed with soy inks on unbleached recycled paper

NATIONAL WILDLIFE FEDERATION

Participants have proven that by working together, we can have a positive impact on our local environment and ease the return of some species that have disappeared from our neighborhoods. City wildlife gardens are especially important as they provide safe havens for wildlife to thrive in an often hostile environment.
—David Mizejewski, Program Manager, Backyard Wildlife Habitat Program, National Wildlife Federation

part three

Places to Grow

II

window box, fire escape, & balcony gardens

It's wonderful to sit in your favorite chair with a good book and glance out the window to watch the daily progression of your flowers, herbs, and vegetables. This closeness to nature and ease of proximity for watering, spritzing with a spray bottle, deadheading, and harvesting cannot be surpassed.

PLANTING IN ANYTHING OTHER THAN GROUND

It's called container gardening. You are mimicking Mother Nature by adapting plants to the sunlight that's available, providing water when it doesn't rain, and furnishing the best soil with proper drainage.

Window box gardens send a nonverbal message that people care not only for their home, but for their surroundings. Tourist brochures depicting quaint seaside and his-

toric cities inevitably include photographs of window boxes.

Place Defines Type

Before heading out to a garden center or discount store, or placing a catalog order for a window box, you must keep two crucial details in mind: fit and security. Take exact measurements and make sure you have easy "reachability" for watering and tending the window boxes.

Many window boxes are never installed in windows. City gardeners creatively attach them to terrace walls, hook them inside roof railings and parapets, and hang them on fences. With the owner's permission, you may have a gardening opportunity on a neighboring wall.

Look for choices in plastic, wood, metal, terra-cotta, glazed clay, cement, stone, and cast stone. Fiberglass containers last for years, and catalogs offer decorative planters of lightweight resins that closely resemble stone and terra-cotta but can be moved at whim.

Installation Jitters

Once you've added drainage material, soil, and plants, window boxes made of any material can be surprisingly heavy. If you need to secure brackets into the building, obtain permission from the owner. Bring a picture from a magazine or photograph to show what you're planning. Combat any potential liability concerns by pointing out that air conditioners all over the city would also fall if they weren't properly secured.

Unless you know how, leave the job to someone who has the tools and experience. Tape a note on the front door for the "4th Floor Window Box Gardener" to find out who did the installation, or check with your hardware store for suggestions.

Success using cement nails varies with the type and condition of the wall's surface. A masonry drill or high-powered nail gun and anchors will secure brackets, and lag or toggle bolts are used for plastic-coated metal or L-shaped stainless steel brackets. Wrought-iron brackets must be painted with a rust-proof sealant before installing.

Set the Stage

Check the drainage holes at the bottom of the window box, or drill some for water to escape. Clean the container, and then add a layer of stones or broken clay at the bottom to prevent the roots from rotting.

Recycle a cracked terra-cotta pot by putting it inside a paper bag and, using a trowel, smacking it repeatedly. Check your progress with each smash, since 2-inch, irregular shards are great for drainage. To reduce seepage, place a used, rinsed fabric softener sheet over the shards before adding soil.

Soil Plus

If you squeezed some topsoil in the palm of your hand, you'd wonder how tender seedling roots could grow. Lighten up with a soilless "grow mix" (contains lots of peat moss) or a potting soil blend, and add nutrients with organic fertilizer and compost.

A great no-soil technique is to place a variety of annual plants, still in their plastic pots, down inside the window box. Conceal your secret with sphagnum moss and rearrange at whim.

Plant Choices & Design

Window-box gardens are so versatile. A wide range of annuals and perennials, herbs, vines, and vegetable seeds and plants are suited for window boxes. Replant to change with the seasons or your mood; and replace plants that fade.

Height is a prime consideration with window-box gardens. Know the growing habits of your plant choices, so you can stagger heights and include some that trail. Dusty-miller (*Senecio cineraria*) adds height and a silvery white accent to annual arrangements. Don't ignore ground covers and low-growing, creeping varieties of flowers.

Individual Needs

Every flowering plant has distinct aspects—when it will bloom; life span; shape, height, and color; foliage texture; spreading habits; color and length of bloom; and fragrance. Be aware of your plants' sun, soil, and watering needs—an aloe vera plant would be miserable sharing a home with impatiens and a tomato plant.

Do ignore the recommended spacing directions on the plant labels for a fuller effect. Spacing of 4 to 6 inches apart is not intended for container city gardening.

Don't forget vegetables! Follow a lettuce crop in the spring with patio tomato, bell pepper, basil, and parsley, and save seed for a late lettuce harvest. Enjoy eating tender lettuce leaves as you thin them. Crop rotation in a window box!

The Nature of Color

Color choices are as diverse as your imagination and preferences. From color coordinated (all red flowers or just blues and yellows) to mood-enhancing arrangements (pale to deep pinks with small touches of white for an old-fashioned romantic look), the individual selections you make will have a definite impact.

Flowers naturally bloom in colors ranging from the "hot" yellows, oranges, and reds to the "cool" purples, blues, and greens—and in hundreds of shades, tints, and tones in between. Variations in foliage provide background, add contrast, and unite plantings. Note the color combinations that please you; the best tool for color design is your own eye.

Seasonal Changes

Keep in mind that many perennial flowers, bulbs, and herbs—like lemon-scented geranium (*Pelargonium crispum 'Major'*) are delighted to be growing in your window box, but may not survive winter in such a small space. Harvest what you can, or find room indoors.

Southern gardeners don't have to worry about this; but if you have a terra-cotta box, remove the plants and soil before it freezes, wash it with detergent and a little bleach, and store it for next year. With other window boxes, simply cultivate the soil, add compost and a layer of mulch, and anxiously wait for spring.

Although it may be the end of your gardening season, your window box can continue to be a visual pleasure. Green markets, nurseries, florists, and even the corner delicatessen carry natural decorations to add interest and color. Darrell, our local Christmas tree vendor, makes his annual trek from Vermont with a wide array of trees, wreaths, roping, and dwarf Alberta spruce (*Picea glauca* 'Conica'). After gracing our window box through the winter, the spruce trees go to our local park garden, where we replant them in spring.

FIRE ESCAPE FINESSE

Many a room has been rearranged to take full advantage of the floral view afforded by created outdoor plantings. All varieties of containers are workable, but you must never forget the primary function of the fire escape. When placing your window boxes or containers, imagine people scrambling up or down the escape. Nothing can block the way.

Where anything can fall off, or the wind can blow down, there is potential for injury or death; such areas must be secured. Climbing plants such as passionflower (*Passiflora* × *alatocaerulea*) vine will also need to be reined in.

Permission Is Crucial

If you do not own your building, then you must find out if gardening on the fire escape is allowed. Although a window box suspended over the street may appear safe, hang it on the inside of the railing so it won't hurt anyone in case it falls.

Great Beginnings

My husband and I took our maiden voyage in "city farming" with a fire escape garden. An eclectic assortment of coffee and restaurant-size aluminum cans soon had holes punched in their bottoms with a nail and hammer. This "kitchen garden" outside the bedroom window expanded to include string beans, basil, cilantro, arugula, radishes, lettuce, and bush cucumbers.

Our tomato and pepper seedlings seemed to thrive on this south-facing fire escape, but we were upset to notice that they were all listing toward the west. Then it dawned on us that they were literally just following the sun. Stretching certainly didn't stop an abundant harvest!

You can't change either the configuration of your fire escape or the path of the sun, but you can adapt by placing plants in the most effective arrangement. Grow tall plants that call for full sun, but know they will stretch toward the sun. You can place shorter partial-sun plants underneath the leaning flowers, and then place shade-loving plants behind them. Watch that you are not dripping water onto your neighbor's windows or passersby below.

Don't Be Shy!

Once you have the green light from the building's owner, get dramatic! Think up! Many climbing vines, both perennial and annual, will wrap around iron bars—for example, try growing a passionflower (*Passiflora* × *alatocaerulea*). Clematis is a hardy, multizone perennial that enjoys sun to partial shade but loves to have its base moist, mulched, and shaded by the foliage of surrounding plants. Since many vines can reach to 15 inches and higher, you'd best speak with your neighbors upstairs.

BALCONY BRILLIANCE

The romance of a balcony is undeniable. Even if you never stand on it and gaze down into your beloved's eyes as he woos you with song, this distinctive architectural detail exudes fantasy. Often constructed of stone and incorporating columns in the railing, balconies are a showcase for delicate, trailing vines that flow downward toward the street below. The city of New Orleans is famous for its balconies and terraces edged with lacy, ornate ironwork railings overflowing with flowers.

By definition, balconies project from the building; and they are generally too narrow to hold a chair. But what your space may lack in width is made up for by its potential for incredible impact. Small plants bearing single blooms are not for you. The spaces between your balcony railings can be bursting with flowers and ornamental grasses.

Add dimension and create an illusion of a lush, more spacious balcony by slipping decorative planter "feet" or bricks under your containers' drip trays to stagger heights. Elevating your planters improves drainage and offers air circulation. Jostle the planters a bit to make sure that they're sturdy.

Trailing Plant Ideas

You can let plants and vines freely flow, or you may want to do a bit of training. Tendrils will wrap themselves around thin fishing line; string it between the container and a fence or other support.

The wind can play havoc with trailing plants. Wrap a bit of clear tape, loose enough

1. Butterfly bush surrounded by columbine (add a trellis for clematis)
2. Hybrid tea rose surrounded garlic and garlic chives
3. Phlox surrounded by creeping and lemon thyme
4. Lemon balm and sweet and lemon basil
5. Daylilies and white alyssum
6. Lamb's ear and lobelia
7. Parsley and oregano
8. Rosemary and sage
9. Lamb's ear and lobelia
10. Coreopsis
11. Trailing nastortiums in front, ivy in front corner, and snap dragons
12. Trailing nastortiums in front, ivy in front corner, and snapdragons
13. Cornflower

Sunny Balcony

1. Astilbe—red
2. Astilbe—white
3. Astilbe—pink
4. Bleeding hearts—white & pink, surrounded by white impatiens
5. Astilbe—pink
6. Astilbe—white
7. Astilbe—red
8. Hosta—gold and foxglove
9. Impatiens—pink
10. Cinnamon fern
11. Impatiens—white
12. Lily-of-the-valley, primrose, and ivy in front corners
13. Impatiens—white
14. Lady fern
15. Impatiens—pink
16. Hosta—blue and foxglove

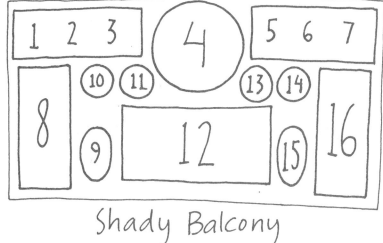

Shady Balcony

for growth, near the end of the vine tendril to add some weight.

Pesky Pigeons

Some city residents see these birds as "flying rats"; others see them as so sweet that they risk paying fines to feed them. But to a city gardener tending new seedlings, pigeons are the devil incarnate.

A temporary solution is to have a spray bottle or child's water pistol handy to startle the pigeons. Deter them from landing by "planting" chopsticks between plants and around the edges. Smear a thick layer of vegetable shortening or petroleum jelly anywhere they sit. Hang a small wind chime on a plant stake in a container, and dangle small mirrors. Install iron points on roosting ledges, and crunch chicken wire underneath air conditioners. Call your city's animal control phone number to inform yourself about possible humane solutions.

Having a container rose garden out on our fifth-floor fire escape extends the decor of our bedroom, and the river breeze brings the fragrance inside. It's great that everyone can clearly see the roses from a block away.
—Neil Koch, fire escape gardener, New York, New York

garden your city

12

terraces & roofs

Rome wasn't built in a day—and your garden won't be, either. You wouldn't want it any other way. You need time to explore ideas, make decisions, reposition things, change your mind, and be flexible to adjust to a plants' growth and external conditions.

Gardening on a terrace can afford increased sunlight, additional space for planting, and more privacy than a roof. Often constructed as a visual extension of a living room, and unlike a balcony, terraces usually have room for a patio table and chairs to enjoy an interesting view. If yours doesn't, there are tricks to turn your terrace into a destination of its own. Despite size or view, a terrace affords a special respite and gives city gardeners room to expand their talents.

TERRACE—SPLENDID SPACE W/MEDIOCRE VIEW

It can't be all bad. At least you can look up and see some stars. But, you face a brick wall or look out on architecturally boring buildings, roofs, or warehouses. Add places for plants to grow by adding a fence of latticework, or secure a trellis or two on the sides of walls. A vine covering a fan trellis will easily block an unsightly view of a graffiti-scrawled chimney.

Bring two terrace chairs out with you. Sit down in every possible position. Once you've found the best view, decide where the other chair will live. It may be up against the outside railing and facing into your living room! Once that's decided, you have already completed the core of your garden design. Keep these two optimum views of your terrace garden in mind as you design your garden. Planters can edge paths leading into "rooms" and/or position plants on either side of your seating.

Take Stock

Your terrace may have a railing, wall, and floor space offering plenty of places to hang baskets, window boxes, and planters.

Take complete measurements and map it out on paper.

The Wind Factor

More terrace gardeners complain about the impact of the wind than do those who have full roofs on which to putter around. Maybe it's because of the way the wind wraps around buildings, or because terraces jut out into the natural flow of the wind. In any case, city residential buildings often feature terraces that catch the wind in varying degrees.

Plants that are damaged by windburn are common on unprotected terraces. The best solution is attaching Plexiglas to protect plants from wind gusts and to allow you to see through. Since drilling may splinter Plexiglas, ask the dealer to place holes at least an inch from the edge of the sheets, so they can be secured to your terrace railing. Twist sturdy wire through and around the railing, or have a professional install.

Hang On . . .

Use solid walls to secure a trellis. Leave a 2-inch space between the back of the trellis and the wall's surface to give vines plenty of space.

Put up some shelves and flowerpot holders with the right hardware to hold the weight.

. . . and Up!

If there's another terrace above, suspending a trellis from the ceiling to your floor is a possibility. Hooks can be inserted to enjoy baskets hung at different levels. Create an herb basket high enough to get full sun but low enough for easy tending and picking.

Water Considerations

Two factors to consider with a terrace garden are the weight of the containers and how to water the plantings. Unless an outside spigot is available for installing an irrigation system, you'll need an attachment for a hose to run to the nearest faucet, or you'll have to use a watering can.

If business or vacation trips will take you away during the growing season, you'll need to call on neighbors to water the terrace plants—or, you can invest in an irrigation system with a timer. Unless your terrace is completely exposed to the sky, the direction of rainfall may not give your plants the water they need. Take advantage of rainy days; set out a decorative vase and ladle to collect and use rainwater.

A 1,000-square-foot rooftop garden can easily hold several hundred pots of plants. Container gardening in Houston can be vicious since plants must withstand exposure to both freezing winter temperatures and sweltering summer sun with humidity hovering at 80% and temperatures in the 90s. In spite of the rule to water only in the morning, I found that watering just before or after sundown is best. The need for roots to have moisture far outweighs the risk of fungal infections! By soaking the sides of the clay pots with the hose, much more water goes to the plants instead of being wicked out of the soil by the dry clay. Of course, the larger the pot, the less water required. Herbs perform much better in pots 10 inches or larger and [large pots] allow more space for interesting plant combinations.

—Kyle Wallace, rooftop gardener and owner of
Gaia Garden Design, Houston, Texas

Drainage trays underneath your containers conserve water by allowing the plant to absorb the water through its roots. Trays below your containers also halt stray drips.

high-rise apartment towers. Place window boxes on the floor up against the open railing, and plant at varied heights for a lush appearance.

Suspension Suspense

Can your terrace withstand the weight of that planter you are considering for a peach tree? If you do not know the weight guidelines (often based on pounds per square foot), you may need to consult an engineer. For you, your plants, and people below, safety must come first.

Design Decisions

If the décor in your living room is minimalist, are you going "English Cottage" on your outdoor room with wicker rockers and floral patterns on a little round table? Consider function, such as dining, or using an easel or telescope; view the terrace from all interior views.

Viewed from Afar

Some terrace gardens can be seen from the street, others only glimpsed from other

Plant Clusters

Terraces are ideal for creating beautiful groupings of plants. Use the maximum space

As my first gardening experience, I had a high-kill experimentation rate. But I learned where the summer sun shone, ranging from five to three hours along the 33-foot terrace, and I'm now very successful with lilies, roses, herbs, and vegetables. We love the leaves of the 4-foot crepe myrtle tree that turn brilliant autumn colors. What amazes me is that weeds and aphids find me ten floors up. Come winter, I hose down shredded newspaper around perennials and shield them with chairs. Mussel and clam shells saved from restaurant meals go on top as mulch!
—Liz Shieldkret, East Side of Manhattan, New York City

that you have for soil surface by pushing square containers into the terrace corners. Place a round container on one side and a rectangular window box on the other; fill in with assorted sizes and heights of round planters for a full corner planting.

Grow It All!

If it grows in the ground in your city, you can certainly grow it on your terrace. Your plant list is limited only by the amount of sun shining down. Tomatoes are very happy with six hours of sun; lettuce thrives in containers; and many seed catalogs offer dwarf and bush sizes of vegetables, including cucumbers and string beans. Corn would be very tricky, since it likes a lot of company for pollination; but if you have the room, why not?

ON TO THE ROOF!

Your great outdoors is just a few steps or an elevator ride away. There's only one reason, as you look out on all the vacant rooftops of your city, that they are not gardened. Leaks and the valid fear of expensive roof repairs keep many a gardener at bay. In general, roofs were not originally constructed to carry the weight of people's feet, never mind planters filled with soil.

Before gardening, you must ask about the roof's current condition, past repairs, and if there's a history of leaks. Obtain permission from the landlord, or if you're in a co-op or condo, speak to the managing agent.

Drainage Do's

Planters without drainage saucers should not be placed directly on the roof surface. Water forming a puddle on the surface is asking for problems. A more substantial surface, such as stone or cement pavers or a raised deck may be in order.

Where does the rain go? Look around the roof to find the drainage hole, which usually has a raised grate around it to catch debris. Concentrate your planters where the water drains best; the road least traveled is best.

Stress Benefits

Costs involved in roof improvement are considerable, and many factors determine the weight your roof can hold. Structural questions include where load-bearing walls and supporting beams are located, date of the last waterproofing or replacement, and roof warranty.

If you can convince the building owner(s) that the financial and quality-of-life benefits far outweigh the initial costs, you are likely to succeed in gaining permission. The insurance coverage on the building should already cover the roof since people must be able to go there in case of emergency. Have a real estate agent confirm that when a common garden is added, rents are higher and resale values increase for rental, shareholder, and condominium units.

Nuts & Bolts

Once you have gathered facts about the condition of your roof, you need to know the law. If you are a shareholder in a co-op, read your proprietary lease for references pertaining to the use of the roof or concerning planting. Right behind your building's policies are your city's codes, which dictate permits, zoning restrictions, and specific fire statutes.

Your engineer or landscape architect will conduct precise measurements and determine what kind of deck and surface can be constructed. Your design ideas, what the roofer will guarantee under the warranty, and the engineer's plan may totally clash; but communication will result in a safe and stunning roof garden.

Safe & Secure

An alarmed push-bar on a roof door is a common exit in case of fire. Every second counts and trying to remember a code or looking for a key or card could easily jeopardize lives. A professional locksmith should be consulted for ideas.

A three-digit combination key pad can be installed to bypass the alarm. There is no need to distribute keys or cards. Residents can easily be informed of a combination change.

Light the Night

City roofs often have enough ambient light so people can see fire escape openings and not run into planters. Choose lighting purposefully, without ruining the views that only city roof gardeners know and love. Since a roof is a windy environment, consider only candles that are encased, such as inside a hurricane glass.

Fences for Good Neighbors

Walk around the perimeter of your roof. If you can step, climb, or jump to the next one, you may want to consider incorporating fencing into your design. Your local police precinct may have a crime prevention officer who can point out security flaws, and a locksmith can make specific recommendations to save you anguish and money.

But Other Roofs . . .

Look out from your roof, and you may notice others with decks, ladders, and fences you know to be illegal. Don't even think about it. All it takes is one complaint from a neighbor, or a visit from the fire department, or a guest falling, and you could be facing hefty fines if not a lawsuit. Enjoying your gardening experience without the fear of its removal or legalities will give you real piece of mind.

Costs

Each aspect of designing and building a roof garden has variable costs. Depending on roof conditions and the cost of your dreams, it could range from a couple of hundred dollars to over $100,000 for a relatively small, 3,000-square-foot roof.

Professional fees may include a landscape architect, engineer, and structural engineer. Add all material costs, contractor's labor, security and intercom system, lighting, irrigation, electrical outlets, furniture, planters, soil, and—oh yes, plants!

Add More & More

Incorporating features into your roof garden saves money if they're designed before construction. Additions such as privacy partitions, elaborate arbors for roses to climb, and water fountains, spas, and pools require expert advice.

Roofese

It helps to "talk the talk" as you go through the process:

- *Cap flashing,* often made of copper, is installed in an L-shape from the surface of the roof and run up the parapet.
- The *parapet* is the wall around the roof's edge.
- A *base flashing* is often added with a sealant so water doesn't seep up.
- A *waterproof membrane* is a surfacing material placed on top of the roof to protect it.

Design Decision

Do you prefer a square, elongated rectangle, an L-shape, or a curved deck? Where is the "natural" traffic pattern? Will the dining area enjoy the best views? Where are the optimum spots for sunbathing and for reading in the shade? Could an arbor be attached to the bulkhead? Which are the best places for containers to get

optimum sun? When you're using the garden hose, will the table be in the way?

Draw the shape and dimensions of your roof on paper to save time, avoid mistakes, and aid in exploring your options. Draw the roof as precisely as possible, including any physical structures, and make copies.

Which & Why?

Inform yourself on the newest materials, and listen to the experts on material choices and construction methods. Untreated wood can be brushed with a nontoxic sealant to extend wear and beauty. Deck materials made from recycled plastic offer a splinter-free surface that needs little care.

Calling All Artists!

A trompe l'oeil painting can add class, humor, or a realistic or fanciful architectural detail you'd love to have. The structure housing the building elevator's motor, known as the bulkhead, can be an ideal canvas. Create a sense of false perspective by painting a meadow scene as viewed through a bay window, or palm trees seen through an open door; or really trick the eye with a garden path that meanders past a gate into an endless garden.

Paint a large window, and use mirrors as windowpanes to reflect the garden and sky. Mirrors are great fakers, making it appear there is more to see when there's not. Confuse and delight the eye by placing plants so they are reflected in the mirror as people walk over to that area, or so they can be viewed by sitting in a particular chair.

Trompe l'oeil Mural on Bulkhead

Is Everybody Happy?

Educating people will help allay any fears. A roof garden adds an amenity for all residents to enjoy and increases the value of the whole building. If it's a shared space, start a garden club and get people involved. Find out favorite flowers, herbs, and vegetables and announce a garden party!

The Water Connection

Whether a hose is hooked up to a spigot, or a pipe must be run up the side of the building, water is truly a necessity. Watering your plants creates a bond; it gives you time to watch their growth and check for weeds and pests.

As on terraces, on roof gardens it makes sense to have a watering system in place if you

I used to look at those bathroom and kitchen mechanicals on the roof with disgust, as hideous eyesores. That was until discovering that when I grouped planters around to conceal them, the warm air emanating up allowed me to winter over my not-so-hardy perennials. I am able to put my tomato seedlings out three weeks before anyone else in the neighborhood!

—Jo Ann Macy, West Side gardener, New York, New York

can't be there. Including an irrigation system and timer in your roof garden's budget is recommended. Thin black rubber "spaghetti" hoses are placed inside of piping and run underneath the deck to each planter. Mulch can disguise most of the wires.

Expand Designs

A garden's design aesthetic always works if there is visual balance. Using plants of different heights, or varying textures among plants of the same color, both work nicely. Even in a roof planter, you can overlap foliage to mimic how plants grow.

Lighten Up

Soil, that is. Don't expect healthy plants without a healthy growing material. You want excellent drainage plus a mixture that holds onto moisture. Adding compost will add some "meat," but organic fertilizers add the nutrients your plants need.

Another benefit for city gardeners is that the soil in your roof's containers heats up quicker in the spring, and stays warmer later in the fall, than soil in the ground does.

Plant It!

Concerns over all the rules and regulations, and thoughts of every conceivable problem, will melt away when you kneel down to plant that perfect perennial in that gorgeous new soil. As you step back after watering to admire your work, a feeling that you are gardening on "safe ground" makes all the legwork and hassles fade.

Another benefit of roof gardens is that you can add to your repertoire plants from a higher zone. For northern gardeners, start your roof garden's first growing season right by recording in your journal the first and last frost dates up on the roof.

Sky Gardeners

Gardening is a meld of agricultural practice and botanical science. Successful gardening is also the art of growing vegetables, flowering plants, and fruit for pure pleasure, decoration, or use. There are so many choices; but as a city gardener limited to such a special, finite space, give major thought from the start about the vision for your garden in the sky.

HOT TIPS

It's hot up there, and sun-loving tomato plants need plenty of moist soil to keep producing. Add mulch and basil. Combinations are beautiful and useful. Annuals work beautifully around tall perennials, vegetables, and shrubs. The purple tips of spreading ajuga or blue lobelia are striking around white or bright pink rosebushes. Don't forget herbs! Parsley thrives under pepper plants or with scented geraniums. Sow some trailing nasturtium seeds in front of climbing plants and vines.

Theme Planters

Design by color. If you adore purple, then plant purple basil and purple sage with purple morning glories, clematis, lavender, and campanula. The list is as vast as your wallet, planting space, and time will allow. Note the start and the length of the blooming times for each flowering plant.

A 3-foot-square planter can be your salad container. Position a tomato cage around a large determinate and an indeterminate cherry tomato plant; then surround the tomatoes with bush cucumber, heat-resistant lettuce (where the tomato vines and support cast some shadow), parsley, and basil.

Is iced tea your summer drink? Plant a mint garden with some lemon balm. Add some whimsy by using iced-tea spoons or cocktail stirrers as plant supports.

Grow all your favorite herbs in one place. With garlic stalks in the back, add oregano, sage, parsley, thyme, basil, rosemary, and other favorites. Remember to plant those garlic chives in a metal coffee can, or they will completely take over.

Go gourmet and plant an all-basil planter. Get on all the catalog mailing lists, and revel in basils from diverse countries and with scents such as cinnamon, lemon, and anise. Create a snacking planter. Grow edible flowers such as chives with their lovely round purple tops, salsify, violets, nasturtiums, and borage.

Back to Rome

Your new garden won't look "finished" during the first gardening season. Your mind's eye will see the potential of that little sage plant. It will be thick, rounded, and over a foot wide—next year.

It's a worthwhile goal to have flowers in bloom throughout your growing season. Unless you have—or make—the time to plan meticulously what to plant, there will be gaps. Thankfully, plenty of annual plants are available for city gardeners to fill in spaces with color.

Winter Blues

If you experience winter in your city, there is a ritual of preparing for this dormant stage. Remove all dead plant material, cultivate the soil, add compost, and pop in some spring bulbs. Then, it's time for mulching; at least 3 inches is the norm.

During the winter months, especially if precipitation has been low, don't forget to water your plants once in awhile. If you can move your planters, place them away from the prevailing winds and under any protective awning. Protect the roots by wrapping the planters with burlap or black plastic. Use bricks or rocks on the edges to hold the wrap down.

Garden Furniture

Umbrellas offer welcome shade, but must be weighted to ensure they don't become airborne in high winds. Some umbrellas are sold with iron bases, or with a base to fill with sand or water. Don't tempt fate. When no one is using the roof, close the umbrella.

What do you want to sit on, and why? Would you prefer to have plantings with barely enough room to walk by, or space for a bench or large dining table and chairs?

Unless there is a tornado or extreme gust of wind, most furniture designed for the garden should be heavy enough not to blow off the roof. Cast iron garden furniture is decorative and certainly heavy enough, but it does need maintenance. Cast aluminum, which is lighter than cast iron, is available in many styles. It is comfortable, wear resistant, impervious to chipping, and will last a lifetime.

Fun Stuff

Who would say that a flying-pig weathervane spotted on a city building is peculiar? Weathervanes of any kind are mounted through the bulkhead or installed by attaching an eave mount.

Paint a compass on the bulkhead or on a planter. Come up with a name for your garden, or have a contest and give a prize for the best name. Make a sign and have a party to make it official.

What would be more fitting than displaying a flag or a wreath for all to see? Religious holidays or secular celebrations can come alive from your rooftop. Depending on your roof's lighting and height, your decorations can be seen for miles!

Parties & Protection

At your garden party, you see two people who are smoking wandering over to the planters filled with ripe tomatoes and bush beans. One calls over, "Can we pick some?" What do you do? Unless you have soap handy, give a big smile and say. "No." Then go over and explain that tomato and bean plants just don't like nicotine, and offer to pick a vegetable for them. Never assume that others have basic gardening know-how. I saw an entire plant lift up in the air when a friend tried to pick one bean. A bit of healthy paranoia is essential to enjoying your garden party.

I love to be enveloped in green. It's so quiet and relaxing on the roof that I experience a fantasy that no one can see me, although the trellis doesn't truly conceal me. To cut the heat, I hose down the deck, then sit under the umbrella and enjoy the cool produced by the evaporation of the water. The transformation from water to vapor requires energy/heat. That's why it is always cooler at the water's edge.
—Marsha Sayer, M.D., East Side gardener, New York City

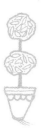

13

sidewalk & entrance magic

As you walk around a city, what makes one block stand out from the rest? It is a mix of pleasing architecture, a sense of order and cleanliness, a perception of safety and serenity, and—of course—flowers.

EYE TO ENHANCE

Cross the street and take a visual inventory of the whole streetscape. No one takes notice when a block is graffiti free, but it sticks out like a sore thumb when one mailbox is defaced with scribbled paint or there is litter in the curb. The sidewalk and street may be stained, cracked, or need serious repair. Notify your city and ask them to correct these conditions; the impact of a beautiful street tree planting is lost when there's a large pothole next to it.

Wouldn't a tall, round planter fit perfectly to the right of the front doors? How is the lighting; does it show off and protect your plantings? Let your eye and imagination roam, finding locations for hanging baskets, climbing vines, or window boxes.

Who Owns What

You can't go outside with a sledgehammer, open up the sidewalk, and plant a street tree without getting permission or a permit from your city. You could hit a gas line! Most municipalities own the sidewalk, but the property owner is responsible for repairs. Other cities have a "shared effort" policy for repairs and liability. Call public works or your department of transportation to find out where your property line ends and learn how much space is required for foot traffic.

Why Here?

The sidewalk is to the city dweller as the driveway is to a suburbanite. Pride in where you live doesn't end inside your apartment door.

Your building's hallways and vestibule or lobby send a message, as does the exterior appearance. Having pride in your community expands to the pride you have in your city.

Show Off!

Whether you're a renter or an owner, it behooves you to want your building to look its best. Write to the landlord or board to discuss gardening improvements. The most obvious place for beautification is at the entrance. Consider planters at least a foot tall for drainage, soil, and room for plants to grow.

MAKE AN ENTRANCE!

Whether the effect is positive or not, a building's exterior reflects the people who live there. Walk in and out of the front door a few times. Be objective. Is there a spot that no one can trip over? Can a 10-inch-round pot or small window box fit on the stoop?

The classic look of matching planters with identical plantings on either side of a door frames the entrance. Shelves or brackets a foot below first-floor windows are ideal for matching window-box plantings.

Dramatic Doors

Is there space over the front door for window boxes? Add a lip to the edges of a shelf to hold the window box in place, and add some trailing plants for more impact. Wrought-iron and plastic flowerpot holders are made with

hooks for attaching to exterior ironwork on windows and doors, and you can secure them to the building's exterior. Make sure there is room for both the pot and saucer to fit securely inside the box. Keep in mind how you plan to water your window boxes.

Half-moon wire baskets are easily nailed to a wood door. Purchase a secure inner liner to prevent dripping, create an outer layer of sphagnum moss, add potting soil, and plant away!

Does your front door have an awning that has seen better days? A custom arbor would be the talk of the block as climbing roses and vines grow from planters on either side.

Stunning Steps

Flowers cascading out of a simple round planter on a top step are engaging. If you have a brownstone or several steps leading to the front door, pots can be placed off to the side of each step. Vary the amount and size of the pots for visual interest. If your steps are wide enough, place pots on both sides.

Hang It All!

Hanging baskets overflowing with flowers—installed near front windows, entrance lighting, and above eye level by the front door—are dramatic day and night. Use antique iron sign holders, simple brackets, or decorative elongated hooks to hang. Use them on your terrace or backyard wall, or hang them from a post in your community garden.

SIDEWALK PLATFORM

Have city approval before putting anything on the sidewalk. Design a platform to highlight your container planting where it won't cause people to trip or prevent people from opening a car door. Decide on the container shapes, and then adjust the number of bricks or stones so the platform will show from all sides. Before you cement it in, put the one layer and planter in place. Would another layer look better?

A park bench is functional and attractive. Window boxes can be placed underneath and planted with partial-sun or shade-loving plants. Check gardening catalogs for benches that come with planters attached on both sides.

If soil can be put inside of something, such as a child's wheelbarrow, a gardener can consider it. As with art, people will view your creations as dazzling or offensive. If in public space, it's open to criticism. In any case, be sure to secure your planters from detractors or admirers.

Add Ornamentals

If you get the go-ahead for a curbside planter, a whole world of ornamental trees and shrubs opens up to you. A tree container should have 3 feet of soil, be wider than it is deep to maximize rainfall, and have a few inches of mulch to reduce surface evaporation.

Dream away with the help of catalogs and websites. Check the planting zone, estimated height, and any maintenance demands. Wouldn't a delicate dogwood, a purple- or white-flowering lilac, a crabapple, or a flowering cherry look marvelous?

Take a whiskey barrel that's been cut in half and turn it on its side. You don't need drainage holes. Stretch out a four-foot piece of galvanized wire [mesh] with small openings and form inside the bottom of the tipped barrel. Secure with small nails or a staple gun. Place a thick black trash bag on top, poke a few small holes, and pour on the soil. Add more inside the barrel and slope it down to three inches. Form the wire edges to hold the soil in. It should look like the soil spilled out of the barrel. It works great packed full of impatiens. The end result stops people in their tracks. It looks as though the flowers were knocked over and kept on growing.

—Yvonne Polson, Belleville, Illinois

Living Sculpture

Topiaries have been popular since ancient Roman times. Most creations are quite formal, but you can ignite those artistic fires and create more casual and whimsical styles to suit your taste. Very formal topiaries can be found in front of some of the fanciest hotels and buildings in your city. Geometric shapes, such as three round balls of increasing girth, are common.

Check your closest garden center, or head out to a nursery with an assortment of yews and other evergreens. Topiaries are a bit time consuming, but the effect is well worth the effort. Arm yourself with a sharp pair of shears, and shape a boxwood shrub into an orb or pyramid. Carve a juniper into the shape of a rabbit or free-form waves. Bend thick wire, or purchase a wire support, and train ivy into giant swirls. The wire should securely fit the inside of the container, or you can bend it around the bottom and cover with rocks and soil to secure.

Up the Bars

If you have stair railings, you can set a large pot at the base or off to the side. Plant it with honeysuckle, a black-eyed-Susan vine, or a combination of sweet peas and moonflowers to climb up the railings.

Do you have ironwork at the front or side of your building that separates garbage cans? Slide in a window box at the bottom, where sweet peas can attach.

Keep It Going

If light shines into your vestibule, consider blocking it with a plant on a table or shelf. Will a bracket fit for a hanging basket? Beware of placing any plant near or above a radiator.

Lamppost Projects

City streetlights can be very boring. Dress up the standard ones, or compliment historical lamps, by installing solid or open wire half-planters with substantial liners on either side. Before attaching and planting anything, make sure to get permission and have your watering plans in place.

garden your city

Improve What Is

Street furniture—newspaper boxes, trash containers, and bus stops—is a reality of city life. Is there room for a small container of annuals nearby? As long as it didn't interfere with a function, pedestrians, or paid-for advertising, wouldn't a climbing vine beautify?

Coal to Coleus

Residential construction in the mid-1800s included coal-bin doors flush up against the building. These raised platforms afford room for an assortment of containers. Check from the basement to see if the shaft opening has been sealed, or stomp on it with your feet to gauge its sturdiness.

Container Covers

Hide unsightly garbage and recycling cans with flowers, shrubs, and vines. Many are enclosed behind iron gates, affording opportunity for intrepid gardeners to turn sidewalk eyesores into places of beauty with flowers, shrubs, and vines.

History Inspires

Horses have played a vital role in our country's transportation history, and cities once provided water troughs on sidewalks to quench the horses' thirst. You can search the Internet, stonework yards, and antique stores—or build a replica water trough and plant it!

A good customer, Lynn Allyn Young, delights in reminding new gardeners that Chicago's motto is Urbs in Horto, *which means "City in a Garden." The biggest trend in Chicago is to install "carriage walks" between the sidewalk and street. Used since the 19th century, the 1-foot-wide brick or stone paths reduce maintenance and give passengers a place to exit their carriages, excuse me, cars, without ruining plantings.*

—Michael S. Thompson, owner, Urban Paradise Landscaping Co., Inc., Chicago, Illinois

14

the rare backyard garden

Who knows how many hidden gems are tucked behind residential buildings on any given city block? If you don't already garden in the backyard, this may sound obvious, but check out all the exits to your building's property to see if there's any outdoor space. Depending on the building's configuration and ownership, backyards are either private, reserved for those living on the ground floor, or common areas open to all residents.

Many backyards in the heart of the city seldom have "real" soil, but container gardening and taking full advantage of surrounding fences and walls can create incredible planting spaces. Take heart in knowing that all of the soil for Inverewe, an extraordinarily beautiful 60-acre garden in Scotland, was imported to its once barren site!

Backyard gardens are much more than summer enclaves; you can enjoy year-round use and visual interest by planting evergreens, grasses, rhododendron, and shrubs such as the 7-foot Westonbirt dogwood (*Cornus alba* 'Sibirica') with red branches in winter. Don't

forget shrubs like the red chokeberry (*Aronia arbutifolia*), which produce berries for beauty and for the birds.

TAKE INVENTORY

Pencil and paper in hand, sketch out your backyard space. Include doors leading in, water spigots, drains, windows, stairs, and street exits. Bring a measuring tape with you, and then comb the walls for existing fixtures, nails, or hooks to work with. Look for the placement of clothes-dryer exhaust vents that could emit hot air and lint onto unsuspecting plants.

Is there an unattractive feature or site that needs repair, paint, or camouflage? For example, to cover some sloppy cement work on a brick wall, try strategically placing a wooden fan-shaped trellis. Plant some scarlet runner beans (*Phaseolus coccineus*) and two hyacinth beans (*Dolichos lablab*); within two months, the bean vines will have covered the flaw.

Paths with Purpose

Even a 10-foot-by-12-foot backyard garden needs a path. It doesn't matter whether the "destination" is to view a fountain on the wall, smell an iridescent orange rose, or sit in a cushioned chair.

Though the most direct route between two points is a straight line, garden paths call for some turns or bends. Once you decide what features to incorporate, plan the optimum path or sightline for enjoying them.

Stroll Strategy

People walk in natural patterns. We have all seen cement sidewalks curving to an entrance; yet a narrow dirt path crosses the once pristine lawn for the most direct route.

Your paths can meander, but as the garden designer, you must be aware of natural traffic patterns. Having to maneuver around a long concrete planter will be irksome to you and your guests if the dining area is clear on the other side. No one wants to negotiate a maze or carry cumbersome trays of food and drink across tiny stepping stones either.

Pathway widths should be practical. Space is desired for strolling around, receiving soil and plant deliveries, and rolling the barbeque into place. Paths should be at least 3 feet wide to accommodate people who use wheelchairs.

Try out different routes by drawing them with children's sidewalk chalk. Chalk won't survive a rainstorm, so if you like what you see, get it down on paper.

Rooms with Views

Set aside different sections of the backyard for specific uses. Do you want a place to sit and read, enjoy the garden at night after work, and entertain? If the backyard is not your own private space, call a meeting for input. Or, tuck a "garden survey" (with a response deadline) under your neighbors' doors.

Designer Dos

Lining up chairs and planters against walls is uninviting. Even if a thin, rectangular-shaped yard is your "canvas," you can trick the eye. Let a pencil make the first mistakes. Tall plants placed in corners soften and expand boundaries.

Keeping the best views in mind, draw in seating for conversation. Should the lounge face the prevailing breeze or the entrance? What is the first thing guests will see? Add the illusion of space and visual interest by altering the levels of the backyard. Raise one of the "rooms" by adding a brick or wood deck for a patio table and chairs, and raise a small area to highlight a sculpture or unique plant to give it more importance.

Shapes, size, and color add to the illusion of space. A path that decreases in width draws the eye in. Hang a decorative birdhouse high up on the wall to give the whole area a sense of height. Blue and purple flowers appear to recede in the garden, while red ones move toward you.

Dining Alfresco

There's nothing like it. If some bugs are spoiling the ambiance, light a citronella candle at least 10 feet away, so the scent doesn't overpower your food. Call or check your city's website for information concerning use of gas and charcoal grills.

The garden at night is best enjoyed with subdued lighting, whether electrical or candle, and don't forget the light given by white flowers. Attractive outdoor and solar fixtures allow for a relaxed mood without glare, and placing votive candles under interesting foliage creates mysterious shadows.

A Word on Pre-Winter Chores

Cultivate your soil, add some compost, and mulch a few inches deep around the perennials, even though the backyard is protected somewhat from harsh winds. Prune broken or torn branches, examine planters for cracks, and see if any trellis repairs are needed.

Yes, Garden in Soil

Even if your garden's floor is all cement, you can create "soil outcroppings" among the planters. Where two walls meet is a perfect place to build out an earth-filled planting area. You will need to build a retaining wall out of brick or rocks, making it at least 10 inches high to allow for drainage and enough soil to sustain the roots. Put up the wall, add the rock, and pour on the soil!

Proper drainage is vital; add enough gravel, rocks, or marble chips to at least 2 inches. Does that corner seem to call out for a delicate dogwood tree? Since the planting area is too shallow to sustain tree roots, build it up by adding another foot of retaining wall

right on top of the soil. Create drainage holes for water to flow from the raised tree area to the rest of the soil. If you are using large rocks, you can add the initial layer of soil, and then use a trowel or shovel to push back the soil to position the rocks. Natural gaps between rocks are all the drainage you'll need.

Whatever material you decide to use, keep the surrounding colors and textures around you in mind. Lay a piece of rope or a garden hose on the ground to try different shapes for your planting area. Look at it from all angles; gentle curves will serve as a great foundation for your plants. Once you've added the soil, peat moss, compost and/or balanced organic fertilizer, you need to place flat rocks—or two bricks—together as stepping stones for reaching your plants.

Using Walls

You have them, so take full advantage of the walls around you. Take note of where the sun is shining, since that's the direction the blooms will be facing. If the wall is not in good condition, think about painting it. You'll need to patch up or repair the worn-out areas, then use a solid-colored paint as high up as you can comfortably reach—or, paint a scene you love.

After checking to see that rain is not forecast, use a scrub brush to clean the wall with bleach and water. After the wall is dry, tape the area you want to paint with wide masking tape. Paint on a coat of any light-colored, water-based latex paint. Paint on your scene with acrylic paint and let dry. If the sun shines directly onto the painting, give it special protection by brushing on clear polyurethane.

Training Is Fun

Vines are funny growers. It seems to take forever for the first tendrils to start, literally, to reach up for something to wrap themselves around; but once they grab hold, they grow!

Take the time to read up on any perennial vine you want to grow. Pay particular attention to its sun requirements and anticipated height before deciding where to place the vine's container.

The hardy climbing hydrangea (*Hydrangea anomala petiolaris*) is slow to start, but if it gets half a day of direct sun or is growing in (curiously enough) a north- or west-facing partially shaded site, it should take off in two growing seasons.

THE SOFTNESS OF ROCKS

You may think the idea of "soft rocks" is an oxymoron, but it rings true in a well-planned and well-planted rock garden. No, no one is going to think you have a geological wonder in your 50-foot-by-10-foot city backyard, but they can be impressed by the shapes and colors of the rocks and diminutive plants you chose to complement each other.

Naturalistic rock gardens are created directly on the ground, or you can go vertical by using an existing stone wall that has gaps for tucking soil and plants inside. Make sure the rock openings are tilted up, so that rain falls into the crevice. Holes in cinder block can be widened with a hammer to create small openings for plants.

There are no hard-and-fast rules for "today's" rock gardens; just guidelines. The prime factor is creativity and knowing the growth habits of the plants you choose. Some plants grow in tufts; others may be erect, or droop, or creep. Buy rock garden plants from local nurseries, catalogs, or you can grow them from seed. A rock garden is perfect for adding interest, contour, and height to a flat surface.

Plant choices abound, but don't ignore the varieties that are native to your region. Explore decorative, small-stature ferns. Tiny purple iris (*Iris reticulata*), varied colors of flowering mats of saxifrage, and sedum are only three ideal rock garden plants. Try desert plants, bulbs, and dwarf heathers. Look for dwarf, creeping, and low-growing conifers and yarrow, alyssum, wormwood, pinks, alumroot, phlox, speedwell, and thyme.

The Hunt's On!

Suitable rocks are not lying around on city streets; but keep your eyes open at vacant lots and construction sites. Ask everyone you know who heads out of the city to scout for rocks; vacation destinations to the country or beach offer great collecting opportunities.

Build It!

For a natural look, bury a portion of each rock and push the soil against it to keep it secure. Now for the special rocks. Avoid plunking them 6 inches apart, or they'll look like planted polka dots. Lean one against the other, create a crevice for a plant to poke out of, or have groupings that almost touch.

Perfect Plants

Keep an eye on invasive spreaders such as mints or hens and chickens. The wonder of rock gardens is that as you walk around, you can see bursts of colors or interesting foliage tucked behind and between the rocks. Look for varieties that spread, mound, or hug onto rocks. Keep in mind how plants "interact" with rocks in nature.

Authentic Rock

Natural rocks were first used in landscaping by the Chinese, and even Kublai Khan's garden stressed the beauty of rocks. Showcase shiny quartz, contrasting colors, striated patterns, and rocks that have great memories. Go to the largest park in your city, and notice in which direction the stripes in the rocks face. It is amazing what impact a glacier's markings (strata) can have in your own backyard!

A POND!

Does building a pond in your city backyard garden sound fabulous—but unrealistic? Essential for irrigation, water was the main component of ancient Egypt's landscape design. The Chinese, and later the Japanese, perfected the art of incorporating water into the garden. With its energy, sound, movement, and light-reflecting qualities, water has a place in every garden.

An Aboveground Experience

When my husband and I first suggested this idea at a co-op board meeting, the other members thought we'd lost our minds. But we were convinced that a raised pond was not only feasible, but a wonderful addition for all residents to enjoy.

The pond was built up instead of down into the ground. The perfect location was easy to determine. A drainage hole already existed 5 feet out from the building, so it was the perfect northern boundary for the pond; the other drain became the eastern edge of the pond. Large rocks, some measuring 2 feet wide by more than 1 foot high and deep, were obtained from a construction site 30 miles north of the city. Club members hauled them home in a van.

An initial layer of cement was placed on top of the existing cement floor and against the building. When it was dry, the new floor was coated with a waterproof seal. The rocks were placed according to the garden club's gentle kidney-shaped design and cemented in. Additional cement was used to plug up gaps and create the sloping walls of the pond. More waterproofing was the finishing touch.

Since rain was forecast, a run to the local dry cleaner provided plastic to tape over the pond. After waiting a full warm day for the waterproofing to dry, we reached the moment of truth. The hose filled up the pond, and we found one leak. More cement, more waterproofing, and the seal held for over two years. Since then, we have raised the pond and installed a liner to accommodate more koi.

If you just can't see yourself gathering rocks, there are sturdy plastic forms that

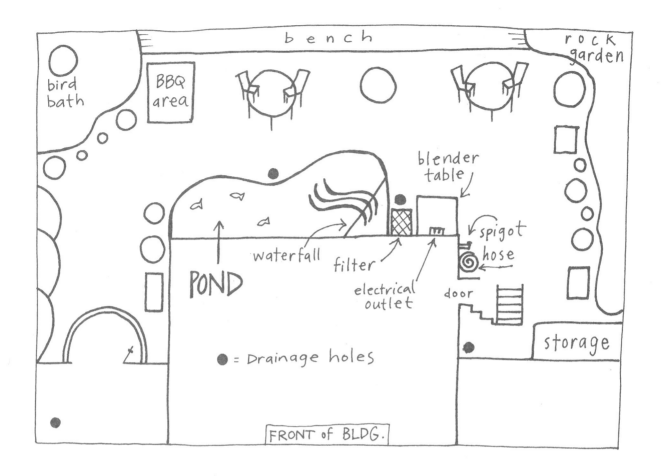

The labels in the diagram read:

- bench
- rock garden
- bird bath
- BBQ area
- blender table
- waterfall
- filter
- spigot
- hose
- electrical outlet
- door
- POND
- ● = Drainage holes
- storage
- FRONT of BLDG.

When reconstructing the edges of the pond, I looked carefully at every rock. Each one had something special about it. The flatter rocks gave a finished look to the top, others were chosen for their coloration, and the massive tall rocks with flat bottoms were meant to form the base of the waterfall.

—Jeff Jenssen, chiropractor and
co-op garden club member, New York, New York

perform well. If you have soil in the back-yard, preformed fiberglass pools are also available.

So there you are, gazing at your pond full of water. Well, how about a waterfall, a bubbling millstone or cascading water (these call for more rocks and a pump, which needs an electrical outlet); water lilies and grasses (via catalog); and a few graceful, colorful fish (also available via catalog or a trip to the pet store)?

Let's Hear It!

The sound of water is truly mesmerizing, and a waterfall that has overlapping or jutting rocks for the water to flow across is visually hypnotic. Many Japanese gardens contain shishi odoshi. Water drips through bamboo tubes; and as they fill up to pour out the water, they spring up and hit a rock. This makes a "thunking" sound meant to scare animals away. Bamboo spouts can also direct the movement of water from one tube to the next when you place them opposite each other.

Sounds of city traffic dissipate, with the waterfall functioning as "white noise." You can even adjust the intensity of the sound. For a quieter presence, add a few more rocks to divert the stream. Look for rocks with a natural scoop at the end. Adjust the placement of the rocks so that the stream flows in a back-and-forth movement. For a more intense sound, raise the waterfall higher so the water drops directly into the pond.

A pump is absolutely necessary to carry the water up, so you'll need a source of electricity. The size of the pump is determined by how many gallons of water your pond contains.

To figure the square feet of the pond's surface, measure the length and width of your pond and multiply those numbers. To get the number of gallons, multiply the square feet by the depth of the pond (in feet), and then multiply that sum by 7.5.

The ideal situation is to have an electrician install an outside outlet near the pond. In the meantime, run an outdoor extension cord out the nearest window of your apartment. Place plants to hide the wires!

The Cleaning Crew

Don't be horrified to see your clear water cloud over with algae. We thought something was dreadfully wrong, but it's Nature doing her thing. Algae are not unhealthy for the fish, but we wanted to see the fish. A quick search on the Internet resulted in some solutions.

Explore "going natural" with algae-eating pond cleaners like submerged plants and Japanese black snails (*Viviparus malleatus*). Purchase one snail or tadpole for each square foot of the surface of your pond. Tadpoles (*Rana catesbiana*) are also scavengers, but unless you want to share your backyard with bullfrogs native to your region (and there are ten different regions in North America), hold off on this purchase.

Submerged plants will clean the water naturally and beautifully. The fish love to hide and spawn in these plants, and they provide a healthy snack. Plant a bunch of these maintenance-free submerged plants for each square foot of your pond's surface. You can also use them in a water tub.

It's Crystal Clear

Impatient for nature to work its magic? Install a biological filter for incredible results. Face it, fish go to the bathroom. Excess fish food, silt, and other debris can also ruin clear, healthy water.

A mechanical filter connects to the pump that can also run your waterfall. Cleaning and changing it depends on the amount of fish you have for the pump to run efficiently. Biological filters remove all suspended materials and neutralize ammonia and nitrite.

There's an exhaustive array of gizmos. Ultraviolet sterilizers promise algae-free ponds, and there are vacuums, skimmers, and even dyes to make the water look blue.

Goldfish and Koi

Fish are not only fun and beautiful to see swimming around, but they maintain a healthy balance of gases for your pond's plants. They inhale oxygen and breathe out carbon dioxide, which the water plants absorb. The plants then release oxygen into the water.

Koi, or nishikigoi, originated in eastern Asia and China. Known as fancy koi, their descendants are from the black common carp, a species over 2,500 years old. First bred for food, koi's color mutations and cross-breeding became popular and profitable. With air travel, koi-keeping outside of Japan increased dramatically.

Strangely, koi grow to adapt to the size of your pond. The bigger your pond, the bigger the koi! They get along swimmingly with goldfish. Goldfish known as comets are deep bright orange and are ideal for pond living.

Speaking of size, before you even think about getting koi, think about the depth of your pond. Koi can swim vertically, not just horizontally, and will become couch potatoes if they can't. The ideal depth is 5 feet or more. Well, that's the ideal, but ponds with happy, fat fish abound in cities across the country.

Seasonal Cheerios

Koi eat the most when the water temperature is over 60 degrees and the water quality is good. As the nights get progressively cooler in northern states, check the water thermometer every day and watch as your fish start to slow down. It will soon be time to stop the regular fish food, switch to some Cheerios, and then stop feeding altogether when the water temperature falls below 43 degrees. The koi will huddle near the bottom and survive by living off their body fat.

Never allow ice to completely form over the whole pond. Maintain continuous circulation by keeping the waterfall going and by plugging in a de-icer or attaching a heater to the water filter.

As spring arrives, your fish will become more active, and their metabolic rate will increase. It's time to toss in more Cheerios until they can handle their high-protein diet again.

A floating pond thermometer is handy to check if it's time to switch on the heater or cease feeding as winter approaches. A nylon net large enough to hold your fish is vital to safely remove them from the pond when you need to make repairs or change a liner.

Safeguards

Beware of natural predators. It is doubtful that a fish-eating bird will swoop into your backyard or that a raccoon can visit, but many cities are just a few miles from wildlife (peregrine falcons nest in the Chrysler Building in Manhattan).

Turtles can take a hunk out of your fish, and even frogs have been known to do damage. Beware of the resident who lets her cat loose in the backyard, since tabby can quickly pounce on your favorite koi.

Pavlov Fish

Wherever you bought your fish, you should find a full complement of food choices. There are floating and sinking varieties of pellets, flakes, and sticks. Have a bit of patience, and you will have koi literally eating out of your hand. Hold a koi pellet or small piece of lettuce in the pond, just barely under the water's surface. Be still and they'll come; koi can also see you when you're behind them.

Silly Stuff

Your idea of what's hysterically funny may make another person cringe. Wait for agreement on an "authentic" shipwreck with bubbles, or a hunk of lime-green coral. One thing the fish certainly enjoy is a bridge to swim under for shade. Two equally tall rocks and one flat one laid across suffices nicely.

WATER TUBS

If you get at least two hours of direct sun, a whole world of water gardening awaits you with fragrant, beautiful water lilies. Call nurseries and comb catalogs for containers and recommended species for your planting zone.

WALL FOUNTAINS

The sound of water adds a special feature to any area of the garden. Whether it is a lion spewing water from its regal mouth, a fish spitting up in the air, or sculpture of a young boy relieving himself in the basin, the sight of water is a marvelous addition.

Get creative and, with the aid of a small electrical water pump, hang a decorative watering can and have it appear to be tipping off a shelf and sprinkling water into a galvanized oval tub. While letting your mind roam, remember to use materials that will withstand the outdoors.

RAILROADS?

Forget the small trains we grew up with, the ones circling around the Christmas tree or up on plywood boards in the basement. These are club cars that your cat or toy poodle can ride in! Garden railroads are a backyard hobby that combines the love of running a railroad with gardening.

The plants of choice for landscaping include dwarf varieties of conifers to give realistic scale and proportion to the size of the railroad cars. As with every aspect of horticulture, garden railway clubs have formed to promote this growing craze. In the San Francisco area alone, there are over five hundred family members (www.bagrs.org) of the Bay Area Garden Railway Society.

There's that special feeling one gets when you put your faith and your hands in Mother Earth—knowing she will reward our many senses. My grandmother taught me about the garden and its wonders and would always say that you'll get back twice as much as you put in. It's so true.

—Wyatta Roberge, backyard gardener, Dallas, Texas

15

street trees—the urban forest

As nature's wind sock, their leaves alert the watchful eye to an impending storm. They draw birds to perch and build nests. Their branches are natural shade structures that cool nearby buildings and hot sidewalks. In northern climates, they clearly announce the changing seasons and allow sunlight through in the winter. Healthy trees add beauty, and living on a tree-lined street is a benefit touted in real estate classifieds.

Our best street trees are well adapted to our temperature extremes that reach from in the 20s or lower, to 110 degrees. Planted in the street-side here in Tucson are dark green Texas ebony (Pithecellobium flexicaule) *evergreens that grow to 25 feet, and 20-foot ferny accent trees with wide canopies called feather bush* (Lysiloma thornberi). *But a favorite is the sweet acacia* (Acacia smallii). *Their very fragrant and beautiful yellow-orange puffball flowers remind me of Juicy Fruit gum!*
—Brian Gallentine, Tucson, Arizona

TAKEN FOR GRANTED

Three things to do for the well-being of your trees: remove any litter, loosen the soil around them, and make sure they receive adequate water.

Street trees absorb and transform carbon dioxide into oxygen, filter against dust and pollution, and act as noise reducers and wind blockers. They also mask unattractive views, give a visual break from cement, brick, and glass, and create pleasing sounds as wind passes through their leaves.

CITY FORESTS

Your city's Parks and Recreation, Urban Forestry, or public works department strives to preserve, protect, and plant new urban-tolerant trees. The City of New York Parks & Recreation, with 3 million trees (2.5 in parks; half a million street trees), has a wonderful phrase in its mission statement: to "replace pavement with green space."

Because of their ability to survive in and screen out air pollution, species chosen for street trees are inclined to be very hardy. Many can not only withstand the salt thrown from snow plows, but are tolerant to the extreme heat that comes off city pavements. It's a wonder so many survive.

Using a computerized street tree inventory, Cleveland, Ohio, identifies spaces available for planting and chooses particular shapes of the best species to match. Portland, Oregon, joins many other cities by incorporating tree planting requirements into all new

development, including future tree care paid by the developer. Roadways in Portland, in Milwaukee, Wisconsin, and along Manhattan's five-mile Hudson River Park were designed with wide medians allowing for tree protection and growth above and below the soil.

YOUR TREE

If you want to garden in your street tree bed, use a trowel and see if the soil is hard as a rock or moves around easily. Are the trunk and branches in good shape? The tree's roots need to get as much water and nutrients as possible; brick and cobblestone commonly laid on top of the soil are not beneficial. Most grates and iron cages installed around or at the base of trees will constrict their growth.

A positive trend is to plant trees in long, rectangular plantings or "nature" strips; but you probably have a tree planted in a 3-foot-square space, or less.

Soil Improvement

What to add depends on the quality and kind of soil you have in front of you. But if the soil has been compacted, then compost and peat moss will certainly help. Work it in carefully to avoid damaging the roots. Two forms of organic fish emulsion, liquid and pellet, are ideal. Read the label for the feeding amount, then dilute it by half and apply twice a month if your tree bed is brimming with flowers, herbs, and, even vegetables.

were taking all the nutrients from the tree. Actually, we were planting beautiful water meters. When the leaves of salvia or impatiens start to curl slightly, you know the tree needs water! Although adding fertilizer for the tree is not recommended unless there is an identified problem, compost is always a positive.

Smart businesses provide their street trees with an internal injection system. Not only do these systems save watering time and expense, but they provide a consistent amount of water to safeguard the company's investment.

Soil-ology

Trees have a tough time in cities. People wrap bicycle chains on them, and they allow their dogs to relieve themselves there. People step on the tree bed's soil, compacting it as hard as cement so that life-sustaining rain just washes away.

Before you combat the sociological issues involved in protecting trees, be aware that improving the soil is the immediate dilemma. Saturate the ground with water 2 hours before working on the tree bed. Depending on the severity of the problem, you may need to borrow a shovel, hoe, or even a pickax. If a neighbor or the superintendent doesn't have one, call your Parks Department to borrow one.

Unthinking people dump motor oil, and they clean sidewalks with bleach. If you see oil or other gook on the soil, sop it up with paper towels and remove the saturated soil. Flush the tree pit soil with water if cleaning products were

Watering

The odds are in your favor that your building has a spigot facing the sidewalk for attaching a hose or filling a watering can. It benefits your street tree to get a lot of water once a week, rather than getting it in dribs and drabs. Most roots are growing within 3 feet below the surface. More than just the tree's anchor, the roots absorb water, nutrients, and oxygen; and they store food reserves.

The early morning is the best time to water, especially in hot temperatures or drought. Water deeply once a week, and slowly add from 10 gallons for a small tree to 20 gallons for a larger tree. Increase the watering schedule to every four days if there has not been any rain.

Having plants in your tree bed is positive! Don't let people dissuade you. A local curmudgeon once said the plants we had added used. Educate the unthinking person or business if possible.

Northern cities add root-damaging salt to tree beds when de-icing sidewalks and streets. Once the soil thaws and dries out in early spring, flush it out with lots of water a few days apart. Using sand around trees is preferable.

Most informed, tree-liking people recoil in horror when they see "decorative" strings of lights attached to live trees. The obvious damage to tree branches during installation and removal is only worsened when they are ignored and left to restrict growth. Strangled by ignorance and lengths of dainty white lights wrapped around their branches, the urban trees experience a new cause of death.

Sometimes, there is just nothing you can do to save a tree from disease, infestations of insects and worms, and damage caused by trucks, car doors, or storms. When a tree dies in a forest, who is there to notice; but when a dead street tree is removed on a residential city block, it leaves a gap that cries out for another. Your city should replace it, or assist you in obtaining sources with the best species for planting.

Your city will help identify your tree, mail information on tree care, and assist you with questions. Ask if there is a street tree advocacy organization.

Pruning

As new growth begins, you may notice miniscule little leaves midtrunk or at the base of the tree. Simply snap them off. But, when the tree you are gardening is three stories high and a branch is dead or the thunderstorm just snapped a branch that is dangling, what do you do? Call your city and ask them to send out an expert to remove it.

Pruning is an art, science, and business. Unless you have the proper tools and are certified by your city to prune street trees, removing their branches requires a permit. Check to see if a licensed tree-pruning contractor is allowed. Check references, prices, and their workman's compensation insurance; improper tree pruning is dangerous to both people and trees.

The average life for a newly planted street tree is less than ten years. With your interest and attention, your new tree will enjoy good health and beautify your neighborhood for many decades to come.

Tree Guards

Look around at what other people have come up with for guarding their trees. Tree guards prevent people from walking on and compacting the soil, and cars from hitting the tree. Tree guards send a visual message to dog owners that something is keeping Fido away from the tree trunk. They also deter people getting out of cars from smacking their door into the trunk or stepping on your plants.

Installing any fencing is better than having none. Guards of iron, brick, stone, or wood are commonly used. Lining the edges of your new street tree pit with seashells, rocks, or cobblestone also draw attention. Increase planting space by having the ironworker install the guard just inside the corners.

Legalities

An out-of-state driver tried to sue a block association for damaging his car. He not only lost the case, but had to pay for repairs to the wrought-iron tree guard.

Although technically seen as "trip hazards," fencing or guards around street trees are usually universally accepted. Street tree gardeners must realize that their garden may be on public property—or, depending on your city's laws, the sole responsibility of the property owner. Be thoughtful about the design and construction of your tree guards.

Bad Dog Owners

It is not the dog's fault. It's the owner who allows, directs, and even pulls their dog straight toward trees. "Save our tree. Curb your dog." signs may deter, but don't expect miracles. Explain that salts in dog urine are toxic to plants and trees.

Theft Proofing

Their 2-foot-tall stakes are painted dark green to match the wood-frame fence and edging. Neatly nailed into each stake is a laminated postcard-sized note that reads, "Welcome to our Block! Help us be kind to our trees and flowers. Remove litter, discourage your dog, and add some water! Thanks. Flowers and tree guards contributed by our Block Association. Yes, we gladly accept donations." A corner deli's name is included.

This system works, because it shows group effort and "reasonable" plants that are not conducive to theft. Impatiens in a wonderful assortment of colors line the shady south side, and the north is packed with varied colors of cockscomb, white geraniums, red salvia, yellow marigolds, and nasturtiums.

Garden Security

Theft may happen, but try keeping a positive attitude! Creative signage shows that someone cares. Use humor, fact, and pleas to get your point across, such as "Don't Touch—Bad karma," or "This garden is monitored. Smile for the camera."

Single white tulips are never touched, yet red and orange flowers go. If you have a theft problem, grow bushier, compact, and difficult-to-yank plants. Perennials are seldom disturbed and, despite their bright colors, annuals such as impatiens, begonias, marigolds, and dusty-miller stay put.

Gardening around Trees

Yes, ivy is pretty, and variegated ivy is nicer; but it is far from the only plant that will thrive under a street tree! How about basil, cantaloupes, or pumpkins? Anything goes, but it's grown on a very small scale.

Since the soil is already prepared, look in the white pages under State Offices or the county listing of your Cooperative Extension, U.S. Department of Agriculture office. Ask them to mail you a list of recommended plants and vegetables for your city.

Unique Tree Gardens

What a great space to show off your creativity, since so many people are passing by your tree!

If you are getting a new tree, consider those that do not grow too high. If you have window boxes, it can really cut your light source. Seeing a row of trees gives a warm, comforting feeling to the block. Because they grow in such small areas, you must take the time to cultivate and nourish the soil. Yes, they require attention, even during a dry winter they need water, but they give back so much with their beauty, and by attracting birds."

—Aaron Fears, New York City

How about all yellow flowers (coneflower, sunflower, coreopsis, black-eyed Susan, daylily, marigold)? Or make them all the same plant, but select different flower colors (geranium, zinnia, astilbe, begonias) or foliage (hosta in blue, deep green, and variegated tipped in gold).

Consider visual, tactile, or fragrance themes. Plant all low-growing plants, groundcovers, all white-and-silver plants, or all herbs.

Think up! Hang colorful birdhouses and a feeder in your tree. Make sure you can reach up for easy refills. If you use sunflower seeds, expect to see them growing next year.

One day, my husband and I walked toward a street tree surrounded by a short white picket fence. The tree bed was filled with a variety of neatly planted and mulched flowers. In the corner facing the sidewalk was a plant stake bearing the words "Look down." We looked to see a mirror between the plants; and painted on a dark rock nearby was the word, "Smile!"

Consider a rock garden for a fuss-free, Zen-like planting around a tree. Take an idea from Japanese gardening and use a small rake to create straight lines and gentle swirls in your soil after you water. One fern and a dwarf evergreen shrub look perfect up against a rock stood on one end.

Let your imagination wander. Recent sightings inside of tree gardens include terracotta quail, a pink flamingo, and others with miniature plastic frogs and dinosaurs.

garden your city

Sun-Loving Perennials for Street Trees

Please remember that trees grow and, depending on the shape and density of your tree's leaves, you will not have the full sun you have now. Look for low-growing varieties of phlox, yarrow, heather, and periwinkle. Bulbs planted in fall in the north include crocus, snowdrops, tulips, daffodils, narcissus, iris, grape hyacinths, lilies, and fragrant hyacinths.

Sun-Loving Annuals

Wax begonias are carefree and nonspreading. Delicate flowers in pink, white, or red hues and striking foliage thrive in full sun to shade.

Geraniums have decorative foliage and impressive flowers of red, pink, or white. Your only chore with geraniums is to remove the flowers when they start to fade. Reach down to the bottom of the flower, slide your hand to where the flower's branch meets the main stem, and snap it off.

Parsley, sage, and thyme look great; but due to passing dogs and engine fumes, they should not be eaten.

Shade-Loving Annuals

Impatiens is grown in a range of colors and combinations. Each plant spreads and stays in full bloom until frost. Your only concern with impatiens is to ensure

Modeled after programs in Austin, Texas, and Roseville, Minnesota, the program appears to work well for any size city. Collected through our water billing system, we have a 3–4% participation rate that involves community groups in the planting process and provides seed money for grants. I wholeheartedly recommend this as a way for cities to involve their community in a positive image program.
—William A. Harrat, Parks & Recreation,
City of Durham, North Carolina

that they don't dry out. They also enjoy partial sun.

Sweet alyssum prefers partial to bright shade in order to spread, and it stays in bloom past the first frost. Their tiny, white flowers (also shades of pink and violet) grow in compact clumps and fade in hot summers; but grab the shears to cut halfway down for renewed blooms.

Vines

Each flower of the huge white megaphone-shaped moonflowers (*Ipomoea alba*) blooms for one night, but their fragrance is worth it. Plant the seedlings 6 inches out from your tree. Since they develop many buds and get heavy, moonflowers need a trellis or twine to climb.

Aaron Fears has been city gardening since the 1980s. His plantings in the West 40s of Manhattan include street trees, flower beds in Hell's Kitchen Park, and those that grace his home. Flowers cover the front and back yards, window boxes, and steps of the Fears's brownstone. His moonflower vines consistently give a nightly show for weeks on end.

Other successful vines seen crawling up street trees include scarlet runner beans, cucumbers, morning glories, clematis, and squash.

GREEN SUPPORT

Some cities raise funds specifically to plant new trees. In Durham, North Carolina (population 187,000), residents and businesses are asked to agree to "round up" their monthly water bill to the next whole dollar amount, add a certain amount per month, or contribute a lump sum. For example, a $25.75 bill is automatically rounded to $26.00, and the quarter is allocated for Durham's Tree Planting Donation Program.

Funds from the "Round-Up for the Environment" program in Roseville, Minnesota, go toward planting trees, flowers, and shrubs in parks, along streets, and in other public places. As the first city to try this program, Roseville also encourages residents to submit beautification ideas.

Households and businesses in Abilene, Texas, are asked to add a dollar to their monthly water bill to support their parks and modernize playgrounds. It took a decade, but by 2000 the city had planted more than 116,000 trees. Keep Abilene Beautiful continues to encourage the care of the trees planted with public and private involvement.

CITY OF DURHAM
TREE PLANTING DONATION PROGRAM

Durham's Tree Planting Donation Program gives each water user an opportunity to contribute funds for tree planting on public property through the City's monthly billing process. The money collected through this Program will be added to existing funds, allowing the City to plant more trees throughout the community.

The Tree Planting Program is a convenient way to donate money to a worthy cause—making the City of Durham a more attractive place to live in and conduct business. Small amounts donated by individuals can add up to large amounts annually.

The form below offers you the opportunity to sign up for the "Tree Planting Donation Program". Complete this form and mail it to:

The City of Durham
Revenue Billing and Collection Division
101 City Hall Plaza
Durham, NC 27701

For more information about donating to this program, you may call the Revenue Billing and Collections Division at 560-4411. For more information regarding tree planting and other questions concerning trees, please contact the Urban Forestry Division at 560-4355.

Help Us Build Upon the Positive Image of Durham, NC
Participate in the Tree Planting Program

City of Durham
TREE PLANTING DONATION PROGRAM
Sign Up Form

Yes, I wish to participate in the City of Durham's Tree Planting Donation Program and contribute funds to provide for <u>tree planting projects</u> on City property.

I authorize the City of Durham to: (please check one of the following)

❏ Adjust my monthly water bill to the next highest whole dollar amount.

❏ Add $_____ to my monthly water bill.

❏ Add $4 to my monthly water bill (enough for one small flowering tree per year).

❏ Add $8 to my monthly water bill (enough for one large shade tree per year).

❏ Here's a one time lump sum of $_____.

I further understand that this program is entirely voluntary and I may cancel or change my donation at any time by calling 560-4411.

Name:_____Address:_____

Signature:_____Date:_____

Account #:_____ (check water bill for your account#)

My twenty-three-year love affair with trees began when we planted six from the proceeds from a street fair. As a one-man watering squad, I think of my block as my front yard, deserving of all the care I can give. My most heroic rescue involved an attack of elm-leaf beetles. Every June for three straight years we illegally sprayed Siberian elms from 5th-floor windows. Today, they are flourishing.

—Bill Huxley, Tree Program Manager,
Turtle Bay Association, New York City

16

adopt a tree, highway, median, & more

Your city garden is a finite area, but if you're envisioning the entire block's tree beds filled with flowers next year, you'll need to enlist other's support. Efforts involving gardening seem to bring out the volunteer spirit. There are many "wannabe" green thumbs, displaced gardeners, and the curious who would love the opportunity to plant something. Work out the logistics of how best to get others excited about your plan.

CATCHING THE BUG!

If there isn't an organized group in the community, the easiest communication tool is the flyer. Condense it to a few punchy statements. "Garden Club forming Saturday!" or "Our Trees Need Help!" says it all. Add a date, time, and a corner or building address to meet in front of, and you are ready to run off copies.

Is there a community bulletin board, or a store owner who'll let you put a flyer in the window? Ask neighbors to put flyers inside their vestibules. Psychologists could have a field day with the phenomenon of putting up flyers. Whether it's plain curiosity or just defending their "territory," strangers turn into magpies when they see flyers going up.

PUBLIC RELATIONS

Call the editorial department of your local paper about doing a story on your Adopt-A-Tree project, or request that your project be listed in the paper's column on community or upcoming events. They may print your flyer as part of the story or even as a free public service announcement!

Reach out to your city's resources. Tree-Folks in Austin, Texas, and Trees, New York are

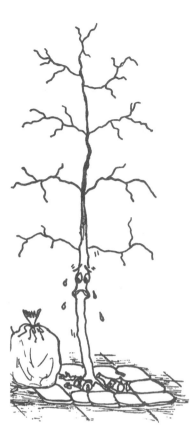

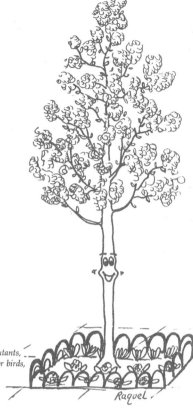

Trees beautify our street, produce life-giving oxygen, trap air pollutants, reduce noise pollution, cut air conditioning costs, provide a home for birds, increase property values, and enhance civic pride.

Courtesy of Racquel Llauger

not-for-profit organizations that promote tree plantings, education programs, and the care of street trees. Citizen Pruner courses are offered by Trees, New York and lead to certification from the Department of Parks and Recreation.

Invite the owners or managers of all buildings on your block. If they seem interested but balk at turning the soil, then don't hesitate asking for a donation. Someone else can volunteer to adopt their tree and garden it, but they can provide some funds for flowers, top soil, and a fence. This is the best time to inquire about water. Where can gardeners attach a hose or fill watering cans?

Gardening is enjoyable to do, and it gives back so much enjoyment. Water and maintain plantings for adoption projects. Set up dates for Spring Cleanup Day, Planting Day, and Prepare for Winter Day; or, if you live in the lap of sunshine, schedule quarterly cleanups. Have a block party and celebrate Arbor Day on the weekend nearest April 25th! Create a tradition for a tree gardening ceremony; spending three or four days a year cultivating the soil, adding flowers, and mulching is a small price to pay for a block full of beautiful gardens and healthy trees.

WINNERS ALL

Sprucing up city neighborhoods with gardening efforts is an extension of personal and civic pride. Have a street tree garden contest

It's amazing to watch the transformation when a community street tree planting is organized. The children are full of energy as they rush to help plant as many trees as they can. The adults work together—helping each other and the children—to plant trees in the empty tree pits in the sidewalk. Children race to water the trees and mulch. Within a few hours, after the flurry of activity is over, the neighborhood is left with a lasting gift of life and hope. The trees are a bonus. The real result is the community spirit fostered from a few hours of hard work and fun.
—Patricia Pyle, Community Forestry Program Director, Parks & People Foundation, Baltimore, Maryland

for best overall design, most artistic, best tree guard, widest variety of plantings, and most imaginative. A gift certificate can certainly be donated by a garden center or retail outlet carrying gardening tools. If your city has a botanical garden, ask their public relations department to send a judge, and bring the press along. Start a friendly competition for the best-looking block.

The City Gardens Contest, sponsored by the Philadelphia Horticultural Society since 1975, offers hundreds of entrants a chance at cash awards, memberships, certificates, and an invitation to their gala awards event. Contact your state forestry agency for details on the Tree City USA program.

CLEAN & PLANT THE HIGHWAYS

It may sound strange, but are you lucky enough to have a highway in your neighborhood? If there's soil along the side, then another gardening opportunity may await you. Thousands of volunteers have joined the Adopt-A-Highway Program. Groups remove trash and plant native plants, shrubs, and trees along their roadsides. Civic groups, churches, sport teams, and corporations adopt a mile or more. Contact your city or state department of transportation since you must have permission.

Residents who live near beaches, rivers, and lakes organize cleanup dates and plant native grasses to protect against sand erosion.

LADY BIRD'S CAMPAIGN

Wildflowers restore the balance of nature to our regional landscapes. As the First Lady known for her efforts to beautify America's highways by influencing passage of the Beautification Act of 1965, Lady Bird Johnson, wife of President Lyndon Baines Johnson, also founded the National Wildflower Research Center in Austin, Texas, in 1982 with her friend, Helen Hayes. The Research Center and www.wildflower.org spread the word on the beauty and benefits of native flowers.

Regional native wildflowers growing along highways and interstates are self-sustaining. There is no need for mowing, chemicals, or irrigation. President Bill Clinton supported regional native planting on roadsides, federal land, and in government-funded landscaping projects. Wildflowers reduce maintenance costs, provide effective erosion control, and add beauty for all motorists to enjoy.

MEDIANS

Many garden designers specialize in creating magnificent perennial borders that can be adapted to a median. When gardening in medians, you have a consideration that no estate gardener needs to fret over: fuel emissions and cars that come way too close as you plant. You do need to take care, but most medians have an interior pathway or buffer for your safety.

The Hyde Park/Kenwood Community Conference designs, plants, and maintains mini-gardens in Chicago, Illinois. To ensure that drivers notice the garden on the west side of Lake Shore Drive, these gardeners concentrate on masses of brightly flowered plants, colored foliage, and diverse textures of ornamental grasses.

You will certainly get lots of words of encouragement and praise from people crossing the street. People stop and regale you with stories about the gardens they have, or had, or hope to have.

ADOPT IT!

You pass by a place and see its gardening potential. You know of a small, triangle-shaped piece of unused land formed where two streets intersect. Whether it's space on an unused pier on the waterfront, in front of a commercial store, or on the edge of a playground, track down the city department or private owner and explore the possibilities.

Small "found" spaces can be filled with roses, ornamental grasses, daisies, and about any plant that thrives in your city. Your elected officials' offices and the Department of Buildings are good starting places for finding city-owned parcels of land that could be gardened.

Other beautification efforts include adopting mailboxes. The U.S. Postal Service's Adopt-A-Mailbox program gives paint and new logos and labels to individuals, groups, and companies to spruce up their local relay boxes (green paint) and collection boxes (deep blue paint). Call your district office and speak with the Customer Relations Coordinator to sign up.

A graffiti-covered mailbox next to a pristine street tree garden doesn't make sense. This is not "art" but pure vandalism. The best way to stop it is to spray or brush some paint over the graffiti as quickly as possible. Disposable sponge paintbrushes cover bright spray paint effectively.

THE FEVER CATCHES

The Parks Department hands out canvas gloves, the local hardware stores donate paint supplies, and the garden center across town gives a great discount on flats of annuals. Why? Because you let them know about your projects enough in advance, because you thank them on your flyers, and because you asked.

The core group can't be shy about picking up the phone or walking into a store with a flyer promoting a community project. Your local Department of Sanitation manager is not a psychic. Call and ask him if someone can drop off some brooms, trash bags, and gloves for your upcoming street cleanup event.

ADOPT-A-LOT

If you see a great open space, don't let the fact that it belongs to a small business or corporate headquarters stop your community group from trying. Who knows, the owners may be planning to leave it vacant for years and would like nothing more than to have it cleaned up. Or, maybe your group would be the perfect tax break. You never know until you ask.

"Professional is as professional does," so approach them by phone, letter, and in person. Dealing with city government is seldom quick and easy, but it can be well worth the effort.

There is a saying here in New York that anything worthwhile takes at least two years. Don't let the time element stop you. You don't want to be standing in front of the same wasted space two years from now, do you?

Trees aren't fluff in the urban landscape, they are as important to our urban environment as are the trees of the rain forest. Too often, people think that once a tree is planted, God is the one who takes care of it. The reality is that good urban forestry practice requires active citizen participation. Planting and maintaining street trees are a crucial form of community empowerment. The impact is immediate. In other words, it's up to us to see that trees survive.

—Barbara Eber-Schmid, Executive Director, Trees, New York

17
community gardening

Because of their benefits and rarity, community gardens are never taken for granted by those who garden, visit, or live nearby. These gardens are appreciated for their opportunities for social interaction and reveal the passionate dedication city dwellers have for their neighborhoods.

As havens for the body, mind, and soul, community gardens improve the air quality of our cities and offer beauty and access to the earth. They are safe places that attract humans and wildlife.

Radish

LET'S MAKE A DEAL

If you do not have a community garden and are determined enough to make it happen, you can establish one. Vacant land isn't plentiful, but your city has a real estate department that tracks, manages, and sells city-owned property. The ideal property may be slated for auction; but you may convince your elected officials that the best possible use for that piece of land is a community garden. Stress that gardeners are developers of the land, and they will do so at no cost to the city.

A private owner may deal for a terrific tax write-off from the city for the donated property. Beware of low-cost lease offers; it is absolutely heartbreaking to have an incredible garden destroyed under a developer's bulldozer.

You could buy the land outright. This is clearly the best way to protect it for the future. There are foundations, grants, and people with foresight and money out there. Does the Parks and Recreation Department have money in its budget to acquire property? Contact your elected officials to earmark their discretionary funds.

Do your homework before making any appointments. What is the population of your neighborhood; and how many open spaces, such as parks and playgrounds, do you have?

CITY POLITICS

Statistics and politics mix well. A compelling argument is to compare your neighborhood's facts to the standard minimum open space/population ratios of 2.0 or 2.5 acres for every 1,000 people. How does your neighborhood compare with others? It helps your argument to be low on the scale; but if numerous playgrounds throw off your figures, stress the fact that there are no community gardens. Gardeners vote, and election years may perk up attention to quality-of-life issues.

ORGANIZE!

After you have secured land, there are decisions to make and likely conflicts to resolve. Community garden "governments" are often run by a committee, where everyone has equal power and input, or by electing officers. Some duties can be shared, such as taking minutes (the recording secretary's duty), so everyone gets a shot at them.

Incorporating the organization gives you clout, can open up the door to more grant and funding opportunities, and protects you from personal liability. As a recognized organization, you should look into low-cost liability insurance for the community garden. It may be a requirement of your license with the city. It will protect your garden in case someone stupidly leaves a hoe on a path where someone steps on it and gets smacked in the eye.

Garden Rules

Rules are not hard to create, but enforcement can be difficult to administer. Having clear and reasonable rules that are readily accepted by the majority of gardeners will have the best chance of being followed. The bylaws set the policies and rules that will govern your community garden's affairs. What are the hours? How do people get a garden plot, when are meetings, and how are members elected to office?

The Common Denominator

Whether they're for a three-generational garden in Boston, Massachusetts, or a brand-new garden in San Jose, California, some rules are basic. Gardeners should garden. If a garden plot is not being used or is being neglected, a telephone call, e-mail, or postcard should warn that, if the situation is not corrected by a set date, the garden will be reassigned.

Consider adding rules allowing no pets, not taking anything except from your own garden, insisting on headphones for music-lovers, maintaining paths around gardens, cleaning tools after use, and contributing toward general maintenance efforts.

It takes a lot to survive in this jungle.

Enforcement

Unless there is commitment to enforce the rules, there won't be any enforcement. All members of the garden must feel empowered to approach anyone and say, "Sorry, but bicycles are not allowed in the garden."

A secure fence and lock, and the lighting from nearby buildings and streetlights, offer security. The best protection is the physical presence of people using the garden.

SITE SIGHT

Check the site history at the library. If residences were there, you may hit a subbasement; so expect to dig out a lot of bricks. Where's the water coming from? Without a nearby water source, you can only consider growing drought-tolerant native plants. This is the single most important must-have for the success of your garden. Hooking up a connection directly to your city's water system is the ultimate solution, and you should work toward that end. In the meantime, your only options may be connecting hoses to the closest fire hydrant or into adjoining apartment building spigots.

OPENING DAY

Schedule your first annual Garden Party, and make sure to take loads of "before" pictures. What a great opportunity to plan ahead, invite the press, and ask the mayor to dedicate the garden. Everybody's happy, and it's a great way to thank all the people who have helped make your garden a reality.

DESIGN DECISIONS

One member was offered thirty free truck tires, and he wants to plant marigolds. Another wants the entire space filled with raised beds with a 6-inch-wide path between them. A respected, talented member wants half the space dedicated to hardy lilacs; and your neighbor wants an edibles-only garden. A cool head and strong leadership are imperative to judiciously guide sensible design ideas. Look to other community gardens' websites for tried-and-true design ideas.

Path Principles

Design the garden pathways for use. They should be wide enough, give or take four feet, for two people to walk down arm in arm. There must be room for wheelbarrows to turn the corners, for people to kneel down to tend their gardens, and for people who use wheelchairs.

Paths can be made of soft materials like straw, pine bark chips, crushed rock, earth, and lawn. Functional paths include cobblestone, wood "stepping stone" disks pressed in sand, flagstone, brickwork, and concrete.

Path designs have a psychology of their own. Straight lines suggest movement, while curves and width changes slow the pace down. All paths need a destination. No matter which path you choose, chores such as weeding between bricks, patching up cracked cement, or raking the gravel need to be considered.

Plot Placement

The path of the summer sun is important in determining the layout of the garden beds. The ideal bed placement would run north to south, so that the sun would shine equally on the east and west sides. In this direction, gardeners can grow taller plants on the north end so nothing is shaded, or grow taller plants on the south side to protect shade lovers like lettuce.

But the realities of gardening in the city include buildings and their shadows. Place the garden plots where you get the most sun. Capture the evening sun for more plots by designing them facing east to west.

Though a rectangle is the standard shape, consider raised beds and children-friendly designs. Go wild with ideas on paper; once

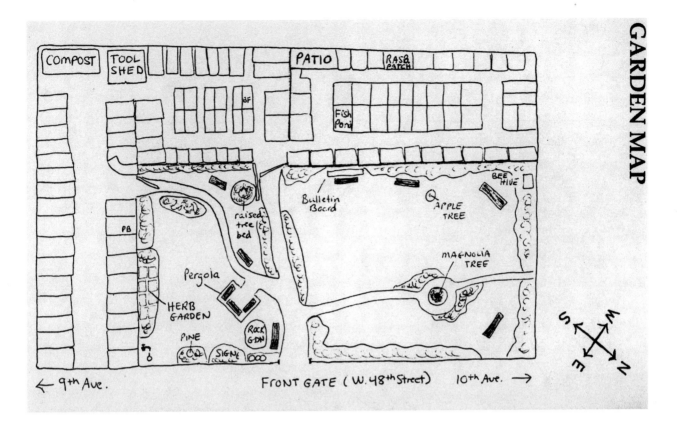

COMPOST | TOOL SHED | PATIO | RASB PATCH

8F

Fish Pond

raised tree bed

Bulletin Board

BEE HIVE

APPLE TREE

PB

MAGNOLIA TREE

Pergola

HERB GARDEN

PINE

ROCK GDN

SIGNE 1000

← 9th Ave.

FRONT GATE (W. 48th Street)   10th Ave. →

it's created, a garden like this is very hard to change. The unique designs of community gardens reflect what is important to their members, but individuals' beds should be at least 4 feet wide by 8 feet long.

A Common Area

Yes, you want individual garden plots, but many people just enjoy looking at the results, not the act of gardening. Set aside an area with benches for people to relax and enjoy the garden. The only limits are space and people's interest in making it happen.

Fence Me In!

Public access to the garden is totally reasonable, but allowing 24-hour access would mean its demise. Do some research to dis-

cover what kind of fence and material make sense for your garden. Chain link doesn't come in just shiny silver anymore, and annual vines quickly cover any fence that allows for tendrils to wrap around. You want to be able to see and be seen. A wrought-iron fence will last a lifetime but is rather expensive. Set your sights for what is best for the site and raise the money.

According to the American Community Gardening Association, "over 92 percent of the money raised in the United States comes directly from individuals and not from foundations and corporations." You should not ignore corporate contributions and grant opportunities; but do not dismiss the grassroots efforts that can raise money, goodwill, and continued support. Raising funds for supplies and projects should be a well-planned campaign involving the entire group.

a sampling of specialized gardens

Herb Garden
Edible Weeds
Butterfly Garden
Shakespeare Garden
Fern Garden
The Sixth Sense Garden
Bird Sanctuary
Shade Garden
For the Bees
The Sensuous Garden
Rock Garden
Conifer Garden
Water Fall Garden
Fish Pond
Heirloom Garden
Animal Garden

Plains & Prairies
The White (or whatever color) Garden
Idea Garden
Rose Garden
Feng Shui Garden
Spring Garden
Fall Garden
The Saints Garden
Native Plant Bed
Children's Garden
Historic Plants Garden
Japanese Garden
Tropical Garden
Five Senses Garden
Garden featuring varieties of one plant
    (i.e., Aster Garden)
Night Garden

the city. Ask for donations (or a discount) and free delivery. Create a garden newsletter or project details on letterhead to lend credibility and to explain what your garden is all about.

TOOLS NEED SHELTER

Building or buying a prefabricated shed is a necessary expense. Put out the word for carpenters and willing assistants. Have members scout magazines, search the Internet, or sketch out their ideal designs.

Once you have figured out your ideal—a cement-slab floor, a shingled roof, a six-foot overhang, a built-in cabinet, plenty of shelves, and beams with hooks to hang tools—compare material prices throughout

Sheds Need Tools

Start with what you need. If you have been borrowing tools from the Parks & Recreation Department or another community garden, they would be the ideal people to ask for recommendations on the best sources, manufacturers, and kinds of tools you should buy.

Depending on the size of your garden, you'll want a wheelbarrow—and a rake, two shovels, forks, and spades, three hoes, and a dozen trowels. Know that good-quality tools are not inexpensive; get the best, and get what you need. Community gardens may need to buy a hand mower, a compost tumbler, and maybe a chipper/shredder. Every purchase should be made with safety in mind. Tool sheds are no place for children; even a cultivator shouldn't be left within reach of a toddler.

Communal Supplies

Everyone will want shredded mulch, bonemeal, dried blood, and an assortment of animal manures for their garden. Compare prices from nurseries, schedule a delivery day, and make an event out of it.

COMMUNICATE!

Reach fellow gardeners and the public by installing a bulletin board to educate people on policies and rules and to announce events. Drilling two holes in plywood works; but a waterproof bulletin board, with a door and a key, will last longer. Start a simple newsletter, using one page folded in thirds and taped at either end. Add your logo and mailing address at the top and a drawing or clip art for visual interest. Run off more copies to hand out at events.

Indicate who gardens where, and identify distinctive collections and garden beds. Develop mailing lists since the more you

grow, the more contacts you'll want to notify. Include gardening tips, planting zone(s), and the last frost date; and announce events, wish lists, and fun news. A question-and-answer column is fun and helpful. Having a website and e-mail is a worthy goal.

JOYS, SORROWS, & PSYCHOLOGY 101

No community garden is problem free. Rules are broken, thefts occur, and the "Quiet Zone" isn't. Networking helps. There's much to learn when you link up with other community gardens—across town, country, or the world. Compare how you resolve problems; how you find sources of materials, plants, and seeds; and how you raise seed money. Larger corporate and foundation grants may be available with joint projects.

PLANT A ROW

Launched by the Garden Writers Association of America in 1995, Plant a Row for the Hungry is a nationwide campaign to help feed people. The premise is simple: Contribute some of your community garden's harvest, or have gardeners plant an extra row of vegetables, to contribute to local organizations that distribute food; or bring the vegetables directly to soup kitchens and senior citizen centers.

DEWITT CLINTON

Located in the community known as both Clinton and Hell's Kitchen, DeWitt Clinton Park is one of the few parks that has lent its name to a neighborhood. Originally stretching to the shores of the Hudson River, the park was named for DeWitt Clinton in 1901 when the City acquired 7.4 acres that was once part of the Clinton farm.

DeWitt Clinton (1769-1828) served ten terms as Mayor of New York City, was a U.S. Senator, and was Governor of New York State for eight years. His most visionary initiative was Manhattan's street grid system (1811) but he was best known for planning and promoting the State-funded Erie Canal.

The park was designed by landscape architect Samuel Parsons Jr., and officially opened in 1905. It featured a recreational and bathing pavilion topped with grand columns, a gymnasium, running track, playgrounds, and curved paths that led to a panoramic view of the Hudson and the Palisades.

The centerpiece was the Children's Farm (1902-32) lead by Director Frances Griscom Parsons, the City's first female park administrator. She oversaw more than 300 children's vegetable and flower gardens and taught young gardeners how to increase their harvests. Raised beds enabled handicapped children to enjoy gardening. This successful program inspired other park gardens and influenced the community garden movement. The construction of the West Side Highway (1931-44) eliminated the gardens and reduced the park to just under six acres.

The striking statue of a World War I "doughboy" was dedicated in 1930 and restored in 1997. The monument is a reminder of all the lives that were lost, many of them local. The memorial is often anonymously decorated with red poppies, which symbolize that remembered heroes live forever.

The 1996 renovation of the aptly named Erie Canal Playground included multi-functional play equipment, safety surfacing, a map of the canal's route painted on the ground, a drinking fountain, and three concrete mules (from "The Erie Canal" song). DeWitt's Dog Run offers pet owners benches and a water supply. There are six basketball half-courts, four handball courts, and parkhouse restrooms just past the frog and arch water sprayers.

Maria's Perennial Garden, a satellite of the Manhattan Botanical Garden, was named for DeWitt's first wife. It features flowers of the 1800s, rock garden species, plants that attract birds, bees, and butterflies, and plantings along the banks of the old "brook." Inside the playground's gate is a serpentine-shaped bed holding Manhattan native plants (growing on the island since the last glacier) and the Five Senses Garden. Come enjoy the Rose Garden at the northeast entrance and the western slope's spectacular show of spring bulbs, including thousands planted as part of The Daffodil Project in remembrance of September 11, 2001.

DeWitt Clinton Park
5.8 acres

© GEORGE COLBERT AND GUNTHER VOLLATH

To get to DeWitt Clinton Park by public transit:
Take the C or E train to 50th Street. Walk two blocks north and three blocks west. By bus, take the M31 on 11th Avenue to 52nd Street, or the M11 on 10th Avenue to 53rd Street and walk one block west.

Hudson River Pier 94

Manhattan

12th Ave

W 54th St

hand ball

basketball

flagpole

Erie Canal Playground

ballfields

Rose Garden

11th Ave

W 52nd St

Maria's Perennial Garden

DeWitt's Dog Run

World War I Memorial

Helpful Numbers

To volunteer or get involved,
call the Manhattan Outreach Coordinator
212.408.0216

To report graffiti, vandalism, or crime
800.201.PARK

Or join us online at
www.itsmypark.org

Map & Guide produced by Partnerships for Parks; map by George Colbert.

He who shares the joy in what he's grown, spreads joy abroad and doubles his own.

—Anonymous

Vegetables, herbs, and flowers are all welcome. It may not seem like much to offer, but these things are much appreciated. Set dates for a volunteer to collect and deliver. Ask your local newspapers to do a story to spread the word to other gardens.

EVENTS/TOURS/ PROMOTIONS/POTLUCKS

Why not have a pumpkin sale or haunted garden for Halloween, a picnic with a string quartet, or host an arts and crafts show? Kids of all ages love games and contests, movies, and talent nights. Have workshops on gardening basics, drawing flowers, or growing exotic or giant vegetables, and have a butterfly release.

An easy event to conduct (donations can be requested) is a tour of your garden. Make it a bigger fund-raiser by organizing a walking tour of a few gardens in the area. Sell tickets in advance at all the sites. Charge a fee for noninvasive photo shoots and weddings. Use your garden's name; or have a logo contest and have T-shirts, mugs, and garden tool bags to sell. Have a party and include door prizes, a silent auction, or a tag sale. Take photographs at all events to file with flyers for cherished memories in the not-so-distant future. Start a tradition by having a formal, yet friendly, guest book to use at each event.

Sell your garden's own cookbook during scheduled potlucks. Prepare one favorite dish and join fellow gardeners in a fantastic mélange of international cuisine. The garden club can provide the paper plates, cups, utensils, napkins, and ice. Make sure to schedule a next-day rain date.

Seed Swap

Come spring, there are plenty of gardeners who overbought on the amount of seeds. Ask people to bring labels, pens, and small sealable plastic bags or glass jars. Write to seed companies well in advance for donations.

Having had the great fortune of being raised on a Mississippi farm, I saw the need for my daughter to be exposed to the environment, even though we lived in the heart of Manhattan. Since 1997, I have taught Saturday family gardening workshops. Now, city families can tell the difference between a bell pepper, tomato, and cucumber plant and aren't afraid to pick up a worm, grasshopper, or praying mantis!
—Annie Chadwick, gardener and herbalist, New York City

Harvest Party

The spirit of competition comes alive when the pride of what people have grown is at stake. Create categories for commonly grown vegetables, flowers, and herbs. Get together a panel of judges; for prizes, give away garden-center or mail-order seeds, or supply gift certificates.

Nature as Teacher

Kids love gardens and lessons can easily be snuck in without their knowing it! Some community gardens designate areas specifically for children, offer art classes, and give tours; but creating gardens on school property is a natural. Environmental courses have become common in curricula at all levels.

FUTURE GARDEN PLANNING

Community gardens are a meaningful addition to urban living, but urban planners seldom consider them as vital as playgrounds and parks are. The expansion of the community garden movement led to the formation of the nonprofit American Community Gardening Association in 1979.

School gardens are ideal classrooms. Half of John F. Kennedy High School is literally in Manhattan; the other half is in the Bronx, where members of the (fantastic) Environmental Club built and developed their "Enchanted Garden." The club started from nothing in 1995 and has turned the space into an enviable garden. An intricate totem pole on the highest ground is carved with symbols representing the countries of the multinational student body.

Winding paths guide the visitor through the impressive plantings of the 1,300-square-foot garden. The bridge over the pond leads past eclectic species and native marsh plants. The club's efforts have garnered awards such as the National Gardening Association's "1997 Youth Garden Grant Winner"; but it should be fully funded, commended, and replicated by educators.

MAKE THE CONNECTION

Corporations and other organizations provide space on their properties and rooftops for employees and members to garden. Many botanical gardens set aside land for the community to garden.

The Denver Botanic Gardens, just ten minutes from downtown, has set aside space and developed fabulous community gardens.

Three garden areas offer 10-foot–by-15-foot garden plots to their members. These 250 individual gardens are also tended by civic groups and community organizations. There are also common beds for cutting flowers and herbs. All gardeners pay a $40 annual fee that includes seeds, workshops, and access to the botanic garden's library.

The children's favorite features at the Botanic Gardens are the sunflower house, secured with morning glory vines, and the bean tepee. Since the 70s, Denver's gardeners have enjoyed being connected to the land, socializing, having potluck suppers, and joining in to work with people, not just next to them. All gardeners are asked to give time to clean up the tool shed and maintain the paths and compost pile.

The community gardens are hooked up to the Horticultural Therapy Program and

Our links to schools enable teachers to incorporate gardening into lesson plans. Kids learn that seeds do not come from packets. They learn how to collect seed to study germination and grow plants in their own school gardens. They get ideas and designs from what they see and learn that the gardeners donate surplus harvest to local food banks.

—Selina Rossiter, Community Gardens Coordinator, Denver Botanic Gardens, Denver, Colorado

Demonstration Gardens. Other beds are raised to be more accessible for seniors, those who use wheelchairs, and for workshops. This link to the Denver Botanic Garden makes experiencing plants accessible to all as a hands-on experience.

NATURE AS HEALER

The garden—what a perfect place to meditate, pray, or sort out life's moments of crisis. As gardeners, we feel such a small part of the greater whole. As the oft-copied sign proclaims, "One is nearer God's heart in a garden than anywhere else on earth."

Healing can also be found in the plants you choose. Herbs can be grown for their medicinal qualities, and signage can enlighten and instruct. Hospitals understand that the sheer practice of gardening has reha-

bilitative applications, and many have on-site gardens with horticultural therapists who were trained at botanical gardens. New York University's Rusk Institute of Rehabilitation has an impressive greenhouse where patients grow and tend a variety of plants.

The criminal justice system has incorporated community gardening programs in prisons. Juvenile offender and misdemeanor community service sentences often include aiding community gardeners while learning.

VEGETABLE GARDENING

Long gone are the World War II Victory Gardens, where vegetables were grown on every available piece of land for the war effort. But in that process, one thing became clear: People could garden in cities!

No occupation is so delightful to me as the culture of the earth, and no culture comparable to that of the garden. . . . But though an old man, I am but a young gardener.
—Thomas Jefferson

It's great being a "city farmer." The north-forty crop may be measured in inches instead of acres; but the joy to be found in eating fresh, organic vegetables cannot be topped.

Don't waste precious space by growing vegetables you don't absolutely love eating. As you page through seed catalogs, the choices will both astound you and whet your appetite.

Different varieties of vegetables are best suited for the earliest and latest planting dates for your region. Get ahold of a regional Urban Garden Planting Calendar from your agricultural extension agent or local gardening organization. Don't forget to ask for their list of recommended heat- and pest-resistant varieties.

Cool to Warm to Cool

Vegetables prefer going into the ground, and enjoy growing, at different temperatures. To ensure success, northern gardeners need to pay attention to the likes and dislikes of their choices. Lettuce loves cool weather, and birds love lettuce. You can keep enjoying salads by covering lettuce with a mesh cover (available through catalogs) to increase yields and extend your harvest. Thwart the birds by forming a protective cage to place over the lettuce seeds.

Think about which cooler-weather crops you want to grow. A full month or more before your last frost date, plant peas, parsley, arugula, spinach, beets, and an amazing selection of lettuce. Two weeks later, sow chard; "designer" and round, red, tangy radishes; and carrots. You need to specially prepare the area for growing carrots by adding peat, sand,

and aged fine compost to increase the drainage.

After the frost date has passed, it is safe to plant tomatoes, pole and bush beans, corn, and summer squash.

Unless you want a stalk or two for decoration, corn joins watermelon as less than desirable crops for community gardening. You need to plant at least three rows of corn in hills at least 2 feet apart to ensure pollination, and the resulting shade will more than annoy neighboring gardeners. If you plant on the north end of your plot, taller plants won't shade out any other crops. On the other hand, to avoid affecting any other garden, plant tomato plants on the southern end to provide shade for more lettuce.

As the soil heats up and you have harvested the early spring crops, there is room for planting cucumber and eggplant seeds. Two weeks after the frost date, add an assortment of colored bell peppers, Hungarian wax peppers, and winter squash.

Seeds or seedlings for fall crops, other than twenty-six-day radishes, need to be in the ground by seven weeks to four months before that first frost. Broccoli, cauliflower, and cabbages need time to develop; and the tenderest brussels sprouts are often picked when snow is on the ground.

COMPANION GARDENING

Try it and see. Once considered as quaint folklore, companion gardening involves intentionally planting certain plants next to

Every blade of grass has its Angel that bends over it and whispers, "Grow, grow."
—From the Talmud

each other to reap particular benefits. Some gardeners swear it aids growth, and the plants complement and protect each other from pests and disease; others shake their heads.

It was true that the lavender-hued rose donated to our community garden was much more fragrant when we planted parsley around the whole base. If your rosebush has Japanese beetles, grow a band of garlic plants around it.

But don't plant cloves of garlic near beans or peas. Some gardeners swear that tomatoes thrive if planted with basil or parsley. Cucumbers like to be paired up with beans and radishes, but keep them far away from sage! Some vegetables just don't like growing next to each other. Onions and peas are two of the earliest crops to plant, but not near each other. Pole beans planted between the onions sprouts grew, but very slowly. Separate these three.

The simple marigold is naturally resistant to insects and stands guard to ward off nematodes that can stunt growth. Tear open a packet of dwarf yellow or gold marigolds, and push three or four of the skinny, extended seeds in the soil every 3 or 4 feet, just a quarter-

inch in and down, from the perimeter of your garden.

The only way to really know whether companions work together is to keep records of where you planted everything in your garden. What looks healthier to you?

SPACE SAVERS

Practice intercropping to conserve space. Plant quick-maturing vegetables between the slower growers; tomato plants don't mind having lettuce growing around them.

Though they are not companions per se, perennial vegetables such as asparagus and rhubarb should be planted at one end of the plot. To avoid the temptation to plant seeds too close, mark the boundaries so you don't interfere with their roots when you prepare and amend the soil year after year.

SUCCESSION PLANTING

The gardening method known as succession planting extends the harvest of the same vegetable, or you can switch to another vegetable to get two crops from the same space. This is accomplished by choosing vegetables to suit their different temperature needs.

Hold back. Don't sow all the bush bean seeds at once. Plant some now, and add more seeds every two weeks to extend your dining pleasure. Just because you can plant beets as soon as you can work the soil, it doesn't mean you should. Northern gardeners can keep planting until midsummer! Read the information on packets and catalogs; they are not making it up. Some vegetables just grow best at certain times of the year.

In the same space, start with lettuce, then plant bush beans, then spinach. Sow peas on St. Patrick's Day; then plant cilantro, harvest it, and plant broccoli. If you enjoy radishes, buy extra packets to pluck where you see any bare 3-inch space—between other growing plants and near the edges of the garden plot.

DON'T FORGET FLOWERS

If your winters are cold, there is always room for spring bulbs and annuals in the garden plot. Southern gardeners enjoy jonquils, lilies, and bulbs that bloom in the fall. In the north, plant an area with all King Alfred daffodils; or combine white crocuses with fragrant purple hyacinths. You really can't go wrong with Dutch bulbs, unless you plant them at incorrect depths.

Stick with dwarf varieties of your favorites so they don't hog too much precious space. Not only are they pretty in the garden and at home on your table, but bees will certainly come to visit. In the fall, use either a bulb planter or your trowel to pop in a few at the corners of your plot to brighten up your spring.

To plant bulbs in a corner of your garden, use a shovel to dig out soil to a depth of 5 inches, extending the hole to about 10 inches out from the corner. In this hole, place the larger bulbs first—such as daffodils, hyacinth, tulips, and lilies. Save space right at the corner for a handful of white and yellow-orange dwarf narcissus, which are short enough not to be knocked into by people walking past.

With your trowel, put back some of the soil; then add some smaller bulbs such as snow drops, crocuses, or grape hyacinth. There are perennial spring and summer bulbs in all colors of the rainbow—and many colors in between. As you enter the nursery or open the catalog, you may feel overwhelmed by the choices. Think of your favorite color and choose others to complement it.

Rambling roses are great for fences or trained up an arbor or wall, but rosebushes and thorns are generally shunned in community gardens. It seems that people unknowingly tend to buy the largest possible species that soon overtakes their garden and heads over to attack their neighbors' gardens or to block paths. A miniature rose or two, a small floribunda, or an upright hybrid tea rose like "Peace" are sensible alternatives.

SOW BY THE PHASES OF THE MOON

Don't laugh until you have seen the difference. Many gardeners swear by the practice of plotting their planting schedules by the phases of the moon. Gardeners point out stronger, more abundant harvests of herbs and vegetables and more vibrant flowers from seed and bulbs.

Seeds for aboveground crops (tomato, peppers, herbs, and flower seeds) should be planted during the time between the first quarter and the full moon (the waxing moon). Plant carrot seeds, a deep root crop, four days before the full moon. Wait until the moon is waning (after the full moon and before the new moon) to sow flower bulbs and other root crops, such as beets and radish.

Never mind just planting your seeds by the moon; transplant tomato and pepper seedlings from your apartment's windowsill after the new moon and before the late afternoon of the full moon!

Because weather patterns can play tricks, sow the root-crop seeds, which would be more protected, first. This allows some time for the threat of a frost to pass and gains you more time to plan exact seed spacing for the room you have left.

CASE STUDY: THE CLINTON COMMUNITY GARDEN

They were sick of looking at the abandoned cars in the vacant lot on their street. The row of tenements on West 48th Street, between 9th and 10th Avenues, had been torn down twenty-eight years earlier; but three vacant lots remained on the residential street.

Discarded appliances, clothes, piles of brick, and weeds covered the unfenced 150-foot-by-100-foot lot. The story goes that in 1977, residents' repeated calls to the city to

Tending my garden gives me a feeling of calm. I believe it has prolonged my life!
—Max Schwartz, retired dentist and community gardener,
Denver Botanic Gardens, Denver, Colorado

remove the cars in the lot were ignored. After residents pushed the cars out into the middle of the street, the city promptly towed the junkers away.

This success was the incentive for the neighborhood to put in hundreds of volunteer hours to clean up the eyesore. But it wasn't until the next year—after sanitation workers suggested that the group plant flowers to discourage further dumping—that the seed, as they say, was planted.

In 1978, twenty 5-foot-by-8-foot individual garden plots were laid out in the west rear corner of the lot, and the Clinton Community Garden was born. Mallory Abramson was the trailblazer who formed a group that, within the next two years, erected a fence and gate along the sidewalk, designed the garden to include a large common area, planted thousands of spring bulbs, and built winding pathways made of bricks that were painstakingly dug up from the rubble and laid by hand.

The current total of 108 garden plots was in place by 1982. The gardeners, organized as a steering committee, obtained a lease from the city through its Operation GreenThumb program; but two years later, the garden committee faced the news of a property auction. The gardeners raised funds by "selling" square inches of the garden for $5.00 each; Mayor Edward Koch kicked off the campaign in April of 1984 by buying the first inch.

The group raised just under $80,000 by November; but less than a month before the scheduled auction, Mayor Koch ensured the garden's future by transferring the land to the Parks & Recreation department. The Clinton Community Garden became the first to receive permanent parkland status. The funds raised by the auction were earmarked for future maintenance and improvements.

Over twenty years later, volunteers continue this garden's policy of member involvement and dedication to the community. Original members still tend their flourishing garden plots, sharing their years of experience with new gardeners.

Mallory Abramson has since passed away, but her presence lingers in each garden bed; and her legacy of tenacity passes to each elected steering committee member. A potluck in Mallory's honor is held every August. One person's vision certainly can endure to positively influence thousands of lives.

As the wheel of the year turns, we also share its fate. We have planted the seeds of our own changes and to grow we must accept the passing of the sun.
—Excerpted from a Solstice Blessing

18

gardening on public land

The surest way to reclaim a park is to use it. Criminal activity and apathy can be replaced by positive action when community groups form to fight back. Cities across the country rallied against drug sales and use in the 1990s and formed working partnerships with their police departments. Paint brushes, brooms, and elbow grease were the tools that led to empowerment, responsibility, and pride. And, as citizens gained control, they pressed for improvements to long-neglected parks.

Nothing unnerves an undesirable element in a park more than seeing a group of people walking into the park with flowers, shovels, brooms, garbage bags, and smiles on their faces.

Sustained use is the key. Teen dances, Halloween parties, puppet shows, barbecues, movies, concerts, talent shows, plays, and caroling under the decorated trees attracts residents back into their park. A park volunteer ran an hour-long "Monday Coffee in the Park" with doughnuts and newspapers for senior citizens that gradually established a meaningful, positive presence. This is where gardening endeavors enter the picture. Nothing makes any place look more cared for than a spectacular display of flowers.

In New York City in the mid-1990s, Partnership for Parks—a joint program of City of New York Parks & Recreation and City Parks Foundation—was formed to promote community efforts to maintain and preserve parks. Volunteer involvement expanded with "Take Back Your Park" and "It's My Park!" campaigns to provide tools and plants for gardening, painting, and cleaning. Informal luncheons and annual events with the Parks commissioner acknowledge volunteer efforts and afford the opportunity to discuss issues. Partnerships for Parks offers small grants, workshops, and practical literature to aid parks' stewards in keeping their parks greener and safer.

GREEN LIGHT FOR GARDENING

It is public land, but it's not your land. Walking into your local park, kneeling down, and planting a flat of annuals may not get you arrested, but your flowers may be uprooted the next day by a park maintenance worker.

If you want to garden in your local park, you'll need permission from whoever is in charge. If your city already has an established gardening program for volunteers, your proposal may be well received. In case you are met by a brick wall, call to get the name of the appropriate person to contact. Ask to meet the park supervisor at the park since it's easier to visualize ideas and less easy for them to say no.

Some parks were designed using expert design principles instead of listening to a community's needs. Is your park overcrowded, or does it lack what other parks have?

GREEN SPACE HUNT

Parks are not the only outdoor spaces that your city owns. Is there a place for a window box or hanging baskets, or a place for a planter in front of the school, library, and local firehouse or police precinct?

PARK PLANTINGS

Cohesive and theme plantings work well in parks. A native plant collection is attractive, wildlife-friendly, educational, and virtually carefree. A mixed-variety sunflower garden looks wonderful packed with giant single heads, multibranched sunflowers, and dwarf varieties growing beneath.

APPLY FOR A GRANT

Grants are usually awarded for a clear-cut, specific project; an organized program; or a garden-related purchase. Grants will underwrite numerous types of costs: operating, capital, project, planning, matching, and seed money. In all cases, your goals should be clear, and your proposal detailed and well written.

Your city's parks department and civic foundations are the first places to investigate for grants to assist your gardening project. Organize the paperwork and save the details to report to the grant donor at project completion. Never forget to write thank-you letters and send photographs and literature in which you mention donors' names, such as a newsletter or newspaper article.

CREATE AN EVENT TO CELEBRATE SUCCESS

Your flowers will soon be in bloom, your park's renovation is coming to an end, and the new benches will be installed by the end of the month. Organize an event to thank everyone who participated. Before setting the date, make sure that the official you really want to thank can attend.

Seasonal Gardening Events

All seasonal must-do's in the garden are opportunities to get the community involved. Flyers throughout the neighborhood can announce dates and times for spring planting of flats of annual flowers and for fall planting of bulbs.

Applaud work well done with an evening Full Moon Madness Party, celebrate the Solstice and Equinox, or throw a potluck dinner to thank the volunteers. Proudly announce your First Annual event on a flyer to impart a sense of history and well-earned importance to your group's reputation.

Our annual Garden Party is held in August, on the evening of the full moon. Begun as a fund-raiser, the party has evolved into an occasion to thank the participants who make the garden a success.

CASE STUDY: A DECENTRALIZED CONCEPT IN CITY GARDENING— THE MANHATTAN BOTANICAL GARDEN

As the first planter was filled with soil and the donated forsythia was planted firmly in place, the dream of a public garden came to life. What a difference this little patch of plant life gave to an old asphalt-and-cement pier jutting out into the Hudson River.

Owned by the City of New York, Pier 84 was once home to oceangoing freighters and luxury cruise ships. Princess Grace left for Monaco from this pier. Thousands of immigrants disembarked onto piers in the West 40s since the waters surrounding Ellis Island were too shallow for large ships. A short ferry ride south brought them to Ellis Island for processing.

Mayor Koch designated Pier 84 a "parklet" in 1979; but over the years, the city granted leases for rock concerts, an amusement park, storage, and parking. Through all these changes, the neighboring residents still found their way to the small public space on the western end to fish, relax, and enjoy river breezes and views.

In 1994, the Circle Line's leased area on the southeastern portion of the pier held cars, buses, and ships' supplies. That summer, when the company locked the gate leading to the public area, 1,700 residents quickly signed a petition and elected officials rallied to demand access to the sole public access to the riverfront for thirty-three blocks. The gate was soon opened, and beautification efforts expanded in 1995 with flower-filled planters at the entrance, down the walkway, and on the popular "end hook."

A few weeks after this incident, news quickly spread of City and State approval for plans to permanently moor the USS *Guadalcanal* helicopter carrier on Pier 84's western end. Views and river access would be lost, and half of the pier demolished, to provide tourist rides taking off and landing every two minutes; the smell of fuel and deafening noise would have rendered the area unbearable.

Elizabeth Rosen

Friends of Pier 84 was formed, and community and local politicians were mobilized. It took two years; but honesty, fact, and rational thinking prevailed. It was community spirit, painstaking attention to detail, and hundreds of hours of determination that saved both Pier 84 and the surrounding neighborhood for future generations.

What could make this 4,500-square-foot garden unique, other than its location over the Hudson River? Since the other four boroughs in New York City had botanical gardens, I felt that Manhattan deserved one too, and the rest of the volunteers and the Friends of Pier 84 board of directors concurred.

Research identified thirty-three plants and grasses that are indigenous to the island and region. The Manhattan Botanical Garden was dedicated by Mayor Rudy Giuliani's Deputy Mayor, Fran Reiter, in August 1996, at the Friends of Pier 84 Second Annual Garden Party.

At our first annual garden party were guests from the east side of Manhattan, where a new garden—named for their most famous community-activist resident, Katharine Hepburn—was being planned inside their park. They were also interested in using native plants.

Working with then Manhattan Parks Commissioner Adrian Benepe to work out the details of gardening on park land, an official Manhattan Botanical Garden contract was developed, stipulating that the garden would be maintained. A plant stake was created for use at the satellite gardens; with the Manhattan Botanical Garden logo on one side and the NYC Parks Department logo on the other, the sign declared: "This area features plants native to our island and is an official satellite of the Manhattan Botanical Garden." Three satellite gardens joined in 1997, and now there are forty-four.

The prototype container garden on Pier 84 combined a number of display gardens, including those labeled as Manhattan Native Plants, Immigrant's Gifts, Neptune's Five Senses, and the Birds, Bees, and Butterflies Garden.

Instant Gardeners

No advertising was necessary. They came, saw the first planter brimming with color out on the breezy pier, and asked to help. Monthly meetings were held to work out watering schedules and plan the garden's growth. The volunteer numbers grew, and before construction was complete, twenty-one official gardeners and assistants were signed up. At an end-of-season party, certificates and T-shirts were awarded for extraordinary efforts.

NEVER TAKEN FOR GRANTED

As with every community project, there are many who make it happen: fellow volunteers; whoever owns the land and provides your garden with water; the organizations that faithfully supported the project; residents, agencies, and groups that donated materials, talents, and labor; and your loved ones for putting up with you. These are the people to thank. Often. To take my own advice: The Manhattan Botanical Garden would never have been established or able to grow without the generous support of the Greenacre Foundation.

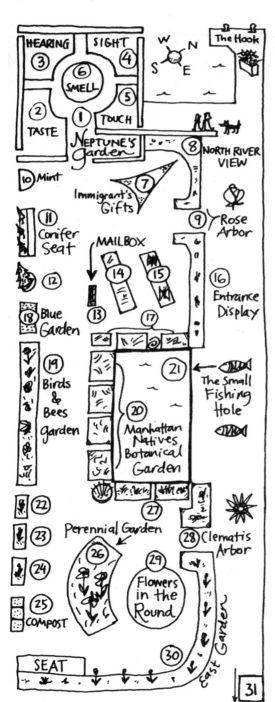

The Manhattan Botanical Garden on Pier 84, 1995–1998

KEY

1. **Neptune's Garden**
   A five-senses garden. Since the Hudson River is an estuary (the Atlantic Ocean's water also flows beneath) it was named for the Roman god of the sea.
2. **Taste**
3. **Hearing**
4. **Sight**
5. **Touch**
6. **Smell**
7. **Immigrants' Gifts**
   Ellis Islands' waters were too shallow. Pier 84 was one of the piers where boats docked for immigrants to take ferries down to Ellis Island for processing.
8. **North River View**
9. **Rose Arbor**
10. **Mint Garden**
11. **Conifer Garden & Bench**
12. **Blue Spruce**
13. **Mailbox Rock Garden**
14. **Herb Garden**
15. **Butterfly Garden**
16. **Entrance Display**
17. **West Display Gardens**
18. **Blue Garden**
19. **Birds & Bees Garden**
20. **Manhattan Native Plants**
    The botanical garden features ferns, grasses, and herbaceous plants indigenous to our island and region. The selection is common to Shallow Emergent Marsh, Maritime Grassland, and Successional Shrubland.
21. **The Small Fishing Hole**
22. **Medicinal Garden**
23. **Coastal Collection**
24. **Yellow Garden**
25. **Compost**
26. **Perennial Garden**
27. **East Display Gardens**
28. **Clematis Arbor**
29. **Flowers-in-the-Round**
30. **East Garden & Bench**
    Regional native shrubs include Honeysuckle, Highbush Cranberry, Toringo Crabapple, Cardinal Autmn Olive, and Silky Dogwood.
31. **The White Planter**

Along with beautification, our gardening efforts seduced many to visit Pier 84 and fall in love with the views, the breezes, the boats, the sunsets, and a real sense of community. In turn, this devotion led to the legislation that created the Hudson River Park and saved Pier 84. The Manhattan Botanical Garden will continue to encourage the use of native plants, volunteerism, and beautification.

lease, a group labyrinth walk, wine and cheese, and gazing at the stars and planets with telescopes. When *Aster novi-belgi* (New York aster) was designated the official flower of the Manhattan Botanical Garden by the Borough President in 2000, we distributed flats of the fall-flowering perennials to the satellite gardens.

CELEBRATE SUCCESS

As mentioned earlier, our annual Garden Party is held on the evening of August's full moon. Guests have enjoyed a Monarch butterfly re-

FATA VIAM INVENIENT: "THE FATES WILL FIND A WAY"

In 1996, Friends of Pier 84 saved the public pier from the privately owned Intrepid Sea Air Space Museum's plan for a tourist heli-port carrier; but the group could not com-

Neptune's Five Senses Garden

garden your city

bat time and the damage of marine borer worms that destroyed the 1920s wooden piles; chunks of the surface gave way and collapsed in 1998. That September, great news came: Governor George Pataki had signed the legislation to create the Hudson River Park—ensuring that Pier 84 would be rebuilt. All the plants were saved, thanks to NYC Parks Commissioner Henry Stern and Manhattan Commissioner Adrian Benepe. They arranged for hundreds of plants to be carefully removed from the condemned pier and transported eight blocks north in a new satellite garden in DeWitt Clinton Park.

No matter what their size, all gardens share concerns such as signage, marketing, design, and security. As Director of the Manhattan Botanical Garden, I have attended and presented ideas at annual conferences of the American Association of Botanical Gardens and Arboreta.

Friends of Pier 84 were involved in the extensive design process and look forward to the rebuilding of the largest, most fantastic public pier in the Hudson River Park. Located at the northeast entrance on the pier will be "The Concept Garden" of the Manhattan Botanical Garden.

GET INVOLVED

It is your city. Look around and see what you can do to improve it with your mind, green thumb, and any volunteer time. Though gardening in public spaces can be frustrating, the rewards are immeasurable.

Never doubt that a small group of thoughtful, committed citizens can change the world. Indeed, it's the only thing that ever has.

—Margaret Mead

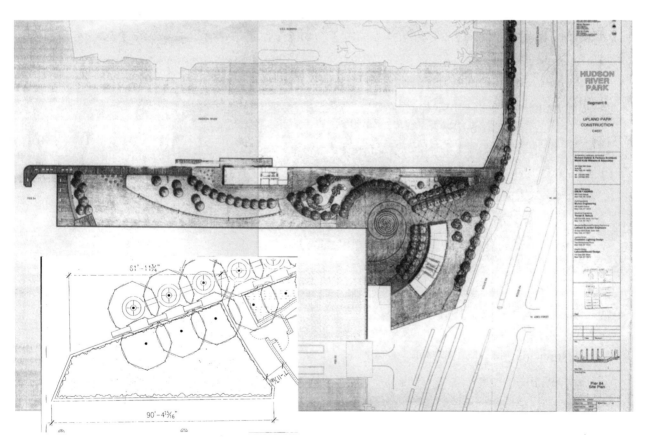

The new pier 84 in Hudson River Park, inset: the concept Garden.
Courtesy Hudson River Park Trust, Richard Dattner & Partners Architects PC, and MKW & Associates, LLC.

part four

City Gardening Resources

19

sources, websites, catalogs, & city parks departments

KEEP LEARNING FROM DIVERSE SOURCES

Pick fellow gardeners' brains for tried and true experiences. Gardeners love to chat, so visit a community garden to learn.

- Internet forums and chat rooms offer solutions, humor, knowledge, and understanding.

- Visit gardens of all types and sizes; play "tourist" in your own city.

- Expand your gardening network—search out seminars; join a club or national association.

- Be part of a volunteer greening project, or organize one.

- Invite a guest speaker from a botanical garden to address your group.

- Review your journal; locate a source for that vine that caught your eye when you were on vacation.

BENEFICIAL WEBSITES

www.aabga.org
American Association of Botanical Gardens and Arboreta

www.communitygarden.org
American Community Gardening Association—shares expertise and resources

www.ahs.org
American Horticultural Society—plants, subjects, clubs, and links

www.akca.org
Associated Koi Clubs of America

www.botanical.com
Herb index, growing, uses, folklore, and message boards

www.bulb.com
The basics, landscape projects, forcing, and buying

www.butterflywebsite.com
Includes a list of plants for a butterfly garden and more

www.cityfarmer.org
Canada's Office of Urban Agriculture's how-to site

www.davesgarden.com
Plants database and user comments on mail-order companies

www.dianacarulli.com
Garden labyrinth design and installation

www.garden.org
National Garden Clubs, Inc.—largest gardening organization in the world

www.gardenclub.org
National Council of State Garden Clubs

www.gardenweb.com and
www.gardenweb.com/vl
Forums, exchanges, plant database, catalog, and garden center directory

http://garden-gate.prairienet.org/
teaching.htm
Organizations & Cooperative Extensions

www.hgtv.com
Click on gardening link and check out the shows

www.labyrinthsociety.org/
All about labyrinths and a worldwide locator

www.mobot.org/cpc
Center for Plant Conservation—restoring native plants

www.nwf.org/habitats
National Wildlife Federation—global to Backyard Wildlife Habitat Program
703-790-4434

www.perennialplant.org
Check out their Plant of the Year list for sure winners

www.treesny.com
Trees New York—street tree information

www.tpl.org
The Trust for Public Land—protects and secures open spaces for parks, community gardens, etc.

www.wildflower.org
Lady Bird Johnson Wildflower Center—native plant image and data

www.fs.fed.us/ucf
Urban and Community Forestry—U.S. Department of Agriculture Forest Service

www.usda.gov/news/garden.htm
Home gardening, conservation, and composting

CATALOGS

Order catalogs by mail, telephone, or on the supplier's website. Many offer extensive online descriptions, photographs, and secure ordering. You can certainly call or e-mail directly for answers to your gardening questions. Most catalogs are free or low cost.

Note: ❀ = Tried and true—all plants grew, or we were very pleased with their products.

Arrowhead Alpines
P.O. Box 857
1310 N. Gregory Road
Fowlerville, MI 48836
517-223-3581
www.arrowhead-alpines.com
Rare perennials, alpine and rock plants, wildflowers, and dwarf conifers

Bamboo Sourcery
666 Wagnon Road
Sebastopol, CA 95472
707-823-5866
www.bamboosourcery.com

❀ W. Atlee Burpee Co.
300 Park Avenue
Warminster, PA 18991
800-333-5808
www.burpee.com
Seeds, heirlooms, plants, supplies

Charley's Greenhouse Supply
17979 State Route 536
Mt. Vernon, WA 98273
800-322-4707
Seed starting supplies, watering systems
www.charleysgreenhouse.com

Comstock, Ferre & Co.
263 Main Street

Wethersfield, CT 06109
860-571-6590
www.comstockferre.com
America's oldest, continuous supplier of flower, vegetable, and heirloom seed

The Cook's Garden
P.O. Box 5010
Hodges, SC 29653
800-457-9703
www.cooksgarden.com
Seeds and supplies

❀ Droll Yankees Inc.
27 Mill Road
Foster, RI 02825
800-352-9164
www.drollyankees.com
Bird feeders

❀ Duncraft
P.O. Box 9020
Penacook, NH 03303-9020
800-593-5656
www.duncraft.com
Wild birdseed, feeders, and products

Dutch Gardens
144 Intervale Road
Burlington, VT 05401
800-944-2250
www.dutchgardens.com
Bulbs, perennials, collections

Ferry-Morse Seeds
P.O. Box 488
Fulton, KY 42041-0488
800-283-3400

www.ferry-morse.com

Flower and vegetable seeds, perennial plants,
bulbs, tools, supplies, gifts

❀ Fox Hollow Seed Company
204 Arch Street
Kittanning, PA 16201-1501
724-548-7333
www.foxhollowseed.com
Heirloom and open-pollinated varieties of
vegetables, herbs, and flowers

❀ Gardens Alive!
5100 Schenley Place
Lawrenceburg, IN 47025
513-354-1482
www.gardensalive.com
Organic fertilizers, beneficial insects, online
pest and disease library

❀ Gardener's Supply Company
128 Intervale Road
Burlington, VT 05401
800-863-1700
www.gardeners.com
Supplies and solutions

❀ Garden Trellises Inc.
P.O. Box 105
LaFayette, NY 13084
800-498-0584
Galvanized steel supports for vegetables,
perennials, vines, and flowers

National Gardening Association Garden Shop
1100 Dorset Street
South Burlington, VT 05403
800-538-7476
www.garden.org

Outdoor and indoor supplies, bulbs,
plants, etc.

Harris Seeds
355 Paul Road, P.O. Box 24966
Rochester, NY 14624-0966
800-514-4441
www.harrisseeds.com
Flower, vegetable, herbs, and supplies

❀ Jackson & Perkins
1 Rose Lane
Medford, OR 97501
800-292-4769
www.jacksonandperkins.com
Roses: hybrid tea, English, floribunda,
antique, climbers, etc.

❀ Johnny's Selected Seeds
955 Benton Avenue
Winslow, ME 04910
800-879-2258
www.johnnyseeds.com
Vegetable, flower, and cover crop seeds

J. W. Jung Seed Co.
335 S. High Street
Randolph, WI 53957-0001
800-297-3123
www.jungseed.com
Seeds, bulbs, fruit, garlic

❀ Miller Nurseries
5060 West Lake Road
Canandaigua, NY 14424
800-836-9630
www.millernurseries.com
Fruit trees, berries, grapes; planting guides
with order

Mingus Dahlias
7407 N.E. 139th Street
Vancouver, WA 98662
360-573-2983
www.dahliasuppliers.com/mingus/index

❀ Native Gardens
5737 Fisher Lane
Greenback, TN 37742
865-856-0220
www.native-gardens.com
Nursery propagated native herbaceous, select
    perennials, wildflowers (plants and seeds)

New England Seed Company
3580 Main Street
Hartford, CT 06120
800-825-5477
www.neseed.com
Flower, vegetable, and herb seeds

Park Seed
1 Parkton Avenue
Greenwood, SC 29647
800-845-3369
www.parkseed.com
Flower and vegetable seeds and plants

❀ Pinetree Garden Seeds
P.O. Box 300
New Gloucester, ME 04260
207-926-3400
www.superseeds.com
Focus on home gardens for vegetables, herbs,
    and supplies

❀ Smith & Hawken
P.O. Box 8690
Pueblo, CO 81008

800-776-3336
www.smithandhawken.com
Gardening tools, plants, furniture, clothing

❀ Stokes Tropicals
P.O. Box 9868
New Iberia, LA 70562-9868
800-624-9706
www.stokestropicals.com

❀ Tomato Growers Supply Co.
P.O. Box 2237
Fort Myers, FL 33902
888-478-7333
www.tomatogrowers.com
Early, main, cherry, and unusual varieties

Van Bourgondien
245 Farmingdale Road
P.O. Box 1000
Babylon, NY 11702-9004
800-622-9959
www.dutchbulbs.com
Dutch bulbs, perennials, peonies, cannas,
    begonias, dahlias, gladiolus

Van Dyck's
P.O. Box 2000
Virginia Beach, VA 23450-2000
800-248-2852
www.vandycks.com
Dutch bulbs and perennials

❀ Walt Nicke Co.
P.O. Box 433
Topsfield, MA 01983
978-887-3388
www.gardentalk.com
Gardening tools and products

❀ White Flower Farm
P.O. Box 50, Rt. 63
Litchfield, CT 06759-0050
800-503-9624
www.whiteflowerfarm.com
Perennials, annuals, flowering shrubs, bulbs,
    vines

❀ Wind & Weather
1200 North Main Street
Fort Bragg, CA 95437
800-922-9463
www.windandweather.com
Weather instruments and vanes, sundials,
    garden ornaments

❀ Worm's Way
7850 North State Road 37
Bloomington, IN 47404
800-274-9676
www.wormsway.com
Beneficial insects, organic fertilizers, row
    covers, composting and seed-starting
    supplies

PARKS DEPARTMENTS— LISTED BY CITY

Atlanta, Georgia
Atlanta Department of Parks, Recreation and
    Cultural Affairs
675 Ponce de Leon Avenue
Atlanta, GA 30308
www.atlantaga.gov
Search for "garden"
404-817-6744

Augusta, Maine
Bureau of Parks and Cemeteries
City Center Plaza
16 Cony Street
Augusta, ME 04330
www.ci.augusta.me.us
207-626-2352

Austin, Texas
Austin Department of Parks & Recreation
P.O. Box 1088
Austin, TX 78767
www.ci.austin.tx.us/parks
512-499-6743

Baltimore, Maryland
Baltimore Department of Parks & Recreation
2600 Madison Ave
Baltimore, MD 21217
www.ci.baltimore.md.us/government/recnpa
    rks/index.html
410-396-0217

Bismarck, North Dakota
Bismarck Parks and Recreation District
400 East Front Avenue
Bismarck, ND 58504
http://bisparks.org
701-222-6455

Boise, Idaho
Boise Parks and Recreation Department
1104 Royal Boulevard
Boise, ID 83706
www.ci.boise.id.us/parks/default.asp
208-384-4240

Boston, Massachusetts
Boston Parks and Recreation

1010 Massachusetts Avenue, 3rd Floor
Boston, MA 02118
www.ci.boston.ma.us/parks
617-635-4989

Boston GreenSpace Alliance
44 Bromfield Street, #403
Boston, MA 02108
www.greenspacealliance.org
617-426-7980

Carson City, Nevada
Carson City Parks and Recreation
3303 Butti Way, Building #9
Carson City, NV 89701
702-887-2363

Charleston, West Virginia
Charleston Parks and Recreation
200 Baker Lane
Charleston, WV 25302
www.cityofcharleston.org/recreation.htm
307-348-6860

Charleston, South Carolina
City of Charleston Department of Parks
823 Meeting Street
Charleston, SC 29403
www.ci.charleston.sc.us/dept/?nid=17
843-724-7321

Cheyenne, Wyoming
Cheyenne Parks and Recreation
210 O'Neil Avenue, Room 205
Cheyenne, WY 82007
www.cheyennecity.org/parksrec.htm
307-638-4356

Chicago, Illinois
Chicago Park District

425 E. McFetridge Drive
Chicago, IL 60605
www.chicagoparkdistrict.com
312-747-2683

Cincinnati, Ohio
Cincinnati Recreation Commission
2 Centennial Plaza
805 Central Avenue
Cincinnati, OH 45202
www.cincyrec.org
513-352-4004

Cleveland, Ohio
Cleveland Parks and Recreation Department,
   Park Planning and Development
1501 N. Marginal Road
Cleveland, OH 44114
www.city.cleveland.oh.us/index1.html
216-664-3284

Columbia, South Carolina
City of Columbia Parks and Recreation
2020 Hampton Street
Columbia, SC 29201
www.columbiasc.net/cofc_pnr.html
803-545-3100

Columbus, Ohio
Columbus Recreation and Parks Department
90 West Broad Street
City Hall, Room 115
Columbus, OH 43215
www.columbusrecparks.com
614-645-8430

Concord, New Hampshire
Recreation Department
1 White Street

Concord, NH 03301
www.ci.concord.nh.us
603-225-8690

Dallas, Texas
Park & Recreation Department
Dallas City Hall
1500 Marilla Street, Room 6FN
Dallas, TX 75201
www.dallascityhall.com/dallas/eng/html/park
    _and_recreation.html
214-670-4100

Denver, Colorado
Denver Department of Parks and Recreation
2300 15th Street, Suite 150
Denver, CO 80202-1139
www.denvergov.org/Parks_Recreation
303-964-2510

Des Moines, Iowa
Des Moines Parks and Recreation
3226 University Avenue
Des Moines, IA 50311
www.dmgov.org
515-237-1386

Detroit, Michigan
Detroit Parks and Recreation Department
65 Cadillac Square, Suite 4000
Detroit, MI 48226
www.ci.detroit.mi.us/recreation/Contacts.htm
313-224-1123

Dover, Delaware
Delaware Division of Parks and Recreation
89 Kings Highway
Dover, DE 19901

www.dnrec.state.de.us/parks/index.asp
302-739-4401

El Paso, Texas
El Paso Parks and Recreation
2 Civic Center Plaza, 6th Floor
El Paso, TX 79901
www.elpasotexas.gov/parks/recreation.asp
915-541-4331

Fort Wayne, Indiana
Fort Wayne Parks and Recreation
705 East State Blvd.
Fort Wayne, IN 46805
www.ci.ft-wayne.in.us
219-427-6000

Fort Worth, Texas
Fort Worth Parks and Community Services
    Department
4200 South Freeway, Suite 2200
Fort Worth, TX 76115-1499
http://ci.fort-worth.tx.us
817-871-5788

Frankfort, Kentucky
City of Frankfort Department of Parks &
    Recreation
407 Broadway
Frankfort, KY 40601
www.cityoffrankfortky.com/cs/pr/co.htm
502-696-0607

Hartford, Connecticut
Hartford Proud and Beautiful
c/o Hartford Arts Alliance
P.O. Box 231436
Hartford, CT 06123-2436

www.connectthedots.org/hpb.html

860-525-8629

Helena, Montana

Helena Parks and Recreation

316 W. Park Ave.

Helena, MT 59623

www.ci.helena.mt.us/text/parks

406-447-8463

Honolulu, Hawaii

Honolulu Department of Parks and
    Recreation

650 South King Street, 10th Floor

Honolulu, HI 96813

www.co.honolulu.hi.us/parks

808-527-6343

Houston, Texas

Houston Parks and Recreation

2999 S. Wayside Drive

Houston, TX 77023

www.ci.houston.tx.us/pr/PicnicSpots.html

713-845-1000

Indianapolis, Indiana

Indianapolis Department of Parks and
    Recreation

City-County Building

200 E. Washington Street, Suite 2301

Indianapolis, IN 46204

http://iapd@ILparks.org

317-327-7275

Jackson, Mississippi

City of Jackson's Mynelle Gardens

4736 Clinton Boulevard

Jackson, MS 39209

www.city.jackson.ms.us/Visitors/mynelle.htm

601-960-1894

Jacksonville, Florida

Jacksonville Department of Parks, Recreation
    and Entertainment

851 North Market Street

Jacksonville, FL 32202-2798

www.coj.net/Departments/Parks+and+
    Recreation/default.htm

904-630-3535

Jefferson City, Missouri

Jefferson Parks, Recreation and Forestry
    Department

427 Monroe Street

Jefferson City, MO 65101

www.jeffcitymo.org

573-634-6482

Juneau, Alaska

City and Borough of Juneau Alaska

Juneau Park Facilities

155 S. Seward Street

Juneau, AK 99801

www.juneau.org/parksrec/facilities/facilities.
    php

907-586-5226

Kansas City, Missouri

Kansas City Parks and Recreation
    Department

4600 E. 63 Street Trafficway

Kansas City, MO 64130

www.kcmo.org/parks

816-513-7500

Minneapolis, Minnesota

Minneapolis Park & Recreation Board

2117 West River Road

Minneapolis, MN 55411-2227

www.minneapolisparks.org/home.asp

612-230-6400

Lincoln, Nebraska

Lincoln Parks & Recreation

2740 A Street

Lincoln, NE 68502

www.lincoln.org/cvb/parks/parks.htm

402-441-8265

Little Rock, Arkansas

Little Rock, Parks and Recreation

500 W. Markham

Little Rock, AR 72201

www.littlerock.org

501-371-6839

Los Angeles, California

Los Angeles City Recreation and Parks
    Department

200 N. Main Street, Room 1330

Los Angeles, CA 90012

www.laparks.org/info.htm

213-473-5888

Memphis, Tennesse

Memphis City Beautiful Commission

664 Adams Avenue

Memphis, TN 38105

www.cityofmemphis.org

901-522-1135

Miami, Florida

Miami-Dade Parks and Recreation
    Department

275 NW 2nd Street, 4th Floor

Miami, FL 33128

www.ci.miami.fl.us

305-755-7887

Milwaukee, Wisconsin

Milwaukee County Parks

9480 Watertown Plank Road

Wauwatosa, WI 53226

www.countyparks.com

414-257-6100

Montgomery, Alabama

Montgomery Parks & Recreation Dept.

101C Forest Ave.

Montgomery, AL 36106

www.montgomery.al.us

334-241-2300

Montpelier, Vermont

Parks Department

City Hall, 39 Main Street

Montpelier, VT 05602-2950

www.montpelier-vt.org/parks/index.cfm

802-223-7335

Nashville, Tennessee

Metro Board of Parks and Recreation

Centennial Park Office

Nashville, TN 37201

www.nashville.gov/parks/index

615-862-8400

New Orleans, Louisiana

New Orleans Department of Parks &
    Parkways

2829 Gentilly Boulevard

New Orleans, LA 70122

www.new-orleans.la.us/home
504-286-2100

New York, New York
City of New York Parks & Recreation
The Arsenal, Central Park
830 5th Avenue
New York, NY 10021
www.nycgovparks.org
Dial 311 for all Parks & Recreation
  information;
outside of NYC, call 212-NEW-YORK
  (639-9675)
and
Partnerships for Parks
www.partnershipsforparks.org
212-360-1310

Newport News, Virginia
Newport News Parks and Recreation
  Department
Attn: Parks Administrator
2400 Washington Avenue
Newport News, VA 23607
www.2.ci.newport-news.va.us/
  newport-news/index
757-926-8451

Oklahoma City, Oklahoma
Oklahoma City Department of Parks and
  Recreation
420 W. Main, Suite 210
Oklahoma City, OK 73102
www.okc.gov
405-297-3882

Philadelphia, Pennsylvania
1515 Arch Street, 10th Floor
Philadelphia, PA 19102-1587

www.phila.gov/recreation/index.html
215-683-3600

Pennsylvania Horticultural Society
Philadelphia Green Program
100 North 20th Street, 5th Floor
Philadelphia, PA 19103-1095
www.pennsylvaniahorticulturalsociety.org/ho
  me/index.html
215-988-8800

Pierre, South Dakota
Parks Department
1201 E. Missouri Ave.
Pierre, SD 57501
http://ci.pierre.sd.us/parks.htm
605-773-7437

Pittsburgh, Pennsylvania
Pittsburgh Department of Parks and
  Recreation
City-County Building, Room 400
414 Grant Street
Pittsburgh, PA 15219
www.city.pittsburgh.pa.us/parks
412-255-2539

Phoenix, Arizona
Phoenix Parks, Recreation and Library
  Department
200 West Washington Street, 16th Floor
Phoenix, AZ 85003-1611
http://phoenix.gov
602-262-6862

Portland, Maine
Portland Department of Parks and
  Recreation
17 Arbor Street
Portland, ME 04103

www.ci.portland.me.us
207-874-8793

Portland, Oregon
Portland Parks & Recreation
1120 SW Fifth Ave., Suite 1302
Portland, OR 97204
www.portlandparks.org
503-823-PLAY

Providence, Rhode Island
Parks Department
Providence City Hall
25 Dorrance Street
Providence, RI 02903
www.providenceri.com/government/parks/
    index.html
401-785-9450

Raleigh, North Carolina
Raleigh Parks & Recreation
P.O. Box 590, 222 West Hargett Street
Raleigh, NC 27601
www.raleigh-nc.org/parks&rec/index.asp
919-890-3285

Richmond, Virginia
Department of Parks, Recreation and
    Community Facilities
City Hall, 900 East Broad Street, Room 407
Richmond, VA 23219
www.ci.richmond.va.us/department/
    parks_rec/index.asp
804-646-5733

Sacramento, California
Sacramento Department of Parks and
    Recreation

4040 Bradshaw Road
Sacramento, CA 95827
http://waterforum.org/parksandrecreation/
    volunteer.htm
916-366-2283

Salt Lake City, Utah
Salt Lake City, Parks
1965 West 500 South
Salt Lake City, Utah 84101
www.slcgov.com/publicservices/parks
801-972-7800

San Antonio, Texas
San Antonio Department of Parks and
    Recreation
115 Plaza De Armas, Suite 260
San Antonio, TX 77023
www.sanantonio.gov/sapar/index.asp?res=10
    24&ver=true
210-207-8480

San Diego, California
City of San Diego's Park and Recreation
    Department
202 C Street—MS37C
San Diego, CA 92101
www.sannet.gov/park-and-recreation/
    index.shtml
619-533-6434

San Francisco, California
San Francisco Recreation and Park Dept.
McLaren Lodge, Golden Gate Park
501 Stanyan St.
San Francisco, CA 94117-1898
www.ci.sf.ca.us/site/recpark_index.asp
415-831-2700

and

Friends of Recreation & Parks

www.frp.org

415-750-5443

San Jose, California

Department of Parks, Recreation &
    Neighborhood Services

4 North Second Street, Suite 600

San Jose, CA 95113

www.ci.san-jose.ca.us/prns/index.htm

408-277-4661

Santa Fe, New Mexico

Parks & Recreation

City of Santa Fe

200 Lincoln Avenue

Santa Fe, NM 87501

www.santafenm.gov/parks/index.asp

505-955-2100

Savannah, Georgia

Savannah Parks and Recreation Department

P.O. Box 1027

Savannah, GA 31402

912.651.6610

www.savannahpd.org/cityweb/webdatabase
    .nsf/spd

912-651-6610

Seattle, Washington

Seattle Department of Parks and Recreation

800 Maynard Avenue South, Suite 300

Seattle, WA 98134-1334

www.ci.seattle.wa.us/parks

206-684-8018

Washington, D.C.

D.C. Department of Parks and Recreation

3149 16th Street, N.W.

Washington, DC 20010

www.dpr.dc.gov

202-673-7693

Even if you're on the right track, you'll get run over if you just sit there.
—Will Rogers

20

a case study—Garrit Stryker's garden

No matter where you are gardening—in your backyard, on your building's roof, around a memorial statue, or in the park—there is history. Ever wonder what was on that exact piece of land in 1850, 1776, or earlier?

Research unveiled a fascinating history in DeWitt Clinton Park between West 52nd and 54th Streets on Manhattan's West Side. At that site, an enchanting mansion had once faced the Hudson River; a sketch of the house, appearing in an article written in *Appletons' Journal* in 1872, gave the first glimpse of the family who had lived there. The mansion was owned by Garrit Stryker, a major general, who created an ornamental garden on the grounds. He tended the garden for fifty years, until his death in 1868 at age eighty.

In 2003, Manhattan Parks & Recreation Commissioner William Castro gave permission to the Manhattan Botanical Garden to beautify the Stryker lot. Starting with a weed-filled hillside, as the garden designer, I continue to follow the clues left behind, in an effort to capture the past. Stryker's favorite species were planted in the parterre; and roses now grow by the "ruin" of his greenhouse, as it was described in 1872. A low stone wall has been built on the hillside orchard, and reconstruction continues on a parterre viewed from the mansion's second floor. Benches were designed to replicate the architectural details of the mansion. The goal of the design is to share the history through plantings, garden design, and interpretive signage. The mission is to honor Garrit Stryker's devotion to the lasting beauty of his garden.

THE STRYKER MANSION

The present appearance of the Stryker
place is very pleasing, in spite of the fall season,
which, however, has not changed the
foliage yet to any great extent, and has
permitted the flowers to linger in the garden.
The parterres are very old fashioned, and the
flowering bushes have usurped somewhat more
space than was designed for them. But the
lawns are pleasant, and the flowers are of the
modern style, even including such comparative
novelties as the canna, with its long
leaves of dark green, and its stiff, orange
flowers, and the caladium, with its huge leaves
shaped like Norman shields. Peacocks strut
about the place, and great maltese cats slink
through the shrubberies, hiding guiltily among
the bushes of box-wood cut in fantastic
shape. There are two tall box-trees, which
have never been clipped by the profane hand
of a gardener. These were planted many
years ago by the tiny hands of Miss Jessie
Benton, then on a visit, with her father, Old
Bullion, the Senator of Missouri, to General
Stryker's famous Hudson villa. One of these
died this year; the other is still in a flourishing
condition. The fish-pond is now in communication
with the river, the gold-fish have
died, or been eaten by finny monsters, the carp
have disappeared, and nothing remains save
great eels, that burrow down in the fat ooze,
and seem to find the place congenial.

TEXT EXCERPTED FROM
APPLETON'S JOURNAL OF LITERATURE, SCIENCE AND ART
NO. 19L, VOL. VIIIL, P. 562
SATURDAY, NOVEMBER 23, 1872.

Appletons' Journal

LITERATURE, SCIENCE, AND ART

Entered, according to Act of Congress, in the year 1872, by D. Appleton & Co., in the Office of the Librarian of Congress, at Washington.

No. 191.—Vol. VIII.]   SATURDAY, NOVEMBER 23, 1872.   [Price Ten Cents.

STRYKER HOUSE, FIFTY-SECOND STREET, NORTH RIVER.

Text and sketch of Mansion, courtesy of Making of America—http://moa.umdl.umich.edu

I like to see a man proud of the place in which he lives; I like to see a man live so that his place will be proud of him.

—Abraham Lincoln

garden your city

garden journal—notes & sketches

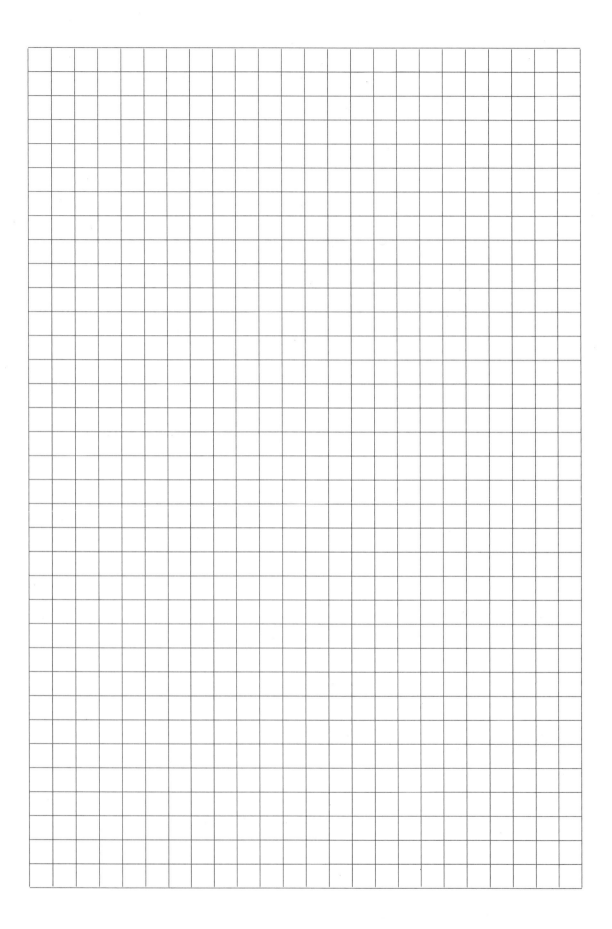

garden journal—notes & sketches

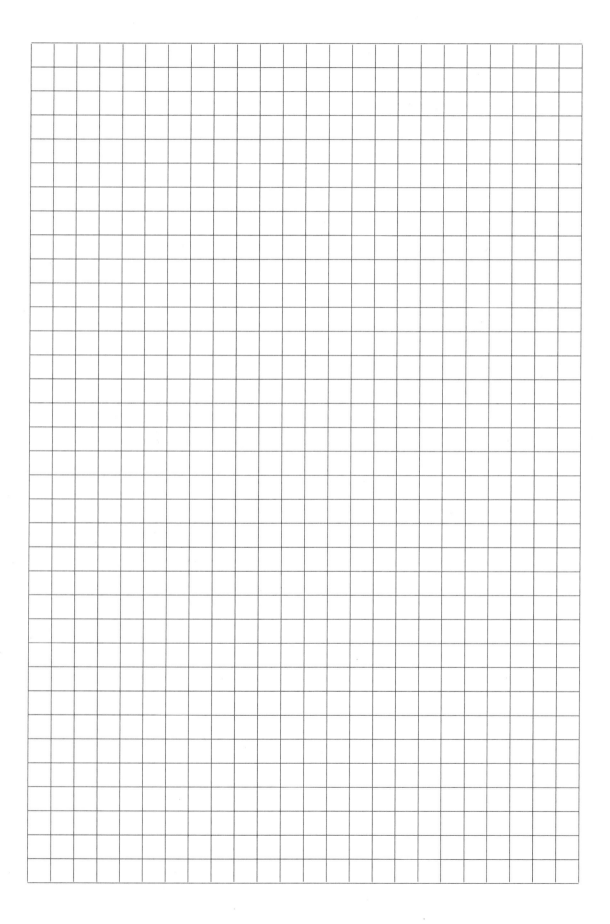

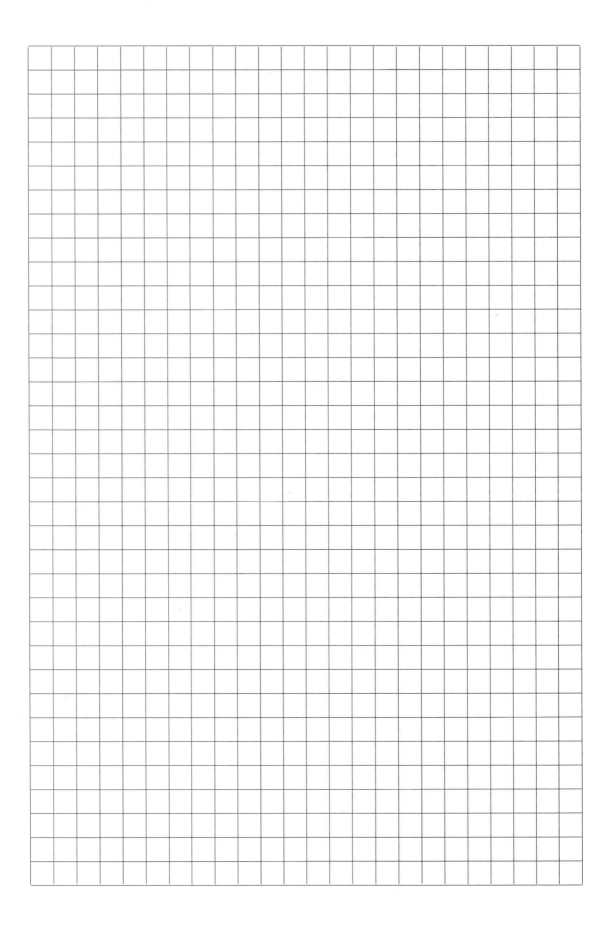

reading list & bibliography

Gardening often develops another passion—collecting books on gardening! Here are favorites off the bookshelf for instruction, reference, and inspiration. If they're not available at your bookstore or library, search on the Internet and scour book sales.

Bartholomew, Mel. *Square Foot Gardening*. Emmaus, PA: Rodale Press, 1981.

Clodagh. "Personal Edens: Outdoor Rooms and Indoor Gardens." In *TotalDesign*. New York: Clarkson Potter, 2001.

Cox, Jeff. *Creating a Garden for the Senses*. New York: Abbeville Press, 1993.

Damrosch, Barbara. *Theme Gardens*. New York: Workman Publishing, 2001.

Favretti, Rudy J., and Joy Putman Favretti. *Landscapes and Gardens for Historic Buildings*. 2nd ed. Walnut Creek, CA: AltaMira Press, 1997.

Graham, Rose. *The Small Garden Planner*. London, England: Mitchell Beazley Publishers, 1991.

Hale, Gill. *The Feng Shui Garden*. Pownal, VT: Storey Books, 1998.

Harper, Peter, and Jeremy Light. *The Natural Garden Book*. New York: Simon & Schuster/Fireside; "A Gaia Original," 1994.

Heintzelman, Donald S. *The Complete Backyard Birdwatcher's Home Companion*. Camden, ME: Ragged Mountain Press, 2001.

Holmes, Roger, ed. *Taylor's Guide to Container Gardening*. New York: Houghton Mifflin, 1995.

Hobhouse, Penelope. *A Book of Gardening: Ideas, Methods, Designs: A Practical Guide*. 1st Owl Book ed. New York: Henry Holt, 1995.

Luebbermann, Mimi. *Climbing Vines*. San Francisco, CA: Chronicle Books, 1995.

Naimark, Susan, ed. *A Handbook of Community Gardening*. New York: Charles Scribner's Sons, 1982.

Nielsen, Signe. *Sky Gardens: Rooftops, Balconies, and Terraces*. Atglen, PA: Schiffer Publishing Ltd., 2004.

Reinhardt, Thomas A., Martina Reinhardt, and Mark Moskowitz. *Ornamental Grass Gardening: Design Ideas, Functions, and Effects*. New York: Michael Friedman Publishing Group, Inc., 1994.

Stevens, David. *Roof Gardens, Balconies & Terraces*. New York: Rizzoli, 1997.

Stevens, Elaine. The *Creative Container Gardener*. Berkeley, CA: Ten Speed Press, 1995.

Strong, Roy. *Creating Small Gardens*. New York: Villard Books, 1987.

Tufts, Craig. *The Backyard Naturalist*. Washington, DC: National Wildlife Federation, 1995.

Yang, Linda. "Not Quite Eden." In Linda Yang, ed., *The City and Town Gardener*. New York: Random House, 1990.

Yang, Linda. *The City Gardener's Handbook: The Definitive Guide to Small-Space Gardening*. North Adams, MA: Storey Books, 2002.

index

about the author

Barbara Hobens Feldt was raised northwest of Manhattan in suburban Demarest, New Jersey. Her love and respect of nature came from spending childhood summers on the ocean down in Bay Head and from growing up beside a woods. Watching red fox cutting through the backyard and putting out salt licks for the deer with her father are vivid memories. Barbara spent every spare hour playing with friends in the crisscrossing brooks, catching tadpoles in the swamp, and running through paths edged with ferns and skunk cabbage. All paths led to Davies Ponds' turtles, waterfall, and abandoned icehouse.

Lessons learned from nature joined with those from her parents, Ronnie and David, as well as from life, love, and a degree in business from Marymount College, Tarrytown, New York. It was her marriage to Fred and move to New York City more than a decade later that ignited Barbara's passion for gardening. One coffee-can tomato plant on the fire escape led to gardening efforts that transformed unappreciated urban spaces into people-friendly, educational, and beautiful gardens. Including native plants, community pride, and volunteerism in all planting efforts, Barbara Feldt has created a unique concept of urban beautification.

Barbara knows what she has grown; her gardening experience was gained by doing. As a member of her block association, as a City of New York Parks & Recreation volunteer park warden, and with the Clinton Community Garden, she organized Adopt-A-Tree plantings, established planting beds in local parks, and wrote proposals for irrigation systems, fences, and soil improvement. As founder and director of Friends of Pier 84's Manhattan Botanical Garden, she used her artistic ability with her sense of place, placement, and history to design and create meaningful plantings. Barbara's professional experience in plant installation and maintenance from Park Avenue penthouses to

Beekman Place terraces and her membership in the American Association of Botanical Gardens and Arboreta led to unique adaptations in design ideas for her co-op's backyard and roof gardens.

Barbara, Fred, and their furry (dog and cat) and slimy (koi and pond fish) kids live in a co-op in Hell's Kitchen/Clinton, just west of Times Square on the island of Manhattan. Barbara and Fred garden whenever they can.